Reading Network Fiction

David Ciccoricco

The University of Alabama Press
Tuscaloosa

Typeface: Minion

∞

The paper on which this book is printed meets the minimum requirements of
American National Standard for Information Sciences-Permanence of Paper for
Printed Library Materials, ANSI Z39.48-1984.

Library of Congress Cataloging-in-Publication Data

Ciccoricco, David, 1973–
Reading network fiction / David Ciccoricco.
p.   cm.
Includes bibliographical references and index.
ISBN-13: 978-0-8173-1589-4 (alk. paper)
ISBN-10: 0-8173-1589-6 (alk. paper)
1. Hypertext fiction—History and criticism. 2. Experimental fiction,
American—History and criticism. I. Title.
PN3448.H96C53 2007
813′.60911—dc22

2007014107

A companion website for *Reading Network Fiction* can be found at:
www.readingnetworkfiction.net/

For Ana,
whose constant warmth and companionship
I could not repay
even with a lifetime of dog treats.
But I'll try anyway.

Contents

Acknowledgments

In 1992 my parents gave me a leather-bound Webster's dictionary with an inscription on the inside cover that reads, "To use in the pursuit of knowledge and ideas to enrich your life." Even though the book has become somewhat outdated, especially as lexicons of digital literature go, its message has not, and after crossing continents and oceans, it still sits beside my desk. I thank them—both distinguished educators in their own right—for their immeasurable support in putting this work together. Effusive thanks also go to Bridgit, who is truly an awesome companion with a smile that remedies all.

Portions of chapters contained in this book have appeared previously in online publications. Grateful acknowledgment goes to Jan Baetens, editor of *Image & Narrative,* for permission to reprint portions of chapter 2, "Network Vistas: Folding the Cognitive Map," that appear under the same title in that journal, and to Joseph Tabbi, editor of the *electronic book review,* for supporting republication of earlier portions of chapters 3 and 4 and, more generally, for welcoming me into the *ebr* community. I also thank John Newton, at the University of Canterbury; Brian Opie, at Victoria University; and Brian McHale, at the Ohio State University for their careful reading and invaluable insight, which greatly contributed to shaping this project. Finally, I'd like to acknowledge the fine work done by all those at The University of Alabama Press involved in bringing this work to publication.

Reading Network Fiction

Introduction

On the History of Network Fiction

In the process of researching a body of work for a full-length study such as this one, it is somewhat unsettling when that body receives a "death notice." It is even more unsettling when it receives two of them. The corpus in question is literature that is written on and for the computer screen, literature that takes the material form of a digital network rather than a printed book, literature that—at least in what media theorist Adrian Miles (1998) has called its first "rosy blushes"—was popularly known as literary hypertext and hypertext fiction. But although *hypertext*, the term, has indeed expired in its capacity to stand as metonym for the diverse field of digital literature, the project of writing literature for screen media has not. Rather, it persists in many forms, one of which is network fiction.

In 1997 Nick Montfort announced that "Cybertext Killed the Hypertext Star" in an essay for the *electronic book review (ebr)* (Montfort 2000). Although the ensuing "Cybertext Debates" in *ebr* involved as much terminological jousting as substantive debate, Montfort's suggestion was both significant and necessary in terms of broadening the field of digital literature to include much more than "literary hypertext." His essay reviews Espen Aarseth's landmark *Cybertext: Perspectives of Ergodic Literature* (1997), which situates literary hypertext in a continuum of "cybertext," a categorical approach that consists of systematic, nonmedia-specific analyses of a text's signifying properties. Despite the shortfalls of some narrow appropriations of cybertext theory early on in the debates—some of which betrayed an obvious bias toward a text's algorithmic potential, or in N. Katherine Hayles's (2001) formulation, mistook "numerosity for analytical power"—Aarseth's model drew distinctions that previously did not exist in digital discourse, and hypertext fiction no longer needed to be seen as the epicenter of a seismic shift from print to digital literature. At the same time, it was by no means clear that the project of using the computer to write narrative fiction had (de)ceased. "Cybertext" did not kill anything; rather "cybertext theory" simply offered a better way to place literary hypertext in a diverse and emergent field of digital art.

In 1999 Robert Coover issued a second death notice of sorts with "Literary Hypertext: The Passing of the Golden Age." Coover was lamenting the demise of a specific body of digital literature: those primarily text-based works that precede the ascendancy of the World Wide Web, "the early classics ... Michael Joyce's *afternoon*, Judy Malloy's *Its Name Was Penelope*, Stuart Moulthrop's *Victory Garden*, and what is perhaps the true paradigmatic work of the era, Shelley Jackson's elegantly designed, beautifully composed *Patchwork Girl*" (Coover 1999). The majority of these works were written in the Storyspace hypertext authoring software, designed by Michael Joyce, J. David Bolter, and John B. Smith. These hypertext fictions garnered a profile in the United States and internationally as a result of their marketing and distribution by Eastgate Systems, a Massachusetts-based electronic publisher. Also referred to as the works of the Storyspace School, they largely constitute a first wave of digital fiction and poetry, since the World Wide Web has brought about enough changes to the reading, writing, publishing, distribution, and accessibility of digital literature to warrant the distinction of a second wave.[1]

Not everyone was eager to catch the second wave, least of all some of the "traditional" practitioners and theorists of digital literature who popularized early literary experiments in the medium. Coover, for one, sees the Web as an inhospitable place for narrative fiction:

> It tends to be a noisy, restless, opportunistic, superficial, e-commerce-driven, chaotic realm, dominated by hacks, pitchmen and pretenders, in which the quiet voice of literature cannot easily be heard or, if heard by chance, attended to for more than a moment or two. Literature is meditative and the Net is riven by ceaseless hype and chatter. Literature has a shape, and the Net is shapeless. The discrete object is gone, there's only this vast disorderly sprawl, about as appealing as a scatter of old magazines on a table in the dentist's lounge. (Coover 1999)

It is difficult to make an argument for a "voice" of literature that is associated exclusively or predominantly with one medium or another (the work of many contemporary print writers would suggest a voice that clearly tends toward the "chaotic"). But Coover does make a more convincing claim based on a media-specific observation. He sees the fear of the *visual* usurping the *verbal* taking on increasing urgency, an observation advanced by the computer's potential for the manipulation, reproduction, and distribution of images, both still and moving. "[F]or all the wondrous and provocative invasions of text by sound and image," he writes, "still, the most radical and distinctive literary contribution of the computer has been the multilinear hypertextual webwork of text spaces, or, as one might say, the intimate layering and fusion of imagined spatiality and temporality" (1999). For Coover the allure of textual webs is lost in the graphical Web.

Coover's "Golden Age" of electronic literature may have come and gone, but it is difficult to accept his view as a telling indication of the course of digital literature in a wider historical, cultural, and geographical context. Historically, it is true that the rate of technological change is dramatically outpacing the changes brought about by the last major innovation in writing technology more than five hundred years ago—the printing press. It is, however, problematic to measure literary experimentation—and the rise and fall of genres—on a strictly technological continuum, and it is even more problematic for an observer to glean a perspective on a historical period when the observer is quite conceivably still *in* it. In the broadest sense John Barth reminds us that "written literature is in fact about 4500 years old . . . but we have no way of knowing whether 4500 years constitutes senility, maturity, youth, or mere infancy" (1982, 38). Coover's partitioning is further limited culturally and geographically. As Roberto Simanowski (2000) points out, "It is characteristic of the German digital literature scene that pure hypertext, as we know it from Eastgate Systems' writers, never really developed. Instead there are mainly two types of digital writing in Germany: one favours interactivity, the other the multimedia power of the digital realm." In the field of digital literature some did not experience the "Golden Age" at all.

Emerging media technologies are continually informing fiction and poetry, both in the sense of "influencing" (not *determining*) and "giving form or structure to." The process reciprocates, evident in the modes of fiction and poetry that were both shaped by and gave shape to the medium of film over the course of the twentieth century. Thus there is little doubt that writers will continue to write fiction and poetry that are informed by the computer medium. With the rapid innovation in computer hardware and software, there is also little doubt that artists who treat the digital medium as a literary medium are bound to use different tools from those familiar to (and, in Joyce's case, created by) the forerunners of first-wave digital literature. The question that remains unanswered—and, in the short term, unanswerable—

is whether writers invested in narrative fiction will continue to compose for the computer screen or, as Stuart Moulthrop has done, simply decide to "let books be books and cybertexts be whatever they turn out to be" (2003b). The movement in the arts away from representation and toward simulation, away from the dynamics of reading and interpretation and toward the dynamics of interaction and play, would indeed suggest that literature as we know it has other worries beyond the power of the image. In a recent essay concerning the state of the art, written five years after Coover's essay and nearly twelve years after his own classic Storyspace fiction *Victory Garden,* Moulthrop writes of a fork in the road: "Beyond this point the traditional narrative interest leads one way, while a second track diverges. We do not yet have a very good name for this other path, though we can associate some concepts with it: play, simulation, and more generally, game" (2003a).

In terms of literary theory perhaps the matter of a few death notices is not such a bad thing. Such announcements tend to serve as checks for more elaborate prophecies, both utopian and apocalyptic, regarding the futures of literature. More important, problematic as they may be, such essays encourage a retrospective glance in a field so intensely preoccupied with what comes next. Montfort's and Coover's contributions to the discourse offer a convenient way to begin talking not about what the digital medium will mean for literature but rather what it already means, and what it has meant. This is not to say that digital fiction has reached its potential or that it has concretized into a stable empirical object; after all, much of its potential resides in its penchant for transformation. The point is simply that the writing, so to speak, is on the screen.

What Is Network Fiction?

In using the phrase *network fiction* to describe the primary works chosen for this study, it is not my intention to add to an already bloated cybercultural vocabulary but rather to apply existing terminology with greater precision.[2] Network fiction makes use of hypertext technology in order to create emergent and recombinatory narratives. It is possible to define *emergent* and *recombinatory* by contrasting network fiction with other forms of digital literature that also use hypertext technology.

Hypertext technology is a tool that allows users to create digitally mediated links between nodes of information; when I refer to *hypertext,* I am referring to the technology. A technological denotation of hypertext runs counter to the current practice of painting "hypertextuality" in broad strokes and across media.[3] But as a way of reading, of writing, and of thinking, *hyper-*

text has lost much of its utility as a descriptive term: rather than connoting a discernible mode of association and juxtaposition that can apply usefully to texts both onscreen and in print, it has come to represent the polar opposite of *conventional*—the privileged term in the binary of liberating/oppressive and new/old. For the same reason, the term alone does little to distinguish different applications of hypertext technology in digital literature.

Hypertext documents fall into three basic categories: *axial, arborescent,* and *networked.* In general terms *axial* denotes a structure situated along an axis; *arborescent* denotes a branching structure resembling a tree; and *networked* denotes an interconnected system of nodes in which there is no dominant axis of orientation. These categories have been applied to hypertext systems but more often with axial and arborescent grouped together as "hierarchical" since both have a main axis. A hierarchical structure sits in opposition to a networked one. These distinctions have several precedents, two of which are particularly relevant to narrative fiction. George Landow (1994, 23) speaks of "axial versus network-structured hypertext." For him axial hypertext constitutes for the most part a "translation" of conventional print texts into digital text, a form of organization "in which references, variant readings, and other supplements to the main text radiate from it in the manner of branches from a tree" (23). The promise of hypertext technology, Landow continues, is realized in network structure, which exploits the "dispersed, multiply centered networked organization inherent in electronic linking" (23). Deleuze and Guattari's concept of the *rhizome* also celebrates the potential of networked structures, though it was only later appropriated as a theoretical framework for hypertext (Landow 1997; Moulthrop 1994).[4] In *A Thousand Plateaus* (1987), a book whose own modular organization is popularly regarded as protohypertextual, Deleuze and Guattari distinguish between *arborescent* and *rhizomatic* forms: "unlike trees or their roots, the rhizome connects any point to any other point, and its traits are not necessarily linked to traits of the same nature; it brings into play very different regimes of signs, and even nonsign states" (21). They see the principles of "connection" and "heterogeneity" that characterize rhizomatic forms as powerful figures of thought and expression for subjects caught in the flux of information society. Both Landow's pedagogically based model and the more philosophical model of Deleuze and Guattari provide technical and rhetorical foundations for literary experiments in digital environments. But these theorists do not make any further distinction between axial and arborescent structures; for them it is more important to establish a networked or rhizomatic form as antihierarchical, with liberating and empowering implications for those who use it.

A three-tiered distinction of axial, arborescent, and networked structures adds greater precision when applied to narrative fiction. An axial narrative can refer to a narrative where digressions are present in the form of glosses or notes that are secondary to the main narrative; typically, a reader returns to the main text after the digression. In *The Virtual Disappearance of Miriam* (2000) Martyn Bedford employs links to this effect in his comical narrative about a disappearing lover. In a passage where the narrator is referring to his absent partner, for example, a text link from "Miriam" opens a smaller window that displays a woman's photograph with the accompanying text: "This isn't actually Miriam, but the resemblance is close enough. Same hair, same skin tone, same top. This picture is from the Next catalogue (Spring/Summer 2000) that's been lying on her bedside table for months. I don't have any photos of Miriam so this one will have to do. She is less 'professionally beautiful' than the model but, if you ask me, all the more attractive for that." The reader closes this window and returns to the main text after obtaining further information about Miriam, albeit indirectly, through this gloss.

An arborescent fiction, by contrast, can refer to a narrative with branches but specifically those that contain mutually exclusive story events or outcomes; a reader of an arborescent narrative makes choices at bifurcating points in the text *and continues on until the end of one of the branches is reached.* Returning to a previous bifurcation in an arborescent narrative is equivalent to rewinding a temporal frame; that is, readers undo and redo the story whenever they decide to go back. In Milorad Pavic's *The Glass Snail,* for example, readers encounter "crossroads" where they must decide which "chapters" will begin and end the story. As the Second Crossroads indicates, "Here again it is up to you to choose where to go, to make your own map of the reading. The chapter <u>Christmas Candle</u> will bring a tragic ending to the story. The chapter <u>The Lighter</u> ends happily." Since they require decisions at branching points that always imply temporal progression at the diegetic level, arborescent fictions share an affinity with another form of computer-based digital fiction that has come to be known as interactive fiction, or IF: the structure of IFs tends to reflect the movement from an Initial Situation to a Final Situation (Montfort 2003), thus reaching the "end" of a given branch.[5]

A *network* narrative, then, differs not only in its nonhierarchical organization but also in that its narrative emerges gradually through a recombination of elements. Writers of network fictions are less concerned with confronting the reader with mutually exclusive outcomes and more concerned with the way narratives emerge in digital environments. As *networked* fictions, they assert Coover's (1999) belief that "the most radical and distinctive literary contribution of the computer has been the multilinear hypertextual webwork of text spaces." Fixed sequence does not play a crucial role in determining meaning in network fictions. Rather, the experience of reading a network fiction is analogous to Hayles's (1999a, 214) discussion of an engagement with complex systems, whereby repeated encounters with local structure give rise to an emergent global structure. The parts, or *nodes*, of network narratives are self-contained semantic entities—and each screenful of narrative material must be combined and recombined in order for a higher level of coherence to emerge. Network fictions are emergent and recombinatory, and they exploit digital technology toward these ends.

Narrative coherence in network fiction, therefore, is not rendered in the strict sense of a coherent *story*. In her discussion of "networked narrative environments," Laura Trippi (2001) writes, "Our understanding of 'narrative,' as a special way of knowing, is becoming disentangled from the narrower concept of 'story.' In gaming and other cultural arenas, this has been happening in practice now for some time. The discussion developing around 'narrative intelligence,' bringing researchers from AI together with those from the arts and humanities, seems to be addressing this." As Trippi suggests, in narrative texts no longer dominated by a singular overarching plot and causal unity, the very notion of *story* recedes as other qualities of narrative, such as pattern and mood, are brought to the fore (Trippi 2003). These elements are not necessarily representational narrative elements, which is to say that they do not necessarily correspond to something that exists or could possibly exist outside of the text itself. Nonetheless, much in the same way that the patterns of a Bach fugue are meaningful to the listener, these nonrepresentational elements can carry the meaning of the text.[6] Pattern recognition is thus implicit in the practice of reading network fiction. As Mark Bernstein and Diane Greco (2004) write, "Patterns allow coherence to emerge when a narrative supports many different possible orderings of events."

Although the present study looks at digital manifestations of network fiction, the distinction of axial, arborescent, and network is by no means exclusive to the digital realm. Axial narratives have obvious precedents in texts that make use of—and possibly subvert—the footnote or marginal gloss. Arborescent narratives have roots in pick-a-path and Choose Your Own Adventure stories in print. There are also print precedents for network fictions, such as the French writer Marc Saporta's *Composition No. 1* (1962). Saporta's "box" of fiction consists of about 150 unbound unnumbered "pages" (Spencer 1971, 210).[7]

Reading Network Fiction

Many early theorists of hypertext (Bolter 1991; Landow 1997; Lanham 1993) claimed that hypertext could liberate its users from a systematic oppression of hierarchies, in both artistic and pedagogical practice, and suggested that it could free literature from the "tyranny of the line" (Coover 1992). Though such critics were arguably exercising a necessary extremism in order to clear ground for a new discipline, the most utopian claims of hypertext as inherently democratizing and empowering have been demystified. Practice has shown that hypertext can democratize and empower only if its users exploit it toward these ends. Notions of "nonlinearity" associated with digital texts have been subjected to closer scrutiny and have gained greater clarity (Charney 1994; M. Rosenberg 1994), with critics making a distinction between the *lines* of a network structure and a reader's *course* through that structure (Aarseth 1997). Furthermore, with the ascendancy of database forms comes a renewed attendance to the merits of hierarchical forms, which, as electronic poet Robert Kendall (2001) points out, offer "complementary rather than antithetical" possibilities for artistic expression.

With the effective collapse of hypertext theory's antiestablishment utopianism and the various liberation theologies it fed, it is possible to consider more realistically the qualities and limitations peculiar to hypertext as a writing technology. And it is possible to undertake a broader study that asks how digital writing technologies, including but not exclusive to hypertext, reinscribe the notion of narrative itself. This book focuses on network fiction, not because axial or arborescent structures necessarily imply a rigidity and oppressiveness said to be inherent in hierarchies, and not because this form is in some way dominant or representative of the field of digital literature. (A survey of the directory of the Electronic Literature Organization of all works included as "Fiction" under the "Hypertext" category reveals that between 25 to 30 percent of the approximately 320 works listed were network fictions).[8] My focus lies where it does because network fictions, more than the other literary instantiations of hypertext technology, have the most dramatic impact on the development of narrative poetics.

In a claim that reads somewhat like a more contemporary rehearsal of the hierarchy-versus-network debate, some theorists posit that narrative, as a cultural form, is ill-suited to the database logic of networked media (Manovich 2001). But "narrative" and "network" are not opposing cultural forms. Networks redistribute narrative—both in shifting the delivery model from *one-to-many* to *many-to-many* (Poster 1995) and in the sense that networks redistribute narrative elements into self-contained semantic units. Moreover, textual networks redistribute the task of ordering narrative, endowing the reader with the responsibility of assembling sequence and, in turn, narrative coherence. *Narrative* itself is medium-independent—what narratology describes as a "universal cognitive structure." As such, narrative does not have a natural relationship to the book; one does not intrinsically fit the other. A study of narrative in network form not only foregrounds narrative techniques that have been either overlooked or inconceivable in print, but it also promises to cast new light on the qualities peculiar to the print medium itself.

It is necessary to qualify discussions of the reader's combinatorial power in reading network fiction. In fact, it is difficult to equate the reader's new responsibility with new "power" at all, since the writer prearranges the paths that exist in network fiction, and the reader's "freedom" is circumscribed—subject to the design of the author-as-artificer. Aarseth (1997, 63) has suggested that the reader has *more* freedom when navigating the pages of a book. But given the body of digital literature that now exists, it is also necessary to question the values associated with—and indeed the desirability of—a reader who can add to and change a work of narrative fiction. Granted, the empowered reader ideal has dramatically different implications for pedagogical hypertexts, which develop opportunities for self-paced and self-directed learning. But mapping the same ideal onto narrative art is problematic and was never embraced wholesale even by the most utopian hypertext critics. Richard Lanham (1993, 220), for instance, defends the "balance of power" between the reader and writer of literature: "Writing gets its power from the *role* it allows the writer to play. The writer seems to speak as we do, but actually speaks from a different time scale, one that condenses years of work and thought into minutes of reading time. The rush we get from reading great writing comes from that sudden, almost instantaneous transfer of power. No writer's role, no transfer of power."

For those who seek a "first-person" mode of agency and experience, one afforded by configuration and play, there is no lack of digital artistry. The persistence of IFs and Multi-User Discourses (MUDs)[9]—a form that has directly influenced the development of online multiplayer games—and the now culturally dominant form of video games would attest to this. Theorists have effectively cleared a ground for such works under the rubric of digital art and culture. Furthermore, in order to set their field apart from traditional literary and narrative theory, some theorists of games and game culture have proposed a discipline of ludology (from the Latin *ludus,* for "game") to describe the study of "games and play activities" (Frasca 2002).

Games studies, under any name, is a significant development and has proven crucial in articulating how games, though they contain narrative elements, are not narratives per se and how games and narratives ultimately yield different kinds of experience. Ludology is problematic, however, whenever it falls prey to a needless insistence on a mutually exclusive approach: either a video game is read and interpreted as a text (which is the wrong way according to the ludologist), or it is treated as a rule-based simulation (which is the right way according to the ludologist). Such a view leads to a circular polemic that fails to acknowledge the role of narrative in both shaping game structure and motivating game play; more broadly, it fails to consider how creative works can make use of narration *and* interaction, representation *and* simulation, reading *and* play. In any case critical efforts to better define interactive or gaming environments in digital media have had the obvious effect of helping us to understand what other forms of digital narrative, such as network fictions, are not.

Network fictions maintain the distinction of reader and writer, even if the notion of the "writer" gives way to a creative consciousness that is often plural and collaborative. But beyond that, they welcome the interpretive role of reader as audience, viewer, and critic. Early hypertext theory valorized a mode of reading whereby the reader became something *more* or something *other* than a reader, and in doing so, it set up a misleading opposition that valued the active (or interactive) reader over the supposedly passive one. Rhetorics of active, empowered, and even liberated reading suffused early hypertext discourse, often only to be confounded, from the very beginning (as was the case with Joyce's *afternoon*), by a closer engagement with actual texts. At the same time, many critics who undertook empirical readings produced readings of digital technology instead of digital literature. That is, much hypertext criticism, even when it involved a particular work, was invested in constructing a metacritical model in an attempt to determine the relationship of hypertext technology to textual comprehension in general—a necessary endeavor albeit one that contributed little to an aesthetic understanding of individual works.

The ability of digital literature to encourage strategies of interpretation, if foreshortened in practice, is by no means ignored by theorists. One of the variables of Aarseth's cybertextual typology is the "user function," which includes an array of interpretative, explorative, configurative, and programmatic practices available to the user. The model makes clear that the "interpretive function" is not just one of several possible functions along a continuum of interactivity; it is in fact obligatory and the only function that is present in all texts (1997, 64). Aarseth describes his schema of user functions as "a cybernetic feedback loop between the text and the user, with information flowing from text to user (through the interpretive function) and back again (through one of the other functions)" (65). In this regard, at least, Aarseth's machinic model of reading makes some provision for the psychological complexity of reading literature, even though it does not have a strong investment in it; this simply means that cybertext theory and literary theory are not as rigidly opposed as some critics suggest. For example, David Miall (2004) overemphasizes cybertext's antithetical agenda but nonetheless rightly observes that "[t]he difficulty in understanding hyperfiction lies in the additional complications that the digital medium places on the work of interpretation." Network fictions can thus be characterized as narratives that are designed to be read, a proposition perhaps less obvious than it at first sounds in a media ecology where exploration, configuration, and programming are familiar practice.

Network fictions are also designed to be reread. Readers become acutely (and, for the uninitiated, perhaps uncomfortably) aware of the need to recombine narrative elements in order for the work to emerge and cohere. They are encouraged to consider the dynamics of repetition as a result. Such awareness reciprocates: among the network narratives readers encounter, both online and off, many share a preoccupation with repetition on an aesthetic, thematic, and formal level. Whether that repetition manifests itself formally or linguistically, as recursion, reflexivity, or refrain, the texts dramatize the various forms of narrative loops and spirals in concert with the repetition of nodes at the level of the interface. This study grows out of the foundational claim that the material foregrounding of repetition in network texts forces each work into a new dialogue with repetition in aesthetic and narratological terms. In turn, network fictions recast concepts that have long informed the composition and reception of narrative fiction but that take on markedly different meanings in digital environments, concepts such as orientation, immersion, excess, and mobility.

Overview

The chapters of this book cover three general areas: (1) critical theory that returns to print-based narratology in light of digital literature; (2) network fictions from the first wave of digital literature published as stand-alone Storyspace applications; and (3) second-wave network fictions published on the World Wide Web. The discussions of individual works each focus on the interplay of the material, formal, and semantic elements of network narrative—an interplay that is framed distinctly by the dynamics of repetition. A focus on this interplay of network textuality furthermore sets the stage for a more specific treatment of issues that have shaped the discourse on digital literature since its popular inception in the late 1980s and early 1990s: orientation (chapter 3), immersion vs. interactivity (chapter 4), excess vs. selectivity and restraint (chapter 5), and mobility—or "processuality" (chapter 6). While the primary concerns of this study are aesthetic and narratological, other theoretical approaches inflect the discussions, such as cybertext theory, systems theory, postfeminist theory, and poststructuralist and deconstructionist theory (when dissociated from early hypertext theory that claimed to literalize, embody, or fulfill it). Rather than formulate and apply a single framework—a "theory of network fiction"—the chapters tend to engage with the theoretical and aesthetic discourses that surface in the individual works.

The first two chapters are theoretically based and organized around the familiar coordinates of time and space. Chapter 1, "The Time and Time Again of Network Fiction," focuses on the temporal dynamics of repetition in narrative and considers the reader's practice of repetition and recombination as integral to (hyper)textual comprehension. Chapter 2, "Network Vistas: Folding the Cognitive Map," focuses on the spatial construction of a network text and the role of repetition in facilitating the reader's engagement with hypertextual structure. It proposes a mode of textual orientation and comprehension that moves beyond the practice of *mapping* the structure of a text to achieve a sense of global comprehension in the mode of a fixed cartography.

The section on first-wave digital literature consists of two works composed as Storyspace fictions. Chapter 3 returns to a lesser-known work of one of the better-known writers of digital literature, Joyce's *Twilight, a Symphony* (1997). "Returning in Twilight" begins by tracing the thematic returns and refrains that dominate the text, such as the "resurrection" of the pianist Glenn Gould and the Goldberg Variations. Gould's music is present in various ways in the narrative and allows "theme and variation" to emerge as both a formal and a contextual device, as repetitions in network narratives can be said to enact subtle variations on an original melody. Building on and in some ways diverging from Deleuze and Guattari's notion of the refrain (or *ritournelle*), the chapter develops the idea of repetition as orientation albeit in a virtual territory.

A classical work of digital literature that perhaps did more than any other to foreground the dynamics of repetition in network environments, Stuart Moulthrop's *Victory Garden* (1991) is the subject of chapter 4, "Tending the Garden Plot." A perennial critic of what he calls the "military infotainment complex" (2003a) in corporate America, Moulthrop often investigates how new writing technologies play with and against this complex. Published in the years following the first Gulf War in 1991 and before the second war in 2003, *Victory Garden* occupies a curious place as both epilogue and prologue, a response to the spectacle of the first war and an ominous anticipation of the second. The chapter explains how this flagship work of digital literature complicates but does not necessarily discourage the sense of immersion in an interactive text.

Chapters 5 and 6 constitute the section on "second-wave" works produced for the World Wide Web, which profoundly changed the face of digital literature, a change that was not an entirely positive one. From a market perspective one might say that the best thing about the Web is that anyone can publish, and that the worst thing about the Web is that anyone can publish. With regard to creating narrative fiction, a seemingly boundless form with a seemingly unlimited potential for digitally mediated connectivity certainly posed an aesthetic problem—if not a practical one—for artists. Chapter 5, "Fluid or Overflowing," considers how Web-based network fictions confront the problems and politics of excess. The chapter is structured as a comparative analysis of William Gillespie, Frank Marquardt, Scott Rettberg, and Dirk Stratton's *The Unknown* (1998–2001), which both epitomizes and celebrates excess, and Linda Carroli and Josephine Wilson's **water writes always in *plural* (1998), which constitutes an exercise in selectivity and restraint.

As underscored by both *The Unknown* and **water writes always in *plural,* the computer medium offers not simply new tools but also new methodologies for creative composition—and, indeed, collaborative composition. Both texts, moreover, reveal an equal investment in the process of making and what is ultimately made. But when shifting the emphasis from composition back to reception, it is clear that the quality of material mobility makes network narratives "processual" in yet another way. The page moves before the reader and the reader moves the page in ways not possible in the medium of print. Chapter 6, "Mythology Proceeding," appropriates the theoretical framework of Joseph Tabbi (2003) and Hanjo Berressem (2002) in reading Judd Morrissey's *The Jew's Daughter* (2000) as a "processual page," a phrase that refers not only to the movement of a digital text onscreen but also to the page in the process of migrating from one medium to another (and back again). Itself a succession of rereadings, or rather reinterpretations, of the narrative situation, chapter 6 considers what a moving page might mean for the process of literary criticism.

As in any literary study that must strike a balance between the number of texts that illustrate a concept and the scope of those individual illustrations, choosing which texts to include and exclude is invariably a challenge.

The texts that are included here were not necessarily chosen for their position or popularity in the field of digital literature or, for that matter, in the scope of contemporary literature writ large, and forthright aesthetic judgments are absent. Nonetheless, after Barthes, just as everything that is noted in the realm of discourse is by definition notable, all of the works are indeed notable—each demonstrating remarkable innovation in what can be called the technology of narrative. Furthermore, even though I adopt the partition of a first and second wave of digital literature, the arrangement of texts in this compressed selection by no means constitutes an evolution of digital fiction. In a sense, their relative newness still does not afford us the luxury of "placing" them at all. In the context of network environments that privilege *connection* over *location,* this perhaps becomes much less of a concern. At the very least, we know that all writing on the screen is evanescent, which is both its pathos and its power.

I
The Time and Time Again
of Network Fiction

Suppose at this point your reader, before going on, has to reread one part of
what comes before, I ask. No one asks why. There are reasons.
—Michael Joyce, *Othermindedness*

In a fundamental sense repetition in art is inevitable, since all representation
relies on repetition. In Plato's terms all art is already the repetition of a repetition, since reality itself, as we apprehend it, is nothing more than an expression of ideal forms. But in Western culture repetition is "conventionally con-
demned as parasitic, threatening and negative" (Connor 1988, 3). Referring to
the culturally commonplace understanding, Brian Dillon (2004) writes that
"there is nothing so predictable, so tiresomely unwelcome, as the ideal copy:
it is a marker of a merely traditional, conventional desire for consistency, a
loyalty to a past that, repetition assures us, has never really gone away. Repetition, as some of our most lingering modern cultural beliefs inform us, is
nothing but a serial disorder: a compulsion equally tragic and pathologi-
cal." These "lingering" beliefs have given way, however, to other conceptions
of repetition that resonate more with a postmodern society and a postmodernist literature. In fact, repetition has come to be seen by some as an operation that provides a key—arguably the key—to artistic creativity. In his study
of Samuel Beckett and literary forms of repetition Steven Connor (1988, 2)
notes that "in painting, writing and film, the modernist imperative to 'make
it new' has been superseded by a desire to recirculate the old or the already
known, if only in the attempt to subvert the grounds of familiar knowledge."
As Connor writes, we do not have to see the movement, as Jameson or Baudrillard might, as the "emptying of life or urgency from cultural activity" but
rather as an exploration of "the problematic interrelationship that exists between originality and repetition" (2–3). In turn, repetition becomes not only
essential to the concept of originality but also a potentially affirmative concept in its own right.

The notion of repetition as constructive and even affirmative is evident
in a thread of contemporary philosophy and theory emerging in the latter

half of the twentieth century. Derrida (1978) notes that repetition simultaneously validates an original and calls it into question. That is, the common understanding of repetition as dependent on something that precedes or preexists it informs the Platonic model of original and copy; at the same time, an original is only understood as such after it repeats in some way. The dependence of a copy on its original thus reciprocates.

Derrida's discussion of repetition arises from his broader critique of what he calls *logocentricism,* the privileging of speech (that which implies presence) over writing (that which implies absence). Religious texts that are understood to represent sacred speech underscore the problems inherent in granting such privilege, for they derive force through reiterations made possible by writing. Even though the repetition, in principle, "aims to cut out every vestige of difference between itself and the original," an origin or center is always displaced (Connor 1988, 4). As Derrida writes, "The first book, the mythic book, the eve prior to all repetition, has lived on the deception that the center was sheltered from play" (1978, 296). The deconstructionist critique indulges in the play of origins. With regard to the binary of speech/writing, it demonstrates how writing itself is more than simply the transcription of thought and speech: writing can in fact give rise to the act of thinking or speaking. The point, however, is not simply to reverse the binary; the significance of the critique lies in the play that emerges through the continual redefinition of its elements.

Like Derrida, Deleuze (1994) speaks of a dual logic of repetition and begins his analysis by delimiting its two forms, which he calls "bare" and "masked": "The first repetition is repetition of the Same, explained by the identity of the concept or representation; the second includes difference, and includes itself in the alterity of the Idea. . . . One is negative, occurring by default in the concept; the other affirmative, occurring by excess in the Idea. . . . One is static the other dynamic. . . . One is a 'bare' repetition, the other a covered repetition, which forms itself in covering itself, in masking and disguising itself" (24). Bare or mechanical repetition acknowledges the force of repetition in maintaining traditional understandings of essence and identity. We perceive difference, in this view, not as an autonomous function but always against a preexisting or preestablished similitude, a variation of identity for instance. Locating difference serves only to reinstate the sense of the original: "Even when difference takes the form of negativity or contradiction, the originating concept still controls and delimits the forms of contradiction" (Connor 1988, 5). Mimesis governs this mode of repetition. In providing obedient copies or representations, it resists distortion or additions. It is a Platonic form of reproduction. By contrast, masked or disguised repetition derives force by "knowingly" imparting difference.[1] For Deleuze, masked repetition enables a critique of the dominant philosophy of representation in Western metaphysics, given that it elevates difference above identity, multiplicity over unity, and diversity over resemblance. As Ian Buchanan (2000, 188) describes it, "The difference between repetition and mere duplication (non-genuine repetition) is this: in practice, the latter induces conformity, while the former institutes difference." Thus, Deleuze suggests that in our traditional understanding of repetition, false objects arise through a false form of repetition.

Simply privileging masked over bare repetition would do little more than reverse the terms of a binary, but Deleuze further develops the concept of *complex repetition*, which can exist independent of and external to the Platonic mode of reproduction. He acknowledges that pure repetition is impossible: even with "the most mechanical, the most stereotypical [bare] repetitions, inside and outside ourselves, we endlessly extract from them little differences, variations and modifications" (1994, ix), an observation shared by Derrida, who writes, "Pure repetition, were it to change neither thing nor sign, carries with it an unlimited power of perversion and subversion" (1978, 296).[2] Conversely, Deleuze's disguised or masked repetition, by perpetually displacing difference, can bring back into view, or "restore," bare repetitions (1994, ix). Such restoration occurs when a thing reminds us of— or "repeats"—something else that is quite unlike that thing but strangely or opaquely resembles it. It comes alive involuntarily, through a process of forgetting or dreaming. J. Hillis Miller (1982, 8) associates this form of repetition with what he (after Proust) calls "involuntary memory." Unlike the visible similitude apparent in the intentional movements of bare repetition, two visibly dissimilar things echo one another, creating an image that carries its meaning not in one thing or the other but in some imagined associative space in between them. For Deleuze there exists no adequate system or category of representation in Western metaphysics to process these transformations.[3]

Derrida and Deleuze both draw on Nietzsche's doctrine of "eternal recurrence" to articulate their models. In *Thus Spoke Zarathustra* (1883–92) Nietzsche, whose own critique of Western metaphysics and Christian teleology anticipates Derrida's, envisioned a world in which there were a finite number of events, ideas, and things, both cosmic and mundane, which played themselves out over time and then repeated. He saw the "entire flux of life [as] a causal nexus" (Higgins 1988, 144). Such a world holds no promise of infinite novelty and has no ultimate goal. The prospect of a cosmic life cycle both enthralled and appalled Nietzsche, especially given the realization that all human suffering was destined toward repetition, not resolution. Critics disagree not only on the meaning of Nietzsche's doctrine but also on its development.[4] But many agree that the idea stands as one of the most enigmatic in Nietzsche's philosophy, an idea given voice by his equally enigmatic prophet-protagonist, Zarathustra. Zarathustra's role is mainly to set the stage for the *Übermensch*, or Overman, who is less the object of a teleological "coming" than he is the subject of human striving, a placeholder for earthly aspiration.[5] Zarathustra, nonetheless, is given the task of articulating the idea of "eternal recurrence": "Have you ever said Yes to a single joy? O my friends, then you said Yes too to *all* woe. All things are entangled, ensnared and enamored; if ever you wanted one thing twice, if ever you said, 'You please me, happiness! Abide, Moment!' then you wanted *all* back. All anew, all eternally, all entangled, ensnared, enamored oh, then you loved the world. Eternal ones, love it eternally and evermore; and to woe too, you say: go! but return! *For all joys want eternity*" (Nietzsche 1883–92/1995, 323). Confronted with the prospect of a moment that has already been—literally, at a gateway called "Moment" (158)—Zarathustra responds by wanting more moments. He preaches a form of positive fatalism: live each moment as if you were forced to relive it for eternity.

The librarian of Jorge Luis Borges's short fiction "The Library of Babel" (1941) exhibits an analogous recognition of, and reaction to, the idea of eternal recurrence: "If an eternal traveller were to cross [the library] in any direction, after centuries he would see that the same volumes were repeated in the same disorder (which, thus repeated, would be an order: the Order). My solitude is gladdened by this elegant hope" (1964, 66). Indeed, Nietzsche's ideas encourage the renegotiation of repetition and difference that underscores the deconstructionist and poststructuralist critique—a critique that considers these concepts in more complex and potentially more affirmative ways. But such renegotiation goes beyond contemporary philosophy. The philosophical and theoretical explorations of the dynamics of repetition go hand in hand with literary and artistic ones.

Repetition and Narrative

Repetition plays an overt role in music and poetry, but it inhabits narrative texts in equally significant if less explicit ways. Narratives have exhibited a long-standing preoccupation with repetition. Shlomith Rimmon-Kenan, for example, cites Cervantes' parody of what narratologists call "singulative logic," specifically, the case of telling *n* times what happened *n* times. In *Don Quixote* Sancho tells the story of a fisherman who had to transport three hundred goats across a river in a boat that could only fit one. As he proceeds to tell of the three hundred trips one at a time, Quixote interrupts: "Take it that they are all across . . . and do not go on coming and going like that, or you will never get them all over in a year" (cited in Rimmon-Kenan 1983, 57).

Only more recently, however, from the early half of the twentieth century to the latter, from James Joyce and Gertrude Stein to Lewis Carroll, Alain Robbe-Grillet, Beckett, and Borges, repetition emerges as a powerful theme and technique in its own right.[6] The aesthetics of repetition, in turn, has received progressively more critical attention. With foundational work in what has come to be known as the field of narratology, Gérard Genette (1972, 1983) and Rimmon-Kenan (1983) systematized forms of narrative repetition constituted by the relations between a story and its expression as discourse. In her study of "ideological novels," or *roman à these,* Susan Rubin Suleiman (1983) broadens the emphasis on repetition-relations arising between story and discourse to consider repetitions that are present either on the level of the story or the level of the discourse alone.[7] An earlier essay by Rimmon-Kenan, "The Paradoxical Status of Repetition" (1980), deals with repetition and difference. It considers three paradoxes that are conspicuously indebted to the philosophical and psychoanalytic ideas put into circulation by Deleuze and Derrida, Freud and Lacan:

Paradox 1: Repetition is present everywhere and nowhere.
Paradox 2: Constructive repetition emphasizes difference, destructive repetition emphasizes sameness.
Paradox 3: The first time is already a repetition, and repetition is already the very first time. (Rimmon-Kenan 1980, 151–55)

Literary critics have dealt directly with repetition and aesthetics. In addition to Connor (1988), Bruce Kawin (1972) looks at the aesthetics of repetition in twentieth-century literature and film; J. Hillis Miller (1982) directs his study of repetition at seven English novels, ranging from Joseph Conrad to Virginia Woolf; and Peter Brooks (1984) draws on the dynamics of repetition to construct a model of narrative desire. Repetition, in the broadest sense, is responsible for the rhythms and patterns that exist both within and between works of literature.

Changing ideas about repetition accompanied changing ideas about origins, originals, and originality. In one of the boldest—albeit one of the most often misunderstood—articulations of these changes, John Barth responds in "The Literature of Exhaustion" (1967) to a perceived crisis of originality. Barth recognizes the challenge of creating original works of literature as twofold—both formal and thematic. Even though his discussion deals specifically with the novel, Barth addresses this twofold challenge in a way that applies to literature in general. First, he concedes that literary forms "certainly have histories and historical contingencies, and it may well be that the novel's time as a major art form is up, as the 'times' of classical tragedy, grand opera, or the sonnet sequence came to be" (Barth 1967/1982, 11); and earlier he includes both "certain forms and certain possibilities" in his discussion of exhaustion and "used-upness" (1). Here he appears to refer not only to the possibility of new forms but also to the possibility of saying something new or original in any literary medium at a time when such an achievement seems more and more difficult. Todd Gitlin writes of the "postmodernist" sensibility: "There is a premium on copies, everything has been done" (1989, 102). Similarly, Fredric Jameson writes, "There is [a] sense in which the writers and the artists of the present day will no longer be able to invent new styles and worlds—they've already been invented; only a limited number of combinations are possible; the most unique ones have been thought of already" (1983, 115). It would seem that Barth's 1967 essay speaks to the same sense of exhaustion. In his essay "The Literature of Replenishment" (1982), however, he qualifies his comments dramatically and claims that his first essay has been "much misread": "The simple burden of my essay was that the forms and modes of art live in human history and are therefore subject to used-upness; . . . artistic conventions are liable to be retired, subverted, transcended, transformed, or even deployed against themselves to generate new and lively work" (38). Barth does not believe that the only choice for contemporary writers is "parody and travesty of our great predecessors," and he says "at once and plainly . . . that literature can never be exhausted—its 'meaning' residing as it does in its transactions with individual readers over time, space, and language" (38). In the second essay he clearly identifies the "effective exhaustion" as the "aesthetic of high modernism": "In 1966/67 we scarcely had the term *postmodernism* in its current literary critical usage . . . but a number of us were well into the working out, not of the next best thing after modernism, but of the *best next* thing: what is gropingly now called postmodernist fiction; what I hope might also be thought of one day as a literature of replenishment" (39). The "literature of exhaustion" (the concept) amounts to Barth's attempt to articulate and perhaps name the emergent body of work that Raymond Federman (1975), several years later in an eponymous manifesto, would call surfiction (from *surreal* and *fiction*) and Brian McHale (1987), in his comprehensive study of works that share a penchant for ontological uncertainty, would reluctantly—albeit by that time more familiarly—call postmodernist fiction.

Barth's "Literature of Exhaustion" is thus meant to demonstrate the impossibility of exhausting literature. He shows how writers of this school, Borges, Nabokov, Calvino, and Barth himself among the progenitors, succeed in deploying conventions against themselves, using the notion of exhausted possibility paradoxically as a point of departure, as a theme with which to generate more literature.[8] To illustrate this point of departure, Barth cites Borges's "Pierre Menard, Author of the *Quixote*," a story in which "the hero, an utterly sophisticated turn of the century French Symbolist, by an astounding effort of imagination, produces—not *copies* or *imitates*, mind, but *composes*—several chapters of Cervantes' novel" (Barth 1967/1982, 6). At one point the narrator compares Menard's *Quixote* with that of Cervantes:

> It is a revelation to compare [them]. The latter, for instance, wrote (Part One Chapter Nine):
> ... *truth, whose mother is history, rival of time, depository of deeds, witness of the past, exemplar and advisor to the present, the future's counselor.*
> Written in the seventeenth century, written by the "lay genius" Cervantes, this enumeration is a mere rhetorical praise of history. Menard, on the other hand, writes:
> ... *truth, whose mother is history, rival of time, depository of deeds, witness of the past, exemplar and advisor to the present, the future's counselor.*
> History, the *mother* of truth: the idea is astounding. Menard, a contemporary of William James, does not define history as an inquiry into reality but as its origin. (Borges 1993, 36)[9]

According to Barth, Borges uses the perceived crisis of originality against itself; that is, he "writes a remarkable and original work of literature, the implicit theme of which is the difficulty, perhaps the unneccessity, of writing original works of literature" (Barth 1967/1982, 8).

For Barth this perceived sense of exhaustion is "by no means necessarily a cause for despair," for the solution is already implicit in the problem (1967/1982, 1). Significantly, his reaction differs from that of early hypertext theorists such as George Landow and J. David Bolter, who see an artistic preoccupation with originality as symptomatic of the impending demise of a literature exhausted by the conventions of print. Such theorists have positioned digital literature as a response to much of the "exhausted" print literature that precedes it. Not only does this model rely on some form of technological determinism (in which conceptual complexity is simply a call for

a more advanced medium), but it also suggests that the works said to anticipate hypertext are somehow deficient in their own right.

Barth's writing on the implications of medial innovation for literature is
unique in that it spans formal and medial innovations that predate and postdate digital literature, with "The Literature of Exhaustion" and "The Literature of Replenishment," followed by "The State of the Art" (1996), which
responds directly to the convergence of digital technology and narrative fiction, as well as his own short fiction "Click" (1997), a parody of hypertextual
writing. (Barth's critique of electronic text is expanded—if not advanced—
in his most recent print novel, *Coming Soon!!!*, which juxtaposes two writers,
one an ageing novelist trying to write his swansong book, the other an up-
and-coming tech-savvy MFA student who is set on releasing his debut novel
onscreen as a hypertext.) It is evident from the first essay in 1967 that Barth
was raising questions about materiality, a term that is perhaps best understood in a nontechnical but lucid description as "the stuff texts are made of."[10]
He states that his literature of exhaustion has little to do with the fate of the
novel per se. To him, whether or not the novel "expires or persists seems immaterial," for he is more concerned with the cultural fact (the "historical datum") this sense of exhaustion or limitation creates (1967/1982, 11). Despite
his "immaterial" stance on the novel as form, Barth makes a significant statement about materiality in the opening of the 1967 essay. Observing the shift
from conceptual experimentation in literature to medial experimentation, he
faults the latter, what he then called "intermedia happenings," for their tendency to lack "expertise and artistry" (1–2). In turn he opens a debate on aesthetics, negotiating a division between gimmickry and artistry in both his
criticism and his own art, between "things worth remarking . . . and things
worth doing" (3). Although Barth sees the virtue—or rather the necessity—
of being "technically up to date," such "intermedia" literary experiments fall,
at least implicitly, under his category of gimmicks.

Repetition and Networks

More often out of necessity than choice, many of the critics and theorists
who have provided the foundation for an understanding of repetition in narrative texts deal in an exclusively print textuality, where textual elements are
fixed both by the material page and by the material dimensions of the book
as a whole. Even for those whose work coincides with the ascendancy of personal computing, the computer was still seen as nothing more than an en-
hanced calculator. For example, in discussing the complexity that arises in
identifying relational chains of textual redundancies, and conceivably assign-

ing weights to the relations, Suleiman remarks that "[a]t that point the use of a computer would become indispensable" (1983, 178). She thus recognizes the computer as an aid in the reception and interpretation of narrative fiction but not as an innovative tool for composition.[11] Although the notion of computers as *literary machines*, after Theodor Nelson (1981), is still by no means common in the arts and humanities, the past decade has seen the proliferation of narrative fiction in dynamic, network environments. The aesthetic and narratological discussion of repetition that has been motivated by these critics needs to be extended in turn.

In digital networks repetition-relations are manifest at the material level of the text in three closely related ways. First, network narratives rely on reiteration for their iteration; that is, *rereading* can no longer be thought of as an epiphenomenon of *reading* in a network text since the rereading of textual elements, via the recycling of nodes, is fundamental to (hyper)textual comprehension. Furthermore, although many print narratives can claim to have no definitive ending at the level of discourse, network narratives make the promise of return at the material level. Finally, the reader of a network narrative initiates iterations and recursions at the level of computer code, which involves a material engagement with the properties of a literary text that can be evoked by but not manifested in book form.

In *Language of New Media* (2001) Lev Manovich asks, "Can the loop be a new narrative form appropriate for the computer age? It is relevant to recall that the loop gave birth not only to cinema but also to computer programming. Programming involves altering the linear flow of data through control structures, such as 'if/then' and 'repeat/while'; the loop is the most elementary of these control structures" (317). To be sure, the movements of network narratives depend, elementally, on repeating loops, an observation that encourages the application of cybernetic theory to digital texts. Cybernetics invokes the loop, or more complex looping structures, to study systems in which a network defines the flow of information. As a theory of the control of regulatory feedback, cybernetics is further relevant in that it is, by definition, a theory of reflexivity—a formative concept in both the thematic and formal makeup of digital fiction. The notion of the loop as an expressive form in digital art is thus not only an appropriate but also a definitive distinction to make. In fact, if the drive to make it *renew* has superseded the modernist desire to "make it new," then one can add to that an ethos apparent in digital art to "make it loop."

At the same time, it is necessary to avoid blurring ideological manifesto with formal innovation. Walter Benjamin (1968, 237) notes that the "history of every art form shows critical epochs in which a certain art form aspires to effects which could be fully obtained only with a changed technical standard, that is to say, in a new art form." And it is logical to assume that a body of work called "hypertext fiction" would not exist without the advent of hypertext technology. Nevertheless, it is not possible to reduce all literary innovation to an aspiration of formal or medial change. As poet John Cayley (2005) writes, "New tools do not necessarily imply new forms, let alone new rhetoric."[12] Early theorists of digital textuality were hampered by this very reduction. As Mireille Rosello (1994) writes, it is "as if hypertext had a life of its own, as if our commentaries were somewhat outside reality, as if the discourse we produce about hypertext had no power to shape its future" (127).

Technological innovation does not overwrite—does not exclusively determine—any and all change in the flux of media ecology. Rather, technology and ideology exert a reciprocal influence, each continually reinventing the other. Manovich's discussion of a "*new* narrative form" errs in attending only to the material instantiation of the narrative loop, treating it as the point from which ideological or artistic innovation can follow. Despite the constraints of print (and film) that limited their material manifestation in narrative, loops have long been used to structure narrative discourse, from classical fictions (such as *1001 Arabian Nights* and Homer's *Odyssey,* the archetypal narrative return of Western literature) to popular films of today (such as *Groundhog Day* [1993] and *Memento* [2000]).

Attempts to assert the "newness" of art forms—forms that require new ways of reading and writing—often result in circular formulations or a technological determinism that makes a new medium result in a new artistic form or genre by default. According to Aarseth, "[h]ypertext is certainly a new way of writing (with active links)," but, he asks, "is it truly a new way of reading? And is all that jumping around the same as creating a new text?" (1997, 78). In these terms it is difficult to see how *reading with active links* would not in itself point to a new way of reading if the criteria for "newness" are to be equivalent for writers and readers. After all, both use digitally mediated hyperlinks, which are absent in print texts no matter how far we stretch the notion of "hypertextuality." It is Aarseth's own cybertextual framework that allows him to assign different criteria to the composition and reception of the text: cybertext creates a template based on textual function that takes precedence over how these functions manifest in particular media. The medium, in this sense, is "immaterial," and the way to read a hypertext document may in theory be identical to the way one reads a text in print if their typological functions are the same.

Cybertext's typological model is valuable not only for its categorical breadth and precision but also in breaking down the binary values associated with digital versus print text: the notion that print is fixed and stable, whereas hypertext is fluid and dynamic. Too much is made of the print/digital binary when, from a semiotic point of view, too little changes when we read words on the screen rather than the printed page. Using *Beowulf* and Wordsworth's *Prelude* as examples, Matthew Kirschenbaum (2001) shows that the opposition of the "radical mutability" of the digital text and the "orderly durability" of print is "patently false, yet has become a truism in the nascent field of electronic textual theory." Kirschenbaum takes issue with Marie-Laure Ryan's list of oppositions describing print vs. electronic textuality (1999, 101–2) and Michael Joyce's (1995) catchphrase, "print stays itself, electronic text replaces itself." Among Ryan's pairings of print/digital are, respectively, durable/ephemeral, centered structure/decentered structure, unity/diversity, solidity/fluidity, and work/play. For Kirschenbaum, Ryan's extended opposition elides more pressing critical-historical questions of "digital preservation": "[In] the long run we do electronic fiction and our critical understanding of electronic textuality no favors by romanticizing the medium through a dated discourse of play that is really only screen deep" (2001). Cayley (2004) puts forth a similar view. On the generation of digital letters from the same "atoms" as digital graphics, he finds that "apart from what is perhaps yet another opportunity for graphic art to patronise applied grammatology," there is actually no great significance or affect arising from the translation from ink to pixel. He instead shifts focus to the semantic, stylistic, and potentially affective quality of the text by asking, "[D]o constraints that are imposed on the manipulation of pixels in order that they produce the outlines of letters tell us anything about those letters or the words which they, in turn, compose?"

The foundation of print does appear solid and enduring, but only when a culture that has naturalized the conventions of print peers through a narrow historical lens. If there is an opposition worth upholding, it rests with the book and the computer as *environments* that accommodate literary structures. Much separates books and computers, in a strictly technological sense, when we refer to their media properties. But as environments for reading and writing literature, the conventions we associate with the two media tend to migrate and, to use Bolter and Grusin's (2000) broad but lucid phrase, *remediate* one another. Bruce Clarke (2003) defines *environments* in systems theoretical terms as "the unmarked spaces upon which systems inscribe their distinctions." Most systems theorists agree that a literary narrative can be thought of as only part of a system, namely the social and cognitive system that processes the literary work. But the notion of an element in a unilateral "space" that is set apart—made *distinct*—from other marked or unmarked elements in that space can contribute to an understanding of network textuality.

This conception of a network environment further moves beyond the poststructuralist preoccupation with transcending textual borders. Poststructuralists conceive of the text (any text) as a dispersed and borderless network, a conception that was force-fed into hypertext discourse early on as an attempt to describe the material properties of hypertext structures. The conflation of material structures of a medium with linguistic structures that are common to all writing resulted in a practice of "literalization," whereby hypertext technology was portrayed as theory-in-practice and a vision fulfilled. The deconstructionist and poststructuralist critique, invested in the inherent instability of all language, did not and does not need a new medium to realize or literalize it.[13] In a digital text, a hypertext, or a network text (material) boundaries are not erased but rather are continually maintained through a process of selection and filtering. In terms of networked literary structures, the border between a work and its environment is renegotiated whenever a link is added to a node that previously did not constitute part of its structure; in turn, when links are added between nodes already present in the structure of the literary work, its internal boundaries are redefined and made more complex. The "node" thus functions as a semiautonomous, self-contained, bibliographical unit.[14]

As N. Katherine Hayles (2002a) points out, in addition to a comprehensive typographical approach, there is a pronounced need for a "media-specific analysis" that attends to how a particular medium not only exploits the qualities peculiar to it but also dramatizes and thematizes those qualities in the process. A focus on materiality, furthermore, resonates with modes of print-based textual and bibliographical criticism that attend to pragmatic problems such as access, obsolescence, and compatibility, which take on a pronounced urgency in terms of computer hardware and software. A media-specific analysis and a cybertextual analysis are not mutually exclusive. After cybertext theory has aided in parsing the semiotic components of a text, it is still necessary to consider what individual texts "have done with the variables they choose to work with in exploring the nuances, complexities, and pleasures of a given configuration" (Hayles 2001).

For example, cybertext theory posits seven "traversal functions," the variables responsible for making textual signs present to the reader. The presence of the capacity for "Linking" is one traversal function in the typology. Another is the "User function," which describes texts as (1) interpretive; (2) explorative (users must choose what paths to follow); (3) configurative (the user can choose or create the signs that appear in the text); or (4) textonic (the user can change the text and/or its traversal functions by adding writing and/or programming) (Aarseth 1997, 64). Network fiction employs linking, and it is possible to say that its capacity for linking is what makes it explorative. With regard to the text's poetical function, the significance lies in the role that linking plays in not only the explorative but also the interpretive mode. In its emphasis on the machinic functioning of the text, cybertext theory stops short of identifying the aesthetic implications of an exchange across or between functions. With regard to narrative poetics in particular, the dynamics of repetition underscore the ways in which active links must be considered as integral not only to the technological and material constitution of the text but to its formal and semantic constitution as well.

Network fictions radically foreground repetition. Recursion, reflexivity, and refrain are all specific modes of repetition that are manifest in literary works. In the context of narrative literature they can be referred to collectively as "narrative returns." Narrative returns in digitally networked environments reanimate aesthetic and narratological conceptions of repetition. Thus, by way of a metacritical feedback loop, digital fiction encourages us to ask many of the same questions about narrative texts in a different context, as must all readers and writers who can no longer take their medium for granted.

Rereading

"Poetry can repeat anything," writes Ursula Le Guin (2002, 104–5), "a stress-pattern, a phoneme, a rhyme, a word, a line, a stanza. Its formality gives it endless liberty to establish rhythmic structure. . . . What is repeatable in narrative prose? . . . Which elements recur, are repeated with variations, to form the rhythms of prose? Those that I am aware of are: Words and phrases. Images. Actions. Moods. Themes." To Le Guin's inventory readers of network texts add the node, a "screenful" of text and/or image, as a reiterative narrative element. In addition to the possible linguistic recurrences of material it contains, a node can recur in its entirety in a network narrative. But what difference does this repetition make? How does the repetition of nodes create a different experience from that which readers get by simply rereading the pages of a text in print?

Nodal repetition produces effects that are similar to those produced by linguistic repetition in print. Two of the most pronounced of these effects are the disruption of temporal frameworks and the signaling of artifice.[15] The relationship of time, narrative, and repetition is an intimate and inalienable one. Temporal progression is a precondition for narrative—"without change,"

McHale reminds us, "there is no possibility for narrative" (1987, 63). But as Rimmon-Kenan writes, time itself "can become measurable only when a repetitive pattern is discerned within it (e.g., the solar year) or imposed upon it by machines constructed to this end (calendar-, clock-, metronome-time). Time 'is,' paradoxically, repetition within irreversible change" (1983, 44). "Like any other aspect of the world," she adds, "the experience of time may be represented in a narrative text . . . [but] time is not only a recurrent theme in a great deal of narrative fiction, it is also a constituent factor of both story and text" (44). Thus, a mutual, or even circular, dependence occurs: repetition mediates (allows us to perceive) time, time mediates narrative, and narrative, because it is a representational form, can both mediate repetition and comment on its mediation. Dillon builds on Rimmon-Kenan's exposition of time, narrative, and repetition. If early twentieth-century formalism and later narratological structuralism instruct readers to identify patterns within (and between) stories, Dillon (2004) notes that the process can work reciprocally; that is, we are attuned to construct stories from the patterns we perceive: "In the simple repetition of a clock's ticking is already the possibility of movement, of a narrative (we hear the actual and meaningless 'tick, tick' as 'tick, tock': a tiny story." In this case repetition mediates a narrative.

Writers have long sought ways to subvert and destabilize time in narrative without abandoning narrative itself. The use of linguistic and poetic repetition offers one such way. For Miller such recurrences can work either "to generate meaning or to inhibit the too easy determination of a meaning based on the linear sequence of a story" (1982, 2). Rimmon-Kenan identifies factors that work against "the irreversibility of text-time" (1983, 45), one of which she describes as "the fact of writing and hence the possibility of re-reading" (137n).[16] We often return to print texts, rereading (along with the contrary practices of skimming, skipping, and jumping ahead) and thus accreting meaning by repeating either parts or wholes. Iser describes the process in similar terms: "When we have finished the text, and read it again . . . we shall tend to establish connections by referring to our awareness of what is to come, and so certain aspects of the text will assume a significance we did not attach to them on a first reading" (1980, 56). Critical (re)reading in print texts is taken for granted as a hermeneutic necessity.

The practice of rereading fiction in print often depends on the notion of a whole: readers can repeat a print text because they can think of it as a discrete object with a beginning and an end. They may reread parts, moreover, in fixed relation to this whole. Network narratives have boundaries and limits, but they do not offer a reliable way to analyze a structural whole: in an obvious sense readers may or may not encounter all of the nodes that exist in the textual database, but less obvious is the fact that even if they do, it is unlikely that all of the possible permutations of the text will be realized. In other words a reader will not move through all of the transitions implicit in the structure of links, which nests rhetorical meanings through continual juxtaposition and recombination. When considering not only meaning in transition—the temporal unfoldings of any narrative—but also the meaning *of* the transition, it becomes clear that the sum of hypertextual parts is greater than its whole. At the same time, a network aesthetic implies neither a modernist lament for the lost whole nor a postmodernist celebration of it. In an interview with Sarah Sloane (2000, 129) Michael Joyce advocates not a disavowal of aesthetic coherence in network fiction but rather a paradigmatic shift in perceiving coherence as something other than a singular organic whole: "In an age like ours which privileges poly-vocality, multiplicity, and constellated knowledge," we might locate such coherence with a shift toward "successive attendings." Through a reader's successive attendings, local unities emerge in addition to—or, in some texts, in lieu of—a singular, organic unity.

Along with the problem of the whole, the idea that network texts insist on being *reread* also requires qualification. When nodes recur (or cycle) on a hypertextual path, a reader does not necessarily decide to "reread" material; rather, the text invites the reader to do so. The (re)cycling of a node is a function of its position subsequent to its former occurrence—it is, simply stated, the way the text goes. Rereading can no longer be thought of as an epiphenomenon of reading in this context, for it becomes fundamental to (hyper)textual comprehension. The notion of prerogative justifies this claim. In a print text it is common to think of rereading as a reader's prerogative, whereas repetition remains the (design) prerogative of the writer, but the distinction breaks down in network narrative.[17] The reader has a hand in the repetition of narrative elements, for she or he can choose to return to a certain node (by backtracking or possibly by using a search function). Narrative returns are often written into the network structure, with a multiplicity of inbound links for any one node.

Network narratives perform their reiterations in two distinct ways: (1) reading the same node in new surroundings—a new "semantic neighborhood" —can endow it with new meaning; and (2) a reader may return to a node much later on and find some of its elements foregrounded by information accumulated since first reading it, a process that can be said to augment the way memory works when reading a work of print. That is, our engagement with the interface can unexpectedly bring information back into consciousness and, unlike the first scenario, its context is recast in a strictly cognitive sense. Both scenarios demonstrate the network's capacity to generate new meaning through a recombination of elements already read.

Bill Bly's *We Descend* (1997) provides an example of elemental foregrounding characteristic of the second scenario.[18] Modeled as an archive, the text contains the writings "pertaining to Egderus Scriptor," a scribe at an isolated Mountain House. Egderus, who lives in the "distant future," has collected documents written by several people regarding some mysteries of the place, which include the unsolved murder of one of the Brothers in the rocky hills surrounding the Mountain House—an event that appears to have precedents secreted away by the senior Brothers. One of the accounts in the archive comes from Aric, a guard stationed at the Mountain House. Aric tells of his furtive pursuit of the Good Doctor, who arouses suspicions by wandering around the hills when all of the other inferior Brothers are confined to the immediate House grounds. Another guard, Gig, accompanies Aric in the pursuit. At one point Gig, whose own behavior has grown wild and erratic after rumors that he witnessed one of the murders, fearlessly and recklessly follows the Good Doctor as he disappears into a crevasse of rock. As Aric recalls:

> Now I was in a spot. I knew I could not follow him. Just the smell of the place! My legs simply would not carry me further into that dark rock. So I shouted that I was going back to the House to take care of the shift change; he could return when he chose. I waited for as long as I dared, then ran back to the road, where I turned toward the Gate instead of taking the shorter route along the lower road. The sun had already touched the high horizon above the bluffs; I needed to get back into the light, onto the broad main road with the open sky above it. ("Now I was in a spot")

The node appears along a prearranged default path that takes readers achronically through many different scenes and character perspectives, what Bly in his preface to the work calls the "tour."[19] The tour, however, raises more questions than answers, encouraging and facilitating the reader's successive exploration of the archive via text links. In a different sequence, readers learn of a mysterious cave-dwelling people who are mentioned at one point in the writings of the Historian, writings that considerably predate Aric's narration and the recent murder on the grounds:

> They wear garments that cover the entire body and head, with a flap for the mouth and nose. A few of the older ones also wear a peculiar

kind of eye covering that shields their eyes from the light, to which they seem extraordinarily sensitive. In fact, this piece of equipment is a kind of badge of seniority, if I am reading aright the way these elders are treated by the others.

I do not think they ever take these garments off, let alone bathe. I am beginning to be able to distinguish individuals with my eyes closed, by their scent. ("They wear garments")

After reading the Historian's description of these cave dwellers, the reader may or may not recall what initially seemed like an extraneous detail in Aric's more contemporary account: "Just the smell of the place!" But a subsequent reading of Aric's node, which readers can return to through a series of bifurcations, can bring the detail back into consciousness in light of the Historian's note. Even though there is no knowledge or mention of the cave dwellers in Aric's present, the detail of the cave's stench allows the reader to see what Aric cannot and, in turn, establish an association between the cave dwellers (who, it becomes clear, may be more than the stuff of *distant* myth), the Good Doctor, and quite possibly the murder. The repetition of such textual elements can occur in varied ways, with anything from a few or a few hundred nodes in between recurrences.

In "Nonce upon Some Times: Re-reading Hypertext Fiction," a chapter of his *Othermindedness,* Joyce (2000) uses a simple chronological story sequence in four parts to demonstrate more specific forms of narrative return and their effects: "[1] Two people meet. [2] They fall in love. [3] They quarrel and part. [4] They reconcile" (134). He supposes that from the fourth part, a link returns us to the second. Joyce then suggests that from this point of the second node, what is now in his example a retrospective look at the lovers first falling in love, there exist only three possible kinds of links available to the writer. They are *recursus* (or cycle), *flashback,* and *renewal.* The *recursus* would involve a loop, with or without an exit, and is a strategy that works in tandem with the familiar discursive forms of "hallucination, déjà vu, compulsion, riff, ripple, canon, isobar, daydream, theme and variation" (135–36). The next possibility is *flashback,* which would entail the continuation of the story (from the second node to an "uninscribed fifth space"), therefore rendering the return as simply "a new look at previous thematic material" (135). Finally, *renewal,* the third possibility, involves the movement from the second node to an entirely new space, which Joyce describes as an escape "inward and outward simultaneously" (135). For Joyce this form of narrative return differs from the other two since it does not involve a weaving of textual elements ("the woven etymon, text as textus") but instead illustrates a "narrative ori-gami." Significantly, rereading makes such folding, unfolding, and refolding possible: "Linking itself—re-reading itself—has discovered and opened a new story dimension" (135).[20] Joyce's exercise is just that—an exercise. It requires a simplified, truncated, and chronological story. But it nonetheless demon-strates how narrative returns operate in different and discernible ways.

As Joyce writes, "Hypertext fiction in some fundamental sense depends on re-reading (or the impossibility of ever truly doing so) for its effects" (2000, 137). Joyce's claim speaks to a distinctive quality of network narrative and recalls the paradox of "pure repetition" discussed by Deleuze and Derrida. Stuart Moulthrop (1992a) agrees that network narratives foreground repe-tition and rereading, and he gestures toward the same breakdown of pre-rogative between the two when he writes, "Hypertextual fictions invite and may even demand recirculation." Citing Peter Brooks (1984, 91), Moulthrop adds that such narrative returns are "nothing very new, since this strategy recapitulates (manically) [Tzvetan] Todorov's famous formula for narrative structure: *the same yet different.*" Moulthrop is correct in seeing an intensifi-cation of a quality already inherent in narrative forms. But if network nar-ratives recapitulate this print-based formula "manically," it is because they first do so materially.

Digital Bliss

The use of the computer as a vehicle for narrative fiction has prompted con-siderations of the relationship between narratology and the aesthetics of digital literature. Aarseth (1997) discusses hypertext aesthetics in relation to Roland Barthes' narratology. In *The Pleasure of the Text* Barthes (1980) in-vokes the rhetorical figure of *tmesis* to describe the playful skipping and skimming of the text that forgoes a conventional allegiance to its linearity and "integrity."[21] For Barthes even "the most classical narrative (a novel by Zola or Balzac or Dickens or Tolstoy) bears within it a sort of diluted tme-sis": "we do not read everything with the same intensity of reading; a rhythm is established, casual, unconcerned with the integrity of the text; our very avidity for knowledge impels us to skim or to skip certain passages (antici-pated as 'boring') in order to get more quickly to the warmer parts of the an-ecdote (which are always its articulations: whatever furthers the solution of the riddle, the revelation of fate): we boldly skip (no one is watching) descrip-tions, explanations, analyses, conversations" (1980, 11). Barthes sees reading as pleasurable, but he also equates *pleasure* with complacency. He articulates two modes of reading—pleasure *(plaisir)* and bliss *(jouissance)*—and associates pleasure with traditional, linear reading, an experience of any given text that conforms to our expectations: "It is the text that comes from culture and does not break with it. . . . [It] is linked to a comfortable practice of reading" (14). *Bliss*, the privileged term, evokes a sense of play, of skipping through the text and chancing on unexpected connections. *Skipping* itself connotes both playfulness (as in skipping rope) and mischief or delinquency (as in skipping school). Hence, Barthes attempts to articulate a way of reading that is deviant or at least deviates from the norm, but more generally, the "text of Bliss" refers to any text that challenges or even subverts our traditional idea of what a text should be: "[It] unsettles the reader's historical, cultural, psychological assumptions" (14).

Barthes' distinction certainly destabilizes the belief that there is a "proper" way to read and, in this sense, his critique seems to anticipate the practice of reading a network text, where readers can struggle in search of linearity and closure—the creature comforts of popular narrative. And the network text certainly asks that readers revisit many of the historical, cultural, and psychological assumptions about textuality and narrativity naturalized by the material trappings of print. So there are notable connections between reading for Bliss and reading in the decentralized, nonhierarchical network. But, as Aarseth (1997, 78) makes clear, to equate "the discontinuous, fragmentary reading demanded by hypertext" with Barthes' tmesis would be a "grave mistake." "Hypertext reading is in fact quite the opposite," he writes; "as the reader explores the labyrinth, she cannot afford to tread lightly through the text but must scrutinize the links and venues in order to avoid meeting the same text fragments over and over again" (78). Ironically, if hypertext technology were to literalize Barthes' subversive mode of reading, it would in turn subvert the subversion readers equate with it; that is, reading "heterolinearly," or against the line, cannot be a subversive mode when it becomes the only mode, when there is nothing from which to deviate. But Aarseth argues that the concept of "homolinear" and "heterolinear" (or tmesic) reading itself is not relevant in a network text, which allows only a "hyperlinear" mode—"the selection of paths across a network structure" (79).

Reading a network text is not analogous to reading in the mode of Barthes' *jouissance*. As Aarseth (1997) makes clear, "tmesis in hypertext will always be limited by the topological constraints laid down by the author" (78).[22] Even though Aarseth identifies the disjunction between Barthes' theory and reading network texts in practice, however, his determination to avoid "meeting the same text fragments over and over again" points, superficially, to an understanding of nodal repetition only in a degenerative sense. This comes as little surprise given that Aarseth focuses on Joyce's hypertext novel *afternoon* as his primary source. Joyce's *afternoon* limits what can be said of reading a work of network fiction because, unlike the vast majority of works that followed, it does not make its links visible to the reader; it is, by Aarseth's own admission, "unrepresentative of the growing body of literary hypertexts" (1997, 85). The invisible links in *afternoon* not only make it difficult to speak of a rhetorical strategy implicit in the linking structure, but they also contribute to a brand of author-imposed disorientation that leads potentially to an antagonistic relationship between narrator and reader. The portrayal of nodal repetition as an unwelcome frustration makes sense in a work that is seen to perpetuate a scheming, "man-behind-the-curtain" mentality.

What's the Frequency?

Markku Eskelinen (1998) also critiques appropriations of print narratology for digital literature, but his discussion is limited similarly by its focus on *afternoon*. Where Aarseth's discussion deals with a specific theoretical concept in Barthes' repertoire, Eskelinen's "Omission Impossible: The Ergodics of Time" engages with a broader narratological model—that of Gérard Genette. Genette treats text time in terms of Order, Duration, and Frequency. *Order* refers to the order in which events are narrated in relation to a chronological story, with *analepsis* roughly equivalent to flashback or retrospection and *prolepsis* roughly equivalent to foreshadowing and anticipation. *Duration* (or speed) deals with the relation between three things: the duration of the extratextual story, the text time (e.g., one minute rendered in one page), and the time of reading. *Frequency* considers the number of times an event appears in a story in relation to the number of times it is narrated in the text, and deals with repetition-relations in three forms: the singulative, the repetitive, and the iterative. The singulative involves the most common scenario of telling once what happened once (and also includes the least common scenario of telling *n* times what happened *n* times); the repetitive involves telling *n* times what happened once; and the iterative involves telling once what happened *n* times. Eskelinen casts doubt on the application of these categories to network narrative: "Hypertext renders the category of order almost useless with the almost tautological exception of achronic texts. The case may seem to be the same with frequency, which could at least be modified both by quantitative and qualitative analysis of link structures. On the other hand, if we think that the necessity of navigation only increases the probability of re-reading and there is nothing special in revisiting a node, then the category of frequency looks as valid as before."[23] Referring to *afternoon*, Eskelinen continues: "If there's only one car accident there's only one car accident. And we can count how many times our middle-aged fraud of a narrator comes back to recount it and quite possibly also how many times his reader bears with him."

Eskelinen claims that "hypertext renders the category of order almost useless," but Order directly affects an understanding of repetition in network narratives. Much of how we understand Order in network narratives depends on whether or not the text in question is written in fragments, which would imply that they are parts of a preexisting whole, regardless of whether they can be reassembled or not. *Nodes* and *fragments* are quite different in this respect, for nodes can function as complete, self-contained entities in and of themselves in addition to playing a role in a network of larger relations. A fragment has a certain autonomy as well, but fragments connote something broken or shattered, whereas nodes connote something that has been or is being built. The order of narration is always variable in network narrative, as Eskelinen suggests, but what he overlooks is the fact that the content of the nodes can indicate where they appear in a causal chain of events, that is, *when* they occur in a story. The distinction overwrites his dismissive claim of tautology, for such a text would not be achronical but rather anachronical. To dismiss Genette's narratology and endorse Aarseth's cybertext theory, Eskelinen does not need to consider semantic material at all, what he "patronizingly calls a content-oriented approach" (Hayles 2001). Hayles asks, "[I]s not content, however postmodern, fragmented, contradictory, deconstructive, or elusive it might be, intimately involved in why most users read texts and especially why they return to them time after time?" Her comments expose Eskelinen's elision of semantics, an elision that is common, and unavoidably so, to cybertext theory in general. Nonetheless, both Aarseth's and Eskelinen's discussions remind us that just because a text makes narrative returns (materially) possible, it does not necessarily make them desirable.

In her thorough reading of *afternoon* Jill Walker (1999) finds evidence of both analepsis and prolepsis in the textual material of Joyce's nodes. She separates the nodes of the text into levels that include analepses, prolepses, and metacommentaries, all of which emerge from the series of events that transpire at a primary level: "The accident happens in the morning. Peter has lunch with Werther at noon, then makes phone calls and visits the site of the accident in the afternoon. He calls Lolly after five o'clock. These, and Peter's meeting with Lolly after the phone call, are in fact the only events at the level of the 'first narrative' in Genette's sense" (Walker 1999). Eskelinen's (1998) comments on *afternoon* suggest that he, for one, sees "nothing special in revisiting a node."[24] As the example of Bly's *We Descend* shows, however, returning to nodes does make a difference in rendering the process of interpretation accretive rather than worthlessly redundant. The one car accident in *afternoon* can be told in different ways and from different perspectives; it can also be told the same way in different formal contexts—in a different "semantic neighborhood" of nodes; finally, it can simply be "retold" in a different cognitive context, as readers in network texts return to textual material they might otherwise not have revisited, and often with the benefit of new information gathered since their first visit. Walker's essay recognizes both scenarios of changed perspective and changed context, first by discussing different tellings of the accident (Peter's interpretation, then Lolly's interpretation of Peter's interpretation) and then by discussing the practice of rereading accounts of the accident. For her, rereadings in network fiction evoke a Nietzschean form of repetition, a visible similitude that nevertheless creates an indelible—if not ghostly—difference.[25] Underscoring the dialogue between the structural and semantic components of the work, Walker treats nodal repetition in relation to the thematics of the text at hand, specifically the notion of returning to the scene of an accident.

In addition to her detailed analysis of *afternoon* Walker takes up the task of what she calls "enlarging" Genette's model of Frequency. Her critique moves from the observation that "Genette describes Frequency of narration, but not of reading," and thus might be understood as a coupling of a narratological model with pragmatics. Since the reader must take responsibility for the course of a hypertextual narration, the coupling is inevitable. In Walker's model the reader of a network fiction can read

(1) once what is told once,
(2) *n* times what is told *n* times (this is how repetitions in codex books are read),
(3) *n* times what is told once (this describes the re-reading of one and the same node in *afternoon*),
(4) or once what is told *n* times. (1999)

The fourth possibility, Walker notes, "could occur if a section of text was duplicated, but the reader only ever came across one of the nodes containing the text" (1999). It represents an anomalous case, much like the unlikely scenario of telling *n* times what happens *n* times. By contrast, the third possibility, reading *n* times what is told once, points to the phenomenon foregrounded in network narrative.

Once narrative returns come to the fore of the reading experience, the expectation of and familiarity with repetition sets up other poetical possibilities. Walker, for instance, speaks of "false repetitions," which consist of subtle substitutions or changes in phrasing that serve to break the reader's sense of expectation and automation. She locates an effective example of false repetition in Joyce's opening node, "Begin." The node contains some twenty links, making it a hub for hypertextual transit, and readers come to expect multiple visits. Despite its indicative title, readers may or may not process the false repetition in a different node called "false beginning." As Walker suggests, when readers juxtapose the two nodes, they see that "false beginning" enacts a near inversion in several places.

From "Begin":

I try to recall winter. <As if it were yesterday?> she says, but I do not signify one way or another.

By five the sun sets and the afternoon melt freezes again across the blacktop into crystal octopi and palms of ice—rivers and continents beset by fear, and we walk out to the car, the snow moaning beneath our boots and the oaks exploding in series along the fenceline on the horizon, the shrapnel settling like relics, the echoing thundering off far ice. This was the essence of wood, these fragments say. And this darkness is air.

<Poetry> she says, without emotion, one way or another.

Do you want to hear about it?

From "false beginning":

I try to recall yesterday. <As if it were winter?> I say, but she does not signify one way or another.

By five the sun rises and the night freeze melts again across the blacktop into crystal rivers—octopi beset by fear, and we walk out to the car, the snow exploding beneath our boots and the oaks moaning in series, echoing off far ice.

This was poetry, she says, without emotion, one way or another.

Do you hear it?

There is only one beginning, just as there is only one car accident, as Eskelinen is quick to point out. That retelling or rereading does not necessarily constitute recurrence of story events is no more problematic in a digital network than it is in a book. But the text of *afternoon* can lead and mislead readers back to the beginning, recombining familiar elements and multiplying meanings in the process.

Circuitous Paths and Pathology

Freud's contribution in the early twentieth century to a psychological understanding of repetition is key in identifying its diverse and paradoxical function in human behavior. His consideration of the unconscious has also informed the field of psychoanalytic literary theory (his thought informs that of both Derrida and Deleuze) and, more specifically, models of narrative theory.

Well aware that the pleasure derived from an experience leads to the desire to repeat that experience, Freud formulated the *pleasure principle,* emphasizing that such desires are often set in motion by conscious drives. Further recognizing that the pleasure principle acting alone is "inefficient and highly dangerous" to an organism invested in self-preservation, he refined this notion with that of the *reality principle,* which does not abandon the attainment of pleasure but rather "demands and carries into effect the postponement of satisfaction, the abandonment of a number of possibilities of gaining satisfaction and the temporary toleration of unpleasure as a step on the long road to pleasure" (Freud 1920/1987, 278). The pleasure principle persists, however, in the manifestation of the sexual drives. Thus, the pursuit of pleasure, in the form of sexual gratification, employs repetition as a linear, end-directed process that projects the organism *forward* through life.

Freud articulates a complex set of psychic relations to explain why the instinctual drive for pleasure does not function as the prime motivation for human behavior. In turn, he transcends the mechanic, unidirectional understanding of the movement of repetition. He develops the concept of the *death drive,* which functions to "bind excitations" and continually return us to an earlier state—before hunger, or sexual arousal, or life itself. For Freud the death drive is the instinctual "urge inherent in organic life to restore an earlier state of things" (308). Freud does not accept that the goal of life can amount to a state that has never and possibly can never be attained. Rather, "it must be an *old* state of things, an initial state from which the living entity has at one time or other departed and to which it is striving to return by the circuitous paths along which its development leads" (310). He makes more of these circuitous paths, for even though all paths return to the same place, it is precisely the impact of our conservative instincts—the control and filtering of external stimuli—that allows us to make "ever more complicated *detours*" en route to death (311). The death instinct does not necessarily blot out all other instincts but necessarily guides them: "Seen in this light, the theoretical importance of the instincts of self-preservation, of self-assertion and of mastery greatly diminishes. They are component instincts whose function it is to assure that the organism shall follow its own path to death, and to ward off any possible ways of returning to inorganic existence other than those which are imminent in the organism itself. . . . What we are left with is the fact that the organism wishes to die only in its own fashion" (312–13).

Repetition brings the life instincts, or pleasure principle, into play with the death instincts. But where the pleasure principle points to a conscious act of repeating, the death instinct involves a compulsion to repeat that arises from unconscious material. In fact, the repetition compulsion attains an insurmountable influence in Freudian psychology, underpinning much of complex human behavior. The repetition compulsion overrides the pleasure principle at every juncture, at times giving "the appearance of some 'daemonic' force at work" (307). Repetition forms patterns from which we do not always know how to escape, even if we recognize them (such as instances where one's social relationships all seem to end badly *and* in exactly the same way). The repetition compulsion manifests the weight of repressed material, forcing us to recall past experiences that can in no way bring pleasure and, quite possibly, forcing us to relive unpleasant experiences without being totally aware of the recurrence. For this reason the repetition compulsion can work as a hindrance to memory, which can complicate therapeutic treatment. As Kawin (1972, 16) writes, the "analyst would like to be able to help his patient *remember* a trauma and see it in the present; but what usually occurs is that the patient acts out his trauma again in the present, without any critical distance—without even being aware that he is in fact repeating earlier behavior."

While Derrida's deconstruction disarticulates the binary of original and copy, and Deleuze's *complex repetition* moves beyond the duality of obedient servitude and defiant disguise with regard to identity, Freud's discovery of hysterical trauma exemplifies how repetition transcends the logic of primary and secondary, thus opening onto another possibility beyond or between the two. For example, if a child is subject to sexual abuse at an early enough age, that child will not understand its sexual context and meaning. Symptoms of the abuse will develop in an ungrounded and, hence, a seemingly ghostly or demonic way. At a later point in life another event—perhaps trivial or at least not on the scale of the initial transgression—will reactivate the trauma, bringing it back into consciousness in the present context. For Freud, when such temporally and spatially distinct events or scenes acquire new significance in a present-tense context (often that of fantasy), a psychic operation that he calls "retroactivity" *(nachträglichkeit)* has occurred.

As many literary critics have pointed out, some in the service of contextualizing the problem of causality in network narrative,[26] Freud's observation of retroactivity is simultaneously a critique of cause and effect. For example, if a patient's abuse is reactivated through therapy, it becomes difficult to attribute a definitive source to the subsequent traumatic feelings. For Miller, Freud's discussion of trauma exemplifies the result of the ungrounded—or what he calls a "Nietzschean"—form of repetition: "The trauma is neither in the first nor in the second but between them, in the relation between two opaquely similar events" (Miller 1982, 9). Thus, the third possibility is the meaning generated from the interrelation of two things, neither of which can make an unproblematic claim to primacy.

In semiotic terms the return of the repressed amounts to an expression of an unconscious-signified through a symptom-signifier. A semiotic understanding, moreover, points to the way in which Freud's observation of psychic operations has been appropriated as an interpretative frame for reading narrative. In developing his concept of "reading for the plot," Peter Brooks (1984) draws heavily on Freudian psychology. As Dino Felluga (2004) notes, Brooks's "innovation" lies in his coupling of the structuralist element of *metonymy* with Freud's *pleasure principle,* and its corresponding element of *metaphor* with Freud's *death drive.* Felluga writes, "The final metaphorical meaning of a narrative retrospectively orders or makes sense of all the metonymical deviations of the narrative that came before the end" (2004). Brooks's narratology, then, depends on the complex interplay between what he calls the "metaphoric work of eventual totalization" with the "metonymic work of sequence" (Brooks 1984, 29). When Freud (1920/1987, 311) speaks of making "ever more complicated *detours*" en route to death, Brooks associates these detours with those that occur in narrative plots, which serve to counteract the sexual mechanics of desire that motivate reading. For Brooks the controlled deferral of "full predication" when we read is what ultimately makes its fulfillment fulfilling. "It is this play of forward momentum and ultimate closure, aligned respectively with Eros (the pleasure principle) and Thanatos (the death drive), that structures the 'erotics' of narrative" (Felluga 2004).

With regard to network narratives Brooks's model is too straightforward, so to speak, on several accounts. Most obvious is the fact that his study involves nineteenth-century classical novels that motivate readers from beginning to end along a singular temporal track. When appropriating Freud's psychology, Brooks must place disproportionate emphasis on the pleasure principle: the linear, conscious drive toward "full predication"—an approach that is, arguably, also an outgrowth of his chosen genre. In his preface Brooks describes plot as the "design and intention of narrative, what shapes a story and gives it a certain direction" (1984, xi). Here it becomes clear that Brooks's model will not accommodate network texts, in which "shape" becomes an arbitrary construction and "direction" becomes an operation of the reader. Furthermore, Brooks states that "narratives both tell of desire—typically present some story of desire—and arouse and make use of desire as dynamic of signification" (37). But if narrative plots can both arouse and represent the conscious, sexual drives of Freud's pleasure principle, then surely they can also arouse and represent the unconscious compulsion to repeat that under-lines Freud's model.

For Brooks all repetitions or returns in a print novel enact "interruptions" of a forward progression (1984, 100). But hyperlinks in a network text do not simply interrupt; rather, they redirect, both discursively and materially. Brooks's model does not support the topological dynamics of network nar-ratives, for in his terms repetition seems to occur along the same axis, on a singular vector temporarily reversed. That is, repetition enacts "a calling *back* or a turning *back*" of the text (Brooks 1984, 125; my emphasis), as if forward and backward were the only two directions available to the narrative line. In a material sense this idea holds true for books, where what Coover (quoted in Landow 1997, 184) calls an "ineluctable page-turning chain" offers a fixed point of reference for plot. But hypertextual plots simply do not move in the same way Brooks describes, and their interminability renders "full predica-tion" an illusion.

The reading interface of a network text suggests a course of movement for the reader that is not only backward and forward (as if west to east on a horizontal plane) but also above and below (as if north and south), as well as inside and outside (as in the Storyspace reading interface, where nodes are contained in or contained by other nodes). The interface of a network nar-rative can further be used to dramatize the effect of moving forward and backward—or even laterally "across" and regressively "inside/outside"—the *temporal* frames of the narrative's discourse in ways that are unavailable to the interface of the book.

Metacritical Retrospection

Narrative art that does not pursue Brooks's "signifying totality" raises some crucial questions: to what extent does a psychologically ingrained form of "narrative desire" shape the way narratives are written? Conversely, to what extent does a literary medium, such as a bound novel, shape the way we read—or shape our desire?[27] Is "closure" in narrative fiction a psychological expectation? Is it, as some have argued, something that allows us to compensate for the lack of closure we experience in day-to-day life? Or is it integral to what a narrative is and how it works? As Henry James has said of the novel, "Really, universally, relations stop nowhere, and the exquisite problem of the artist is eternally but to draw, by a geometry of his own, the circle within which they shall happily *appear* to do so" (cited in Douglas 1994, 159). Clearly, narrative endings are always at least double, a convenient coincidence of a material and discursive terminus. But if we can easily accept James's arbitrary circle, must we think of it only in the singular sense? When we think of digitally networked texts, can we find sense and satisfaction in a multiplicity of local unities (and hence closures) rather than, or in addition to, a single global unity?

Cognitive science supports the notion that we are indeed in some way hardwired in our pursuit of unitary perceptions. In his most recent book, *Wider Than the Sky: The Phenomenal Gift of Consciousness*, neuroscientist Gerald Edelman writes, "What is particularly striking about the operations of the conscious human brain is the necessity for integration, for a unitary picture, for construction, and for closure" (2004a, 126). Edelman's discussion of the cognitive effort that is involved in filling in our perceptual "blind spots"—for example, in our given field of vision (126)—is a compelling account of this built-in drive. The necessity of coherence and closure in making sense of our world, and generating meaning from our perceptions, readily applies to our experience of fictional worlds. But in the context of narrative art such coherence and closure do not necessarily need to be dictated by the *story* per se, and readers might locate closure(s) among its other elements, such as those generated by discrete patterns, concepts, or even discrete moods.[28]

Yet another possibility exists with regard to our experience and expectations of reading narrative texts: instead of more and more determined attempts to locate closure, we might find the practice of exploring—of wandering—more satisfying in itself. Theorists writing on interactivity in digital texts and digital video games have articulated the satisfactions of exploration (see, for instance, Janet Murray's comments [1997, 129–30] to this effect with regard to interactive fiction), and their observations can in turn inflect literary criticism of works in print and onscreen. But here a closer look at network fiction might take this line of inquiry even further and gesture toward a possible extension of the concept of "narrative desire." Moulthrop (1992a, 273), for example, writes of an entirely different sort of seduction of digital texts: "Among other things, hypertextual discourse solicits iteration and involvement. While this is certainly a property of all narrative fiction, one can argue that hypertextual writing seduces narrative over or away from a certain Line, thus into a space where the sanctioned repetitions of conventional narrative explode or expand, no longer at the command of *logos* or form, but driven instead by *nomos* or itinerant desire." A conception of "itinerant desire" might better suit a network text marked by iterations no longer "sanctioned" by conventional narrative and motivated by a desire to wander, explore, and return.

These possibilities aside, the value of a more nuanced understanding of repetition is clear. Changing attitudes toward repetition in literary discourse and changes to the materiality of literature itself have contributed synergistically to a foregrounding of narrative returns. At once formal and poetical, technological and aesthetic, narrative returns play an elemental role in network fiction and encourage further expansion of narrative theory in light of network environments.

2
Network Vistas

Folding the Cognitive Map

> Such harmony only he can relish whose long experience and detailed knowledge of the niches are such as to permit a perfect mental image of the entire system. But it is doubtful that such a one exists.
> —Samuel Beckett, *The Lost Ones*

Temporal frameworks of narratology can help locate the continuities and disjunctions that arise when narrative fiction migrates to network environments, along with the pleasures and pathologies that such a shift implies for reading. Narrative returns provide a significant locus in this regard—at once a recapitulation of extant narrative formulas and a phenomenon that is radically, which is to say materially, foregrounded by digital media. But if, as Moulthrop (1992a, 273) suggests, the network form "seduces narrative over or away from a certain Line [and] into a space where the sanctioned repetitions of conventional narrative explode or expand," then it is also necessary to extend the discourse of "spatiality" as it pertains to reading, and rereading. It is necessary, that is, to move over and away from the "Line" and into the space of the network.

In the Space of Writing

Walter Ong (1982, 76–77) reminds us that writing—the transfer of language as orthographic symbols onto a surface—has always been spatial. But writing has taken on another dimension with the rise of network culture. Spatiality constitutes a metadiscourse of digital art and literature, though critics and theorists have found no pervasive consensus in articulating this spatiality. A lack of consensus should come as no surprise, for whether readers see a digital network, a hypertext, or even the World Wide Web as a virtual space, a cyberspace, a hyperspace, a data-space, a "smooth space" (after Deleuze and Guattari), or a "Netscape," what they "see" behind the screen is irrefutably an *abstract* space. It can in some sense be whatever we want it to be, and writers of network fictions have employed organizing metaphors in the service of interface design that are suggestive of the text's "deeper" shape and structure—for example, a text as a garden (Moulthrop 1991b), as a quilt (Jackson 1995), and as a mass-transit system (Gillespie et al. 1998–2001).

One of the more pronounced debates arising from the study of digital textuality concerns contradictory depictions of network space as topographical and topological, with early theorists such as J. David Bolter (1991) outlining the ways in which the computer offers a genuinely topographic "new writing space" and others, such as Espen Aarseth (1994, 69), arguing that "pure hypertext is actually among the least topographical modes of non-linearity." At the same time, theorists entrenched in the sciences, specifically those versed in what is known as the "qualitative mathematics" of topology, dispute what they see as careless appropriations of their discipline (see, e.g., Achter 1992).

Popular characterizations of cyberspace grow out of a spatial logic that is inherently Cartesian, based on a two- or three-dimensional coordinate grid, and topographical, based on a landscape that can be mapped. Hypertext, specifically, was and in many accounts still is seen as a move from two to three dimensions in the conceptual space of writing, as in Douglas (2001, 50), where readers encounter "interactive narratives as structures suspended in virtual, three-dimensional space." The popular metaphors of the World Wide Web (and the *web* metaphor itself) reinforce this spatial logic by implying a body moving through a fixed landscape. Users "navigate" through cyberspace and "visit" the sites. Such a reader is, as Mireille Rosello (1994, 130) describes it, "a body circulating among fixed, immobile roads." When speaking of "adding a dimension" to the space of writing, one is already adopting the logic of the Cartesian coordinate-based grid and the topographical paradigm.

Given that inherent connectivity, not a landscape of spatially locatable sites, defines a digital network, it is more accurate to discuss hypertextual structure in terms of topology (Aarseth 1997; Berressem 2002). Topology concerns itself not with distances but with the movement of points in a dynamic field. Such movement is not subject to the logic of a quantitative grid. As Hanjo Berressem (2002, 29) points out, a (re)conceptualization of network space as topological runs counter to the notion of a "transparent 3D chessboard extending to infinity" described by William Gibson in *Neuromancer,* the work from which *cyberspace* popularly takes its name. There are at least five definitions of *topology,* several of which apply directly or indirectly to hypertext systems and, in turn, compound the confusion over appropriations that already entail contentious border crossings between the humanities and the sciences. Topology can refer to (1) the arrangement of computers in a network or (2) the arrangement of individual nodes in a hypertextual network (i.e., a data structure). It also refers to (3) the anatomy of any specific bodily area or structure (e.g., brain topology—it is not possible to expose the entirety of the brain even with a three-dimensional mapping for it always conceals parts of itself within its folds). Another definition of topology denotes (4) the study of a given topography over time. And topology commonly refers to (5) mathematical disciplines that are concerned with intrinsic properties of spatial configurations, independent of their location and shape. For example, a rubber doughnut can be stretched and bent without tearing it, which makes the hole of the doughnut an intrinsic qualitative property. In all of its mathematical applications topology has more to do with movements than distances, which is why it is commonly described as "rubber-sheet geometry" against the quantitative grid-based metric of Euclidean geometry.

The topology of a network text draws on an amalgamation of these definitions, but it is clear that a basic understanding of topological space is necessary to conceptualize the dynamic structure of hypertextual systems. In technical terms the structure of a network *is* intrinsically topological; that is, the relationships between nodes remain independent of and unchanged by their location in space. In this sense an investment in *connection* over *location* in a network text is a correlate of topology's broader concern with dynamic linkages between elements over their relative distances or positioning. Still, topographical renderings of network space are not wholly inaccurate. It is possible to *impose* topography and hierarchy on hypertextual structure, as is often done to provide a self-evident method of orientation in network environments, especially in the World Wide Web. Furthermore, topographical renderings of network space inevitably come into play when considering the convergence of digital network and narrative fiction, in which artists create a spatially realizable storyworld. Network narratives do not present nodal topologies in a vacuum but rather always through the representational material to which the network gives shape.

The space of network *fiction* has a dual ontology. On one side computer science conceptualized information as spatial as graphical capabilities evolved. Operating systems came to rely on the user's manipulation of spatial elements through the Graphical User Interfaces or GUIs that users take for granted today. GUIs spawned a corresponding system of spatial metaphors—desktops, folders, and trashcans (or recycling bins)—that superseded the language and logic of the linear, text-based command line interfaces preceding them. As Abbe Don (1991, 386) points out, the premise of the GUI is based on a "false spatial representation" of information developed as a necessary means by which to orient users. On the other side the increasing cultural dominance of the image—what W. J. T. Mitchell (1994, 11–13) dubbed the "pictorial turn" in contemporary culture—encouraged further engagement with the relationship between image and narrative. Some saw this engagement as a resistance to the inescapably linear form of the novel and others as a direct response to the emergence of a truly visual narrative form in the first half of the twentieth century—that of film. Thus, the spatialization of information in computer science coevolved with the spatialization of narrative text in the arts.

It is worth noting that 1945 saw the publication of both Joseph Frank's "Spatial Form in Modern Narrative" and Vannevar Bush's "As We May Think." Frank's essay describes works of modernist literature that require a spatial mode of criticism, one that can articulate a structure comprising the "reflexive relations" among "units of meaning" (1945, 87). For Frank these units of meaning arise from "views" of narrative characters, scenes, and actions, and the juxtaposition of views both allows for and necessitates a spatial perspective similar to Rimmon-Kenan's notion of "supra-linear links" that coalesce into spatial patterns (Rimmon-Kenan 1983, 137n). Bush's spatial scaffolding is based on neuronal functions rather than literary techniques. He sought to externalize and, in turn, augment the space of human memory through mechanical means, and his essay introduces the conceptual blueprint for his MEMEX (MEMory EXtender), a major contribution to the (predigital) origins of hypertext technology.

Amid the rhetoric of spatiality, *time* takes a backseat in contemporary literary theory, especially for theorists intent on exploring (or charting, or conquering) the "electronic frontier."[1] As media theorist Darren Tofts (2001) has noted, it is rare to hear anyone mention "cyber-time." In much early hypertext theory it was more common to render and in turn romanticize a topography than it was to speak more technically of a topology—after all, topology is rendered only in freeze-frame, by suspending a figure in motion.[2] The spatial disposition in the literary arts, moreover, led many to aestheticize what was perceived initially as an intrinsically disorienting hyperspace, endowing it with an electronic aura of drifting and timelessness. In fact, those seeking to reinstate in cyberspace what Fredric Jameson (1993, 82) calls the "narrative stroll" invoked some of literary theory's fashionable wandering aesthetes: Benjamin's urban flâneur became an electronic flâneur, and the body of de Certeau's *Wandersmänn* traced a path through a city of hypertext. These portrayals gained force through contemporary critiques that privileged itinerant forms of subjectivity—most notably the nomadology of Deleuze and Guattari.

But there is a dramatic difference between the wandering aesthete of yesterday and today's cybertourist. For the creative wanderer whose popular origins are found in the nineteenth-century aestheticism of French poets Baudelaire and Rimbaud, time moves so slowly that it is no longer relevant.

In his 1843 work *Either/Or* Søren Kierkegaard's aesthete denies time by arresting it: "Time flows, life is a stream, people say, and so on. I do not notice it. Time stands still, and I with it" (1946a, 20).[3] But if time is no longer relevant for the cybertourist, it is for the opposite reason: the instantaneity and immediacy of the network has contributed to a worldview in which time is simply something to be transcended through speed. Paul Virilio (2001) raises his "cyberspace alarm" for the same reason. Virilio echoes Jameson—albeit with the benefit of bearing witness to the impact of the World Wide Web and other instantiations of technoculture—when he sees a radical loss of orientation of the individual caused by the erasure of "real space" by "real time": "A total loss of the bearings of the individual looms large. To exist, is to exist *in situ*, here and now. . . . This is precisely what is being threatened by cyberspace and instantaneous, globalized information flows" (2001, 24). Indeed, whether it is a train or a computer, we tend to notice speed only when something crashes, an observation that Moulthrop takes even further by tracing the "obsession" with the crash in the thematics of early hypertext fiction.[4] Quite clearly, one cannot "stroll" at speed.

Repetition as Reference Point

What is the effect of repetition on or in the space of the text? As print-based narrative theories demonstrate, repetition destabilizes temporality. In doing so, it also signals artifice. The signaling of artifice in a literary work invites two related connotations of *artifice*—"building" and "falsifying"—each suggesting comparable nuances in the terms *construction* and *fabrication*. Writers of fiction build a scaffolding of allusions and interrelations analogous to Joseph Frank's "spatial form." At the same time, the signaling of artifice complicates the veracity of a transparent storyworld; that is, the proliferation of intertextual and metatextual material casts doubt on the existence of any one *true* text, giving way to a potential regress of fictions within fictions. Readers cannot intuit a singularly coherent storyworld when traces of the textual structure are exposed, and it becomes clear that these traces bear a striking similarity to other textual structures. In *The Exaggerations of Peter Prince* (1968) Steve Katz thematizes the process of signaling artifice. After the sad and disturbing death of Peter Prince's adopted daughter, Katz implores the reader to reread: "If you look at things long enough and hard enough they're O.K. Just go back and read that section over, sentence by sentence. There are some nice sentences in it. What more do you want? Some nice style. Some neat scenes. It's emotionally packed, but it's well written just the same. Read it some more" (cited in McHale 1987, 103). Repetition foregrounds a text's spatiality, for only a perceived dimensionality, not a singular temporal axis, can accommodate or contain the artifice. In a book such a space includes the abstract visualization of (1) formal structure, the organization or shape of the text and its intratextual relations; and (2) representational material, of character, scene, and setting. Thus, when speaking of printed books, textual artifice requires that readers orient themselves in relation to a perceived structural integrity on one hand and a semantic integrity or, more generally, an interpretative meaning or truth on the other.

Unlike a book, however, the structural integrity of a network text is not self-evident. It consists of a data-space (the network topology) that too can lend itself to representation(s). Network fictions, therefore, consist of not only a representation of material but also a representation of structure. Readers must orient themselves "in" or in relation to the structural topology of a network fiction, which is technically adimensional. One of the most common and effective ways to do so involves repetition and recurrence, an experience that can be mistaken by readers and critics as a vice, a malfunction, or at the very least, a frustration.

Repetition delimits. When nodes start to repeat in a reading of network fiction, it is like suddenly finding a wall after wandering with arms outstretched in a darkened room. Mark Bernstein, in his predominantly instrumental writing on hypertextual comprehension, discusses the role of repetition in orientation.[5] Both "Hypertext Gardens" (1998) and "Patterns of Hypertext" (1998) helped to dispel the common misconception of what was known in early hypertext literature as the "navigation problem," which was put forth perhaps most visibly in Jeff Conklin's influential "Hypertext: An Introduction and Survey" (1987).[6] For Bernstein part of understanding hypertext more simply as a defamiliarized medium rather than an intrinsically disorienting space involved reconceiving common understandings of repetition:

> Recurrence, revisiting a place that one has seen before—was once seen as a sign of disorientation, inefficiency, or artistic affectation. As hypertext readers gained experience, however, they came to recognize that recurrence was the way readers perceive structure; if readers never revisit a node, it is difficult for them to imagine the structure of the hypertext or the nature of the paths they have not taken. Although some recent critics have attacked cycles as a symptom of postmodern malaise, it is clear that cycles are important in complex narrative. (Bernstein 1999)

Although a broader understanding of hypertextual repetition came with the online publication of "Patterns of Hypertext" and "Hypertext Gardens" in 1998, Bernstein was invested in clarifying its role much earlier, along with

Michael Joyce and David Levine, in the 1992 essay "Contours of Constructive Hypertext." "Recurrence is not a defect," the authors write; "repetition provides a powerful structural force, a motif which helps readers synthesize the experience of the reading. Rhythms of recurrence announce patterns of meaning" (1992, 163). Two other essays by Bernstein, "Chasing Our Tails" (1997) and "Recurrence Is Not a Vice" (1998c), directly address the need to reconceive repetition in network environments.

The reader's experience of repetition in a network narrative depends, in large part, on the writer's act of implanting cycles. As Bernstein (1997) writes, "Cycles in hypertext create and explain structure. Through measured repetition, we bring order to what might otherwise become an endlessly varied (and thus endlessly monotonous) line of argument." In "Hypertext Gardens" (1998a) he adds, "Just as phrase and cadence clarify the structure of music, cycles clarify the structure of hypermedia." "Hypertext Gardens" is itself an exercise in reflexivity, a network text that does what it says. One page offers "seven lessons of gardening," and the seventh lesson explains how "[r]igid structure makes a large hypertext seem smaller," whereas "[c]omplex and intricate structure makes a small hypertext seem larger, inviting deeper and more thoughtful exploration." As with books, "small" and "large" are relative dimensions, but from a software-design point of view, a small hypertext often becomes a large one when it crosses a design threshold. These thresholds present themselves in the form of material constraints, such as how many nodes in an overview map "fit" on a single screen (without interminable scrolling) and without sacrificing legibility of their titles.

These material constraints are always related to cognitive constraints—our own perceptual thresholds. These thresholds tell us to consider a hypertext that can be read in an hour as small, while a large one could take weeks or more. Bernstein's own hypertext is small by industry standard, containing less than two dozen nodes, but it clearly illustrates how intricate linking patterns, here in the form of localized cycles, create a space that appears "deeper" than would a succession of nodes in a fixed linear chain. The perception of depth results not only from what we have read and read again but also from what remains unread, outside the movement through a given cycle. Readers have an awareness of what remains unread each time they move from a node that contains a link not chosen; the unread material is "missed," both functionally and experientially, and it beckons a return.

Repetition, defined in instrumental terms, becomes an indispensable means of orientation in network environments. But as readers acquaint themselves with the defamiliarized materiality of the network, they must remember that they are not necessarily pursuing the same ends as readers and critics of literature in print. That is, readers should not understand methods of hypertextual orientation and comprehension as simply new ways to account for an elusive whole; they do not simply integrate the transformations of a network text into a complete mental map that offers a comprehensive overview from a fixed perspective. How do readers, then, comprehend and engage with—if not necessarily *visualize*—the structure of a network fiction?

Mapping in Mind and Onscreen

Digital media theory has appropriated the concept of the "cognitive map" as a means of visualizing the space of digital networks and, more specifically, reading hypertext narratives. Often it has been anchored in the context of Jameson's (1993) aesthetic. Jameson's disorienting visit to the Bonaventure Hotel in Los Angeles has served as a paradigmatic articulation of "postmodern hyperspace"—an articulation that has found a place in the genealogy of digital narrative. Jameson's concept, however, does not adequately articulate the dynamic topology of network space. In fact, narratives in networked environments do not underscore Jameson's notion of a disorienting postmodernist landscape. Rather, they call for a means of textual comprehension and orientation that moves beyond the "cartographic paradigm" of cognitive mapping itself.

Cognitive psychology tells us that we index our current location in any given place by maintaining a cognitive map of learned environments—synthesized and stored as "spatial knowledge" in the region of the brain called the hippocampus. The psychologist Edward C. Tolman (1948) took the first steps toward understanding this phenomenon in the 1940s by observing that rodents in a maze, when necessary, could draw on a learned understanding of their environment.[7] The image of rodents, unrelenting consumers that they are, might have suited Jameson as he hammered out his "logic of late capitalism" (1993). But in negotiating mazes of a more global variety, Jameson derives his often-cited aesthetic of cognitive mapping from geographer Kevin Lynch. In his *Image of the City* (1960, 2) Lynch investigates the "imageability" of modern cities by studying the mental maps made by their inhabitants.

Jameson extends Lynch's trope of civic legibility to link urban experience and narrative directly. Following the trend in architectural and spatial-experience theory, he equates "our physical trajectories" to "virtual narratives or stories, ... dynamic paths and narrative paradigms which we as visitors are asked to fulfill with our own bodies and movements" (Jameson 1993, 82). Jameson's account of his visit to the Bonaventure Hotel is meant as a frustrated attempt to tell a story, for the hotel confounds his notion of narrative space. "Emptiness is here absolutely packed," he writes. "You are in this hyperspace up to your eyes and your body" (82). For Jameson the hotel's elevators and escalators, in particular, subvert narrative possibility; "the narrative stroll has been underscored, symbolized, reified and replaced," and he sees the escalator as a "transportation machine which becomes the allegorical signifier of that older promenade we are no longer allowed to conduct on our own" (82). Recalling his thoughts as he stepped into the hotel atrium, from out of one of the elevators that architect John Portman describes as "gigantic kinetic sculptures," he notes that it is "quite impossible to get your bearings; . . . colour coding and directional signals have been added in a pitiful and revealing, rather desperate attempt to restore the coordinates of an older space" (83). Stepping out of that elevator into a space that "transcends the capacities of the individual human body to locate itself, to organize its immediate surroundings perceptually" (83), Jameson steps into the classical postmodernist moment.

But Jameson ultimately directs his analogy not at physical architectures whose coordinates defy ordinary perception but rather at social or informational architectures that were never subject to the same design rules. He argues for a socialist political project that has as its most formidable challenge the task of mapping the "global multinational and decentered communicational network in which we find ourselves caught as individual subjects" (83). Even his mental cartography does not involve mapping in the familiar sense; that is, it refers to "figuration" rather than strict "representation," for there is, literally, no space to represent. Hence, Jameson's aesthetic of cognitive mapping, notwithstanding the hotel anecdote, takes as its primary object not a definable topography but the topological connectivity of a network. As such, his cognitive map diverges markedly from Lynch's mental map and Tolman's psychological model, both of which emerge from *learned physical environments*. Jameson's hyperspace predates the Web. But because both narrative and network intersect, at least implicitly, in Jameson's cognitive map, and his essay explicitly mentions the less-determinate but more spectacular notion of "hyperspace," it is no surprise that media theorists have applied the idea to an understanding of hypertext.

Some have cited Jameson's political project directly. Moulthrop (1989a, 266) sees in hypertext's distributed model of textuality a movement toward a "politically relevant" art and a viable "pedagogical political culture"; what he conceives of as the "topographical" space of hypertext could, in fact, work toward realizing the social space implied by Jameson's cognitive map. The sociologist Sherry Turkle (1995, 44–45) sees hypertextual networks as the objects that could represent the complexity of Jameson's postmodern world, just as the "turbine, smokestack, pipes, and conveyor belts of the late nineteenth and early twentieth centuries" were to a newly industrialized society; that is, "a decade after Jameson wrote his essay, postmodernism has found its objects"—objects with which one could realize the spatial consciousness implied by the cognitive map.

In line with early patriarchs of hypertext such as Vannevar Bush, Ted Nelson, and Douglas Engelbart, who saw hypertext as an externalization or at least augmentation of the workings of the human mind, others have referred to the maps provided by some graphical interfaces themselves as "cognitive maps" (Douglas 2001; Koskimaa 2000). The terminological appropriation has surfaced in a more diluted sense in the claim that "hypertext externalizes the cognitive mapping of disconnected word groups that is pre-requisite for the sense of space in modernist literature, what we might call non-computerized hypertext" (Tolva 1996). These theorists have adopted a view of hypertext as a kind of connect-the-dots of modernist textuality, conflating the spatial form articulated by Joseph Frank with the topological structure of the network text. The conflation is encouraged, however misleadingly, by the fact that linguistic models of textual comprehension, such as those developed by Teun van Dijk (1980), render semantic connectivity in the same way that graphical tools render the topological connectivity of hypertextual nodes. For example, referring to van Dijk's model of textual comprehension, Rolf Zwaan (1993, 27) writes, "As the model processes the entire text, it constructs a network of coherent propositions. This network may be visualized as a graph, such that the nodes are propositions and the connected lines indicate shared referents." The visualization described by Zwaan evokes the directed graphs commonly used to represent hypertextual structure, such as the Storyspace overviews familiar to many first-generation hypertextualists. Thus, rather than source the concept directly to Jameson's aesthetic, some critics internalized a generic understanding of the cognitive map and, with it, the assumption that such graphical overviews (whether text editors for writers or navigational tools for readers) externalize some portion of the cognitive process of writing and reading.

David Herman (2000) and Marie-Laure Ryan (2003) have taken steps to clarify the relationship of the cognitive map and textuality, tilling the field of cognitive narratology that combines discourse analysis, cognitive psychology, and literary criticism. Herman refers to a visualization of the spatial relationships in a narrative text or, more specifically, "a process of cognitive mapping that assigns referents not merely a temporal but a spatiotemporal position in the storyworld" (2000). Ryan, similarly, defines the cognitive map as "a mental model of spatial relations" (2003, 215). They direct their theoretical approach, however, predominantly toward mapping the territory of the represented storyworld, a task that now overlaps with the project of mapping the hypertextual structure.

Herman (2000) is correct when he states that "[i]ntimately related to such processes of spatialization are those of perspective-taking. As one of the principal means of adopting vantage-points on people, places, things, actions, and events, stories index modes of perspective-taking by way of personal pronouns; definite and indefinite articles; verbs of perception, cognition, and emotion; tenses and verbal moods; and evaluative lexical items and marked syntax." The textual and narratological factors in his enumeration help determine how readers know what they know about the people, places, and things in the story; they produce perspective on the storyworld. But in a network fiction the interface produces perspective—or produces a multiplicity of perspectives—on the *structure* of the text itself. Not only does the form of a network fiction require conceptualization, but the conceptualization always to some degree creates the form.

Nonetheless, to say that a conceptualization contributes to the creation of a text's form is not to say that the "map creates the territory"—a notion that is the cause of some unease for Baudrillard (1994) in his cultural critique. In his well-known discussion of the Lascaux caves in France, where an exact replica was built several hundred meters from the original in order to protect it, Baudrillard describes a situation whereby the simulation loses dependence on an original: "It is possible that the memory of the original grottoes is itself stamped in the minds of future generations, but from now on there is no longer any difference: the duplication suffices to render both artificial" (1994, 9). In a network text, however, if maps continually create and recreate a territory, then such representations do not displace or supplant an original territory—as in Baudrillard's model of the simulacrum. The concept of *territory* itself, in the strict sense of a spatially locatable area, region, or terrain, does not apply to the abstract spatiality of network topology (until, of course, we arbitrarily impose one, as with the spatial logic of the World Wide Web, where "Internet Explorers" traverse a "Netscape").

Furthermore, contrary to Ryan and Herman's stated focus, empirical evidence suggests that mapping the spatiality of the storyworld—a topographical *mapping* per se—is not a common or at least a primary form of "mapping" (in the generic sense) when reading fiction. Zwaan's research (e.g., 1993, chap. 4) shows that readers of print texts rarely maintain an "accurate map of spatial relations" in the represented storyworld unless they are given specific instructions to read for such clues. In conducting her own experiment on the "construction of narrative space" by analyzing maps of Gabriel

García Márquez's *Chronicle of a Death Foretold* (1982) drawn by high school students, Ryan herself makes clear that it "takes a specific agenda—such as the present project—to attempt a systematic reconstruction of the 'textually correct' map of a fictional world" (2003, 217); she further finds that readers "read for the plot and not for the map, unless they are literary cartographers" (238).[8]

A cognitive map of a network narrative, then, can refer to either the represented world or the link-node structure of the network. But more generally—albeit not less accurately—it can refer to a global understanding of the text's themes and meanings, which is closer to what Teun van Dijk and W. Kintsch call a text's "macrostructure" (Zwaan 1993, 20–25). An articulation of reading comprehension that has undergone countless revisions and criticisms by linguists and cognitive theorists after (and including) van Dijk and Kintsch, a macrostructure arises from the filtering of sentences and/or semantic propositions through the "gateway" of short-term memory and the subsequent arrangement of information into long-term memory. Reading comprehension, in such a model, amounts to processing "microstructures" toward the formation of a manageable, storable "macrostructure."

Davida Charney (1994) and Jhondan Johnson-Eilola (1991) have undertaken studies of the macrostructure model of reading comprehension in relation to hypertextual documents. Their contributions have served as a corrective for some of the more exaggerated claims for liberation and empowerment in hypertext rhetoric. Contrary to the assertion that hypertext technology "liberates" the reader from linearity, we know that we always *read linearly* and sequentially even if (1) the text presents information in a nonchronological fashion, and (2) the reader chooses the order of that sequence. But Charney and Johnson-Eilola go further by drawing on empirical research that shows readers of hypertexts process network texts in much the same way as they would a text in print; that is, they store information in hierarchies even if they are reading in a user-determined order. In other words, readers cognitively *prioritize* semantic material. Charney adds that since the mind cannot import textual structure directly into long-term memory, the resemblance of a hypertextual structure to long-term memory is irrelevant. In turn, the popular claim that hypertexts are more *natural* reading environments because of their resemblance to neural networks is invalid.[9] Johnson-Eilola also explains how the mental representation that constitutes a cohesive macrostructure of a text is in fact "networked" as well. Repetition provides a key to the process of networking meaning: "the repetition in a text of a previously mentioned element may form a connection between the two related propositions, even if they are at different branches in the hierarchical macrostructure" (Johnson-Eilola 1991, 104). Therefore, if the experience of reading network texts does, indeed, yield an analogous macrostructure, then the foregrounding of repetition at a material level would conceivably facilitate the semantic networking of a macrostructural hierarchy.

Some theorists of digital textuality have fused spatial models of textual coherence with theories of information space, updating the print-based model of macrostructure in other ways. Nancy Kaplan and Stuart Moulthrop (1994), for example, make a clear delineation between the "architectonic" and "semantic" space of textual networks. They equate the architectonic space of the network text with a graphical display—the space of the screen, which often imitates physical space, and where architecture involves manipulating stable objects according to "the rules of geometry and perspective" (1994, 207). Kaplan and Moulthrop's semantic space is, by contrast, not a "built structure," by which they mean it is not observable in physical space (on the computer screen); rather it resembles the cognitive macrostructure "built" during the act of reading described by van Dijk. Semantic space, they write, is "deeply connected to the production of meaning [and] interpretation" and—in contrast to architectonic space, which is more often invoked in the context of writing—"emerges more clearly in the act of reading or reception" (207). Similarly, van Dijk's macrostructure implies the processual act of a reader assembling then interlinking propositions as she or he moves toward a global comprehension of a text.

For Kaplan and Moulthrop architectonic space is "topographical" insofar as an arbitrary structure is fixed in the coordinate grid of the computer screen. Their conception arises in part from the limitations of hypertext authoring software in providing dynamic graphical renderings during the act of composition. The same limitations frustrated Joyce in *Of Two Minds* (1995, 64): "Hypertext software, which forces us to represent contours of interaction in rectangles and arrows plotted on Cartesian space, fails to account for the gleeful vertigo we feel on first coming to see cyberspace and our ensuing desire to shape even discursive space proprioceptively and sensually, ie as the body knows."[10] Developments of graphical overviews (through improved animation and user manipulation) have enabled systems to emulate, to greater degree, the dynamic topology of hypertextual structures. But it is not possible to fully represent any topology (neither the connectivity of semantic relations nor that of hypertextual nodes) in a fixed grid of three dimensions, for grid-based metrics do not adequately account for a system's movement.[11] In their own model Kaplan and Moulthrop emphasize that the architectonic space can never "adequately model semantic space (the narrative dimensions of the story)" (209). Recalling a question posed by a mathematician in a research journal, the poet Stephanie Strickland (1999) states the broader challenge of topological phenomena in succinct fashion: "How and to what extent can a dynamical system be represented by a symbolic one?"[12] With regard to digital textuality, a grid is unable to adequately represent the emergence of a network narrative.

It is possible, however, to "map" movement in points—or in what are known in systems-theoretical terms as *singularities*. Singularities are discrete moments in any continuous process "where a merely qualitative or linear development suddenly results in the appearance of a 'quality'" (Kwinter 1992, 58). In a discussion of dynamic systems that heavily influences the opening chapter of Joyce's *Othermindedness*, Sanford Kwinter (1992, 58–59) writes, "A singularity in a complex flow of materials is what makes a rainbow appear in a mist, magnetism arise in a slab of iron, or either ice crystals or convection currents emerge in a pan of water. . . . Some of these singularities bear designations—'zero degrees Celsius,' for example, denotes the singularity at which water turns to ice or ice back to water—yet most do not."[13] Despite this possible form of mapping, Sandra Braman (1994, 362) notes that in topology theory "the location of a point is less important than how it got there." Her comment further underscores the fact that any point in a topological structure implies a history and thus, in turn, a certain kind of narrativity. In a sense a singularity is the moment at which form or meaning arises from a story that precedes, follows, and indeed produces it.

Clearly, there are difficulties inherent in *mapping* space that is either semantic or fluid, but some accounts further complicate the issue by conflating the notion of "semantic space" with the structural topology of links and nodes. In her essay "Cyberspace, Cybertexts, Cybermaps" (2004) Marie-Laure Ryan comprehensively plots four types of space associated with digital texts: (1) the physical space of the fictional world represented by the text; (2) the architecture of the text; (3) the material space occupied by the signs of the text; and (4) the space that serves as context and container for the text. In her model "textual architecture" refers to "the internal organization of the text, the system of relations that connects its elements. These relations, described by literary critics as 'spatial form,' have traditionally been semantic, phonetic, or broadly thematic, but with the introduction of hyperlinks, the digital medium has added 'accessibility' or 'contiguity' to this list" (2004). This second category conflates textual topology, the material form of network narrative, with what can be called a semantic topology, which is immaterial in that it consists of meaning produced by the processing of symbols and their interrelationships. The problem with Ryan's grammatical construction points to the problem with her theoretical construction. She compares the adjectival qualities "semantic, phonetic, or thematic" with the nominal qualities of "accessibility" and "contiguity"; the former take a referent—*relations*—whereas the latter, as nouns, do not, or at least should not. The nonparallel construction obscures the fact that all *relations* already have a degree of both contiguity (otherwise they would not be related) and accessibility (otherwise we would not know they existed). What is really at stake is the way in which connections are connected and the way in which readers access them.

Ryan rehearses a conflation common among theorists who see digital technology as the fulfillment of contemporary literary theories, which is not surprising given that she herself has said that the aspects of theory fulfilled by hypertext "hardly need explanation at all" (Ryan 1999, 101). Clearly, the links and nodes of a network narrative do not constitute an always already deconstructed semantic space—a structure in which all of the "semantic, phonetic, or thematic" connections have been joined by digitally mediated linkages. If this were the case, a network narrative would amount to nothing more than an authorial schema presented to the reader in lieu of a narrative text. Furthermore, where Moulthrop and Kaplan's model addresses the issue of composition versus reception, or writer/reader—the issue, essentially, of agency—Ryan's model does not. The fact that she lacks a corresponding model of agency for her "textual architecture" adds a degree of indeterminacy to the category: who ultimately is the architect of this space?

Movement beyond Mapping

Although a number of theoretical models have moved beyond unreflective appropriations of the cognitive map, the concept itself cannot be divorced from what can be called the "panoptical impulse" of cartography: the pursuit, through both material and cognitive means, of a globalizing or totalizing perspective. The notion of a panoptical perspective has obvious connotations as a tool of surveillant and oppressive regimes and has been a subject of lengthy critique on these grounds, most evidently in the work of Michel Foucault, whose notion of the panopticon (after Jeremy Bentham) has transcended the domain of poststructuralist theory and entered popular discourse. But as a way of "reading" space the panoptical view has also been the subject of critique in contemporary literary theory on aesthetic grounds.

In an often cited essay, "Walking in the City," in his *The Practice of Everyday Life* (1980), de Certeau traces what he calls "the lust to be a viewpoint" back to medieval and renaissance painting, which was able to portray the city as none had ever seen it before. Looking down on New York City (in the early

1980s) from the 110th floor of one of the World Trade Center towers, the view he sees is a materialization of "the utopia that was only yesterday painted" (1984, 92). At the same time, to him the view holds no real power: in pursuing and culminating a "scopic and gnostic drive" for a celestial viewpoint, the subject, whose body is now wholly detached from what it sees, has become *nothing more than a viewpoint*, for a "totalizing eye" (92) is necessarily a disembodied one. With regard to reading literature, J. Hillis Miller sees the practice of (cartographically) accounting for wholes as an inheritance from New Criticism (1982, 17–18) and adds that it "cannot be detached from its theological basis" (24). These theorists suggest that a totalizing perspective is in itself problematic and incomplete, and Jameson's own cognitive map can be said to overextend itself in its totalizing aim, seeking a formal analogue for a complex, global array of social and political relations. But with regard to network space, it becomes obvious that a God's-eye view can no longer hold the same authoritative power—if it ever really did. An alternative model of hypertextual comprehension is required for what is ultimately an unmappable space. Brian Massumi's (2002) writing on topological space—and, more specifically, the concept of proprioceptive movement—provides an alternative spatial rhetoric that can inform an understanding of network space.

Whereas Jameson loses himself in the architectural tour de force of the Bonaventure Hotel, Massumi gets lost in his own office. He begins his essay "Strange Horizon: Buildings, Biograms, and the Body Topologic" with an anecdote about his shock at realizing that, for two months in his temporary office at the Canadian Centre for Architecture, he was "looking at the wrong street out the window" (Massumi 2002).[14] He explains that from the point at which he went through the side entrance of the building, to the point where he reached his office, his negotiation of the building's winding corridors resulted in a disjunction between where he saw himself and what he saw. That is, he saw himself facing north, and this fact overrode any visual clues to suggest that the scene outside, framed by the office window, was anything other than a north-facing view:

> The sudden realization that my north was everybody else's east was jarring. True, I hadn't paid much attention to the scene. But I wasn't just not paying attention. When it hit me, I had the strangest sensation of my misplaced image of the buildings morphing, not entirely smoothly, into the corrected scene. My disorientation wasn't a simple lack of attention. I had been positively (if a bit vaguely and absent-mindedly)

seeing a scene that wasn't there. . . . When you actively see something that isn't there, there is only one thing you can call it: a hallucination. It was a worry.

Massumi explains that although he had no trouble finding the way from the entrance of the building to his office, his memory of the route was not a primarily visual one; he could not have sketched scenes from the corridors or mapped the route with any accuracy: "I was going on a bodily memory of my movements, one of contortion and rhythm rather than visible form." This bodily memory forms a mode of orientation that we tend to take for granted, one based not on vision but on movement. Proprioception refers to the intuitive awareness of our body in space—it is a sense (some would argue our sixth) that makes sure, for instance, that our feet find their way up or down a staircase without watching each individual step (we habitually revert to visual cues when coming to a landing, where this rhythmic motion is altered). It is what allows us to touch the tip of our nose with our eyes closed. Charles Olson, who applied the concept of proprioception to his own poetics several decades earlier, describes it as "the sense whose organs lie in the muscle" and a process by which "the 'body' itself as, by movement of its own tissues, [gives] the data of depth" (1997, 181–82).[15]

Such movements rely on corporeal habits instead of cognitive maps, which, as Massumi notes, are "built on the visual basis of generic three-dimensional forms [arising from] Euclidean configurations" (2002). An overt difference between the two modes of orientation is that proprioception is a "self-referential sense, in that what it most directly registers are displacements of the parts of the body relative to each other," whereas "vision is an exo-referential sense, registering distances from the eye" (2002). As Massumi's anecdote demonstrates, the two modes are not necessarily calibrated to one another; they are, nonetheless, interdependent.[16] Proprioceptive orientation, because it relies primarily on movement, cannot be measured or mapped in a static geometry or a (Cartesian) coordinate-based grid. Since such movement defies a grid-based metric, it occurs in non-Euclidean or *topological* space, where configurations cannot be considered apart from their movement.

Of course, in terms of biomechanics readers move very little when they move through text.[17] But conceptualizing reading as "moving through a text" is axiomatic, and it is common to invoke internalized modes of orientation for textual comprehension. Rosello has said that "reading, interpreting spaces, and drawing maps are activities so intricately intertwined that it is difficult to separate them" (1994, 129). Mapmaking itself implies a conquest of territory, and here it would imply the mastery of a text-as-territory. Such mastery assumes a panoptical perspective, and it is the same totalizing view-from-above that dominates textual criticism as a default mode, and understandably so. How else can a work of art be subject to critique unless that work is considered, to some degree, objectively, which is to say as an object or objective whole? But when the territory itself remains in flux, even a new map will not remove the disorientation felt on a return visit. The cognitive map as articulated by psychology remains useful as a metaphor for textual comprehension, allowing us to "map" either the represented storyworld or the structural complexities of a text. But since cognitive mapping is not the only—or even the primary—mode of orientation in lived experience, *it should not provide the only metaphorical analogue of textual orientation.*

Readers must attend to their conceptual "movement" in a narrative network differently than they would in a printed book, which provides a stable axis of orientation. As the narrator of Shelley Jackson's *Patchwork Girl* (1995) puts it, "Assembling these patched words in an electronic space, I feel half-blind, as if the entire text is within reach, but because of some myopic condition [that] I am only familiar with in dreams, I can see only that part most immediately before me, and have no sense of how that part relates to all the rest. When I open a book I know where I am, which is restful. My reading is spatial and even volumetric. I tell myself, I am a third of the way down through a rectangular solid, I am a quarter of the way down the page, I am here on the page, here on this line, here, here, here. But where am I now?" ("this writing"). Like the narrator, the only way for the reader to know where "here" is would be to move away from it, to see it in relation to a plurality of other locations, and to see it again later from another point of view. Significantly, the effect of returning is lost with a static, totalizing perspective. Of his own view from the tower, de Certeau writes, "One's body is no longer clasped by the streets that turn and return it according to an anonymous law" (1984, 92).

The movement from one node to another amounts to a series of self-referential movements that evokes the *self-referentiality* of proprioceptive experience. These movements, however prescribed by the literary machinery, shape the text—not the text as it *is* but as each reader discursively brings it into view. The form of the text is perceived, in Joyce's words, "outward from the middle of [a reader's] own movement" (2000, 168). The analogy suggests an alignment of the cartographic drive of exo-referential mapping with a sense of the *text-from-above,* whereas the self-referential mode provides a more intuitive sense of the *text-from-within.*[18] The alignment, in turn, gestures toward an operational difference in reading narrative texts, where the rhetorical and metaphorical notion of experiencing a text proprioceptively translates into practice. If the text-from-within evokes the local coherences or "microstructures" in the text, then network environments redefine "local coherence."[19] For example, if the paragraph and the chapter function as semantically coherent units in print narratives, readers in a network text also process the transformation of "node-link-node" as a locus of meaning. Beyond the node-link-node are the micronarrative readings formed from the parts or wholes of hypertextual paths, what Jim Rosenberg (1996) calls "episodes," which would also reside on the level of hypertextual microstructure. Clearly, hypertextual comprehension calls for more than a finely detailed map, for even "zooming in" will not reveal the meaning in/of the transition. Coherence, in these moments, emerges only as an outcome of a dynamic transitionary movement, similar to the "singularities" that mark the form of a rainbow emerging from the mist of an atmospheric topology.

As Massumi's anecdote shows, exo-referential and self-referential modes of orientation both play essential roles in "the practice of everyday life"—to borrow the title of de Certeau's work. Therefore, if in print texts the relationship between the body and the text is characterized predominantly by the making and viewing of maps, then the relationship between the body and the network text implies a reader who comes to know the text proprioceptively. At the same time, in reading both physical and textual spaces, the relationship between the two modes is one of complementary interdependence.

Textual Kinetics

A network text implies a process of unfolding that is at once temporal and spatial, in the manner of what Moulthrop (1992b, sec. 29) describes as an "object-event." For Michael Joyce hypertextual comprehension, in particular, signals a profound convergence of the space of memory and the time of narrative experience (1995, 159–71). Indeed, in attending not only to the object but also the event of reading, a topologically informed understanding of reading networked texts breaks down rigid divisions between temporality and spatiality common to literary criticism. A reconceptualization of the reader's movement does not, however, wholly address the formal mobility of the digital text itself, which remains largely untheorized in narratology.

Movement or mobility of a text is a familiar topos of literary criticism but one whose rhetorical and metaphorical connotations require redefinition in terms of digital materiality. Unlike William Carlos Williams's "machine made of words," the movement of a network text is a literal mobility; that is, its signifying components do not remain fixed in relation to one another.

There are several reasons why narratology remains reluctant to take up the task of textual kinetics. First, the practice is arguably more relevant to poetry (and visual art) that draws on a rich aesthetic tradition reaching back to the Futurists in the early twentieth century. Such artists were invested in representing or evoking movement on an imaginative plane by using a wide array of typographical and design techniques on a necessarily static plane of expression. This kinetic-poetic drive translated readily into forms of e-poetry that erupted with the use of digital writing technologies.[20]

A crucial distinction with regard to textual kinetics in poetic or narrative texts involves whether the text moves with or without the reader's intervention. This distinction can be broken down further; for instance, movement can occur, with or without reader intervention, from one screen to the next *or* within the frame of the present screen. Another related reason for a reluctant kinetic narratology, then, is the practical problem that arises with narrative texts moving without the reader's intervention, which Aarseth refers to as "transient." Moulthrop's *Hegirascope* (1995), which "pulls" the current screen after roughly fifteen or twenty seconds, has become a locus classicus of this digital form. Quite obviously, "words that will not be still"—to paraphrase the opening of *Hegirascope*—have the potential to move too quickly for the reader. (Outside of artistic media it is more often the intent to calibrate the movement of words across a screen to a reader's ability to read them, which is the governing design schema for moving text on anything from a public announcement bulletin board to the credits at the end of a film). Kinetic techniques can work to the detriment of a contemplative reading experience—though disruption and subversion are often the motivating aesthetic of such an exercise. In general, if it moves, fades, or even disappears before one has finished reading it, the most immediate conclusion is that reading the text is not all that important in the first place or that some other aesthetic or conceptual imperative at least takes precedence.

An understanding of narrative kinetics is further complicated by a form of movement that is already intrinsic to narrative: reading itself acts as a motor of discursive movement, an observation that points to another instance where a rhetorical conception of movement intersects with a literal movement of text on or in relation to a surface. "Discourse time" in print narratives is typically a measure of words, sentences, or pages in relation to the represented duration of the story, which makes it actually more a spatial measure than a temporal one. As Rimmon-Kenan (1983, 52) observes, in print texts the act of reading is the "only truly temporal measure available" and thus provides no objective standard. Digital literature, however, recasts this claim by introducing other measurable phenomena, which could include anything from the time a transient text remains onscreen to the time it takes for an online work to load before it is actually read. Also, in a network fiction a measure of pages is useless when there are no pages per se, and, given the possibility of narrative returns, even if the time of the story is understood or determined to be finite, the discourse time is not. Discursive movement in network fiction is distinct from and at the same time inseparable from textual-kinetic movement.

A redundancy of "movements" requires a retroactive clarification of terms and an expansion of theory but is not in itself problematic. A problem arises only when one form of movement is erroneously assumed to literalize the other. In discussing kinetic text and narrative, the greatest inertia to overcome involves the perceived literalization of mobile signifieds in the presence of mobile signifiers. Early hypertext theorists put forth the claim that the material properties of hypertext systems literalized or embodied the infinite deferral of linguistic signifieds (Bolter 1991, 204); they saw semiotic instability realized onscreen in the hyperlinked signifier, which literally yields or defers to another text behind or beyond it. Aesthetic theories that anticipate digital literature often betray an ambiguous notion of *movement*, which contributes to the conflation of (1) properties peculiar to certain technologies and (2) universal properties of language.

Umberto Eco's articulation of the "work in movement" in *The Open Work* (1989) is a well-known example of an attempt to describe what Aarseth calls the "variable expression" of certain artworks. Eco begins with a discussion of musical works in which the performer chooses a sequence from a number of available alternatives, describing them as "open" in a "tangible sense" (cited in Aarseth 1997, 52). But, as Aarseth's critique shows, Eco shies away from a discussion of literary works with changeable or recombinatory elements, instead shifting his emphasis "from the combinatorics of signifiers to the combinatorics of signifieds" (Aarseth 1997, 52). Aarseth cites Eco's rejection of a truly mobile text, Marc Saporta's *Composition No. 1* (1962). Eco dismisses the work, recalling Barth's criticism of "intermedia," when he states that "the book had exhausted all its possible readings in the very enunciation of its constructive idea" (cited in Aarseth 1997, 53).[21]

Predating Eco's *Open Work* by almost two decades, Sharon Spencer's *Space, Time, and Structure in the Modern Novel* (1971) marks an effort to analyze works of literature where movement is a material attribute integral to the text's expression. Spencer claims that there are two characteristics that endow a text with "mobility": "One is a literal mobility: the interchangeability of the book's parts. . . . [T]he other is its embodiment of the aspiration of continuous creation" (188–89). While an "aspiration for continuous creation" reads like an extension of Eco's aesthetic, analogous to a form of interpretive recombination and juxtaposition of signifieds, Spencer's "literal mobility" clearly transcends it. Even though Spencer's critique deals exclusively in the technology of print, it speaks to the need to distinguish between *literal* mobility and what we can call *literary* mobility at the level of the signified, which the poststructuralists have shown to be in constant motion as a function of language, not of a medium.

The literal mobility of nodes in network texts gives rise to material repetitions, which can in turn allow for creative acts of interpretation through recombination. Recombination implies an interpretive act; moreover, because the act of returning to a node often involves a reinterpretation that builds on a former interpretation, it is possible to speak of *recursion* as well as repetition in the context of reading. A special case of repetition, recursion denotes a process by which a structure operates on itself (or some part of itself) and thus produces a more complex version of its own structure. It can occur in many contexts—in logic, in mathematics, in music, in visual art, and in consciousness—and it typically involves the nesting or embedding of elements. Richard Hofstadter (1979, 127) introduces the concept playfully as "(Stories inside stories, movies inside movies, paintings inside paintings, Russian dolls inside Russian dolls (even parenthetical comments inside parenthetical comments!)—these are just a few of the charms of recursion.)."[22]

Recursive logic often enacts a paradox, as in the classic conundrum "I am lying." Is the statement true or false? As a literary device, recursion is commonly associated with a subversion of *ontological* frames in postmodernist writing (McHale 1987), but Barth (1984) has demonstrated its prevalence in Greek and Roman literature (with regard to *narrative* frames and subframes), and Mieke Bal (1981) has done the same for nineteenth-century novels (in terms of embedded *discourse*). Recursion also has a specific meaning in relation to computer programming. Recursive control flows involve a program that refers to itself in order to repeat a given function, as opposed to iterative flows that contain programming loops that continue until some sort of stop criterion is provided. Since the output of recursive flows produces a more complex version of a function (or of the system that reproduces itself on higher level), it does not involve loops; rather, it is represented in terms of an upward-moving spiral.

The corresponding figures of a loop (for repetition or iteration) and a spiral (for recursion) are applicable to the formal properties of narrative texts in print. For example, a text such as *Finnegans Wake* (1959) follows a loop, beginning again at the end: "A way a lone a last a loved a long the / riverrun, past Eve and Adam's, from swerve of shore to bend of bay" (540 / 3). Narrative recursions involve more complex embeddings, where an embedded narrative is subordinate to an original narrative frame. Narratology has several terms for recursive narratives: an embedded narrative is also referred to as a "hypo-narrative" (Bal 1981, 43), and a frame narrative is also referred to as a "matrix" narrative (from the Latin *mater* for "mother" or "womb"). In Rimmon-Kenan's (1983, 91) model a first-degree narrative is analogous to the frame narrative since it is not contained by any other narrative (at least not in intratextual terms), a second-degree narrative is embedded in the first, and so on. The model extends to narrators that correspond to the narrative degree.[23] Narratology supplies a terminology for movement or shifting between narrative levels as well. Genette (1972), for example, calls the (often sudden and disruptive) transgression of these levels *metalepsis*. Metalepsis can bring two different ontological orders, or "worlds," into direct contact—or conflict.

In network environments repetitive loops and recursive spirals take on added meaning as patterns of hypertextual structure. The direction of recursive movement at the level of narration is always a given in print texts, where it is predetermined by the order of reading. In a network narrative, by contrast, a linking structure and its underlying code ultimately dictate these flows. The fact that repetition can occur both as a function of the interface and of the narration speaks to the need to distinguish between the *material* and *discursive* levels of repetition. In a fundamental sense the distinction elaborates on the interplay between the formal and semantic elements of a literary work by adding an awareness of materiality, as does Hayles (2002a, 31) when she discusses works of literature as "embodied" texts that arise from an interplay of "form, content, and medium."

Such a distinction, though cast into sharp relief in digital literature, is not a product of it. Florian Cramer (2001), in an essay adapted from a conference panel with Robert Coover and Jeff Noon, credits Barth's 1967 essay the "Literature of Exhaustion" as the introduction to what he calls "narrative recursions" versus "code recursions." Cramer states that the essay "matches experimental artist books by Dick Higgins, Daniel Spoerri, and Ray Johnson against Jorge Luis Borges' fictions, concluding that the former perpetuate an exhausted mode of modernism exactly because they put recursion into the object code instead of the meta narrative" (Cramer 2001). Cramer does not entirely do justice to Barth's position; after all, Barth states—if only hesitantly—that medial experimentation "may very possibly suggest something usable in the making or understanding of genuine works of contemporary art" (1967/1982, 4); and Cramer further finds more in the link between such "experimental artists" and an "exhausted mode of modernism" than the content of the essay allows. Nonetheless, he draws a crucial distinction, one that does not rely on the print/digital dichotomy as a precedent.

Despite his historically protracted critique that includes a direct response to digital literature, Barth himself does not experiment with digital writing technologies in his own art practice. In "The State of the Art" (1996, 38) he betrays a "benevolent curiosity" about the possibilities inherent in the digital medium; however, he follows his 1967 dictum in transcribing *only* the "cultural fact" of his curiosity when he writes "Click" (1997), a parody of digitally hyperlinked fiction that reads more as skepticism than benevolence. Published in print and online by the *Atlantic Monthly*, "Click" presents the reader with dozens of blue, underlined words and a parenthetical invitation to "*Click on any word of the above,*" which initially appears as a hypodiegetic address to the characters on their computer screen but later in various ways as a direct address to the reader. But the story has no hyperlinks: they are feigned using the appropriate typography. Barth suggests that he does not need digital hyperlinks or a network form to reveal the "hypertextuality of everyday life."

Even though it is published online (readers must hyperlink to access it), and it emulates the appearance of a World Wide Web–based network narrative, "Click" does not move beyond metanarrative recursion. To apply Cramer's terms, there is no recursion at the level of the "object code." From this platform of narration, which is focalized, ironically, through a Mac computer, Barth's story alludes to various forms of loops but only in a degenerative sense. For instance, the narrator describes the characters' bedroom, where "[t]he mirror (left of center) gives back a view not of the viewer— fortunately, or we'd never get out of the loop and on with the story—but of the workroom door" (Barth 1997). In addition, the narrator's discussion of hyperlinking the word *the* in the phrase "The Hypertextuality of Everyday Life" exemplifies a degenerate use of the hypertext medium itself: "A good desk dictionary will list at least eight several senses of the homely word 'the' in its adjectival function, plus a ninth in its adverbial ('the sooner the better,' etc.)—twenty lines of fine-print definition in all." Rather than consider the ways in which a narrative structure might emerge in a network environment, Barth's story is more invested in putting forth the proposition that— in the words of Theodor Nelson—"everything is intertwingled."

In doing so he simply perpetuates an overbroad definition of *hypertextuality,* defined in the story as "[t]he further texts that lie behind any presenting text" (Barth 1997). A broad understanding of "the hypertextual" is by no means misguided; in fact, the efforts to establish the long (bidirectional) line of hypertextual literature has in many ways provided a valuable counterpoint to linear and hierarchical conceptions of reading, writing, and thinking. And it has allowed for a closer scrutiny of what Glazier (1996) and Marsh (1997) refer to as the "internal orders" of textuality (such as typography, calligraphy, pagination, annotation), which have been naturalized in books. At the same time, hypertextuality that simply posits an acute interconnectivity and an endless semiotic slippage or deferral of meaning leaves a difficult question unanswered. William Marsh (1997) writes:

> If hypertext is nothing but text (in the post-structuralist sense) slightly juiced (thus reduced) in the frenzied point-and-click environment of computer hyperlinks, then little is gained by studying its developments. However, if hypertext can be set into motion not merely as text transplanted in electronic space, but rather as an area of high-density hypergrams (beyondwords, words within words), then the work generated out of this 'motion,' as well as the critical articulation of its method, would surely invite the kind of enthusiasm merited by the emergence of any new form.

Here, Marsh's use of the term *motion* vacillates between a literary and a literal mobility, which is necessary given his support of a " 'hypergrammatic praxis' by which the notions of 'word-as-link' (in web page design) and 'word-as-paragram' (in book page design) are themselves linked, mutually informative, reciprocal" (1997).[24] Nevertheless, if it remains unclear how or if hyperlinks reinvigorate language, then it is at least clear that the network environment is set apart from the book in terms of mediated mobility. Barth's story, which is as static as his hyperlinks, is left to ponder these developments but not perform them.

A more telling experiment with material recursion lies not with Barth's online fiction but with a work written contemporaneously with "The Literature of Exhaustion." The opening chapter of Barth's *Lost in the Funhouse* (1988, 3) contains his "Frame-tale," which reads, "ONCE UPON A TIME THERE WAS A STORY THAT BEGAN." The phrase appears twice (one above the other) with subscripted and superscripted letters and instructions to the reader to (1) cut out the phrase, (2) fold it once horizontally so that one phrase appears on the front of the strip and the other on the back, and then (3) twist it once before joining each end as a Möbius strip (by matching up the corresponding letters). As Cramer (2001) explains, "It thus becomes an infinite recursive story, a story that . . . opens up itself as a narrative subframe which in turn opens up itself as a narrative subframe, and so on." Cramer adds that "Frame-tale" is a rare example "where the code itself—i.e. the letters—loops with the narrative," an observation that resonates with Joseph Tabbi's (2002, xxiii) comments on material systems: "Like a strip of computer code whose structure is itself the instruction for its own assembly (and like New Criticism's ideal poem as a self-illustrating artifact), the material system is its own best description." In "Frame-tale" two distinct recursive systems thus operate in unison. But what is most telling about the piece is its sheer absence of the poetic—the best way, perhaps, for Barth to lay bare the "gimmick" of medial experimentation. In essence the text is not only a degenerate form of narrative by way of simplicity and cliché but also a degenerative form of repetition by way of an infinite loop.

Barth's text is instructive, but rarely are recursive systems that simple. For instance, recursion can give rise to what Hofstadter (1979) calls "Strange Loops." Strange-loop phenomena emerge "whenever, by moving upwards (or downwards) through the levels of some hierarchical system, we unexpectedly find ourselves right back where we started" (1979, 10). Strange loops, Hofstadter adds, occur in systems of "tangled hierarchies." As Laurie Johnson (2002) notes, strange loops imply another sort of paradox because "they bring our notions of the finite and the infinite into conflict. Some object (A) always seems to contain or be the root cause of some other object (B) in a finite relationship, yet B also seems to contain or be the root cause of A, a paradox of infinite indeterminacy."

In a network narrative the "tangle" points to an intersection of discourse and materiality. In a network text it is possible that readers move through a tangled hierarchy of nodes, but such strange loops are not necessarily concomitant with the strange loops that might run through its lines of narrative discourse. Hypertextual structures are not hierarchies that are always already tangled and that readers untangle as they read. A strange loop in narrative text occurs as a function of the narrative discourse. In network environments the technology itself (in the form of a sequence of looping nodes) can contribute toward this end.[25]

Hofstadter points out that any system includes a protected or "inviolate level" that always remains "unassailable by the rules on other levels, no matter how tangled their interactions may be among themselves" (688). But "inviolability" here is not absolute; the operative phrase in Hofstadter's construction is inviolable "*by the rules on other levels.*" It is possible to subvert the machinations of a system by transgressing levels, thereby gaining access to a new set of rules. Moulthrop points to John McDaid's *Uncle Buddy's Phantom Funhouse* as an example: McDaid's work contains a node that, when run as code, actually crashes the HyperCard software on which it operates.

Aptly, the node is a "script poem" about nuclear war. The message "might be that every system has its limits. Any recursive or simulacral structure is subject to intervention and opposition, so we have to watch those men behind the curtains" (Moulthrop 1992a). Moulthrop's example speaks to the interplay of narrative levels as a distinctive quality of network fiction. More specifically, it is possible to say that the materiality of network fiction prompts a renewed attendance to the dialogue between the material, formal, and semantic elements of the text.

A Preface to Interplay

It is clear that digital textuality offers up a staging ground for the convergence of discursive and material complexity. But artists are beginning to question whether increasingly complex interfaces and interactions must inevitably limit or constrain the degree of discursive complexity in a screen-based text. Does one necessarily come at the expense of the other? An artist and researcher of interactive technologies, Matt Gorbet frames the question well: "[U]sing a simple, familiar physical interaction which maintains the users' sense of control, how far can the complexity of the content be pushed? Is there a necessary correlation between simple interaction and simple content? Or is it possible to create a body-centric interactive piece with the storytelling capacity of an epic novel or a play?" (cited in Stefans 2005).

Critics certainly differ in conceiving what kind of literature can result from this convergence. Brian Kim Stefans (2005), a practicing digital poet, suggests that any such constraints are more likely to be governed by broader questions of medium: "My guess is that the simplicity of the interaction does not constrain the degree of complexity of the text so much as might the sum of the parts of the application (particularly the screen, whether it be water or a wall, and the limits of how many lines you can have on it)." Other critics wonder if the convergence of discursive and material complexity might be less than amenable. Tabbi (2003), for one, doubts that literature "can take on such multi-dimensionality and performativity and retain its cognitive richness": "The danger is that complexity in performative media . . . obviates, rather than facilitates, verbal and conceptual complexity in the work of literature." Either way, it seems inevitable that as our interactive tools become more powerful and diverse, so too will the nature of the experiments and interactions that follow.

Relative to the "interface" of the book, digitally networked texts are complex and unfamiliar. But relative to the field of digital art, from kinetic poems to corporeal immersions in full virtual reality installations, the hyperlinked node of network fiction is by no means an example of an extremely complex graphical interface. Network fictions do attest, however, to the verbal complexity and conceptual depth of a body of writing created for the surface of the screen. Further, the analyses of individual works in the chapters that follow will suggest that an effective network aesthetic maintains some form of dialogue between the discursive, verbal, and conceptual on the one hand, and the formal, performative, and material on the other. Maintaining such a dialogue and, more so, finding a balance among these elements, might be an essential prerequisite to creating compelling digital fiction.

3

Returning in Twilight

Joyce's *Twilight, a Symphony*

[I]s not such self-reflective activity of the computer homologous to a Bach
fugue which constantly takes up the same theme?
—Slavoj Žižek, "From Virtual Reality to the Virtualization of Reality"

Of the theoretical problems posed by hypertext technology, the treatment of
orientation was both the earliest and probably the most misguided. Joyce's
afternoon, which popularized the idea of narratives in digitally networked
form, also simultaneously popularized the problem of orientation in them.
Given *afternoon*'s "invisible" links, however, the copious criticism it generated responded to the disorienting effects of what was to become an anomalous work in the field. Misdirected criticism was compounded by attempts to
master and map the "territory" of the network text using the tools of an incompatible cartography. In the decade after the first publication of *afternoon*
(in 1987), updated interfaces and updated theories led to better technical and
critical accommodation of textual topologies; and as patterns emerged from
these topologies so too did modes of orientation that were more intrinsic
to the medium. These changes begin to appear in Joyce's *Twilight, a Symphony* (1997), where patterns of repetition and return shape narrative semantics and structure. Nonetheless, the work places a heavy reliance on the
topographical quality of the Storyspace interface and the potential of "spatial hypertext," a reliance that can, in fact, complicate the experience of reading network fiction.

Magdalena's Return

Twilight, a Symphony is a story of returns. In what Carole Maso has called
Joyce's "lyrical elegy,"[1] a journalist, Hugh Colin Enright, takes his infant son
and hides away from his estranged wife on the shores of Pleasant Lake. There,
Hugh befriends an eccentric Polish refugee and his wife, Magda. Almost a decade later, Magda, suffering from a rare form of cancer, seeks out Hugh and
begs for his help in her search for the Twilight Doctor, who she believes will

assist her in her death. When their search fails, Hugh agrees to help Magda end her own life, a macabre quest for closure that repeatedly and ultimately fails.

While Magda's return from near death frames the broader narrative, her return to Hugh frames its opening. As the introductory node tells us, "The beginning of the story in the present moment finds these two talking, rather operatically (or perhaps in the way of a Socratic dialogue), on a screen porch in Spring. Magdalena may be in remission or simply very near death and silver with pain" ("Our story so far"). Beyond the introduction two further nodes, titled "here" and "there," establish the idea of return as a central theme. Neither node assumes the distinct point of view of Hugh or Magda; instead, the narration weaves musings and memories peculiar to each character with a state of reverie common to both. In "here" a contemplation of corporeality suggests that the narration focuses, if only briefly, on the thoughts of Magda, her own body flushed with disease: "Having been here once here now once again. One could actually reach and touch where in the air there before the eyes the center of the body had been bound by bone staves, heavy kettle of innards slung below corseted bellows; reach where once a winged shoulder moved at eye level, so surely there one could lay one's head against the scent of the past itself, nestle in memory, cradle recurrence between curved palms. . . . I tread here once and am once again. What could this mean?" ("here").

Moments of reverie in the node "there" seem to belong to Hugh, who observes couples passing by, "solicitous and tender to one another. . . . [One man] touches the broad freckled back of his big-breasted handsome wife; their child returns from the dark water." Meanwhile, "another woman whose plump arms seem distinct from her . . . returns from the long dock with her dark-haired mustachioed handsome husband and gently slips her hand into his" ("there"). Hugh's observations reveal his preoccupation with family and, more specifically, his yearning for a sense of ordinary domesticity that haunts him as it eludes him.

The narrative continues, with Hugh questioning the "purpose [of] all this intricate care and mindless passing of time," and concludes with an evocation of Magda, "the fragrance of her returning." The phrase may refer to their present-tense reunion on the porch—Magda may have approached him at that moment in midreverie. But her *returning* also refers to his memory of her unexpectedly revived in the hotel room after the attempted assisted suicide. Hugh's next recollection is a question Magda puts to him repeatedly, and it serves as one of the unifying refrains of the story: "Why didn't you let me die?" ("there").

Although their reminiscence "in the present moment" gives some indication of their past, readers must find paths that will return them to the shared history of the two. In this sense Hugh's and Magda's reunion cues our departure. *Twilight* underscores Peter Brooks's (1984, 37) comment that "narratives both tell of desire—typically present some story of desire—and arouse and make use of desire as dynamic of signification." In this case the reader's desire to return to the past experiences of Hugh and Magda runs parallel but counter to Magda's desire to die. Her desire provides the most overt movement toward a conclusion—Brooks's "full predication" of narrative plot. Instead of a final death scene, however, readers repeatedly encounter reunions and an echo of Magda's lament, "Why didn't you let me die?"

Joyce describes the narrative as moving along different thematic trajectories: "east toward life (though in the past) and west toward death (though in the future)" ("Our story so far"). The western arc toward death is still by no means a *forward* progression, toward the "signifying totality" described by Brooks. Though at first it would appear that the aptly named node "the end" might offer at least a quasi ending to the narrative, it instead enacts another, quite dramatic, return: "When it was over he wasn't clear (he never has been) whether he panicked or simply misjudged how much it took to die (he knew one day she would ask him)"; the paramedics and the constable "watched her return in giddy silence" ("the end").

A Return to Gould

In "From Afternoon till Twilight" (1998) Raine Koskimaa argues that, unlike *afternoon*, *Twilight* "is not even attempting to offer different stories but rather different readings of the same story." Koskimaa's observation is also a recognition that *Twilight* falls readily into the category of network fiction, whereas *afternoon* exhibits the qualities of an arborescent fiction with what at least appear to be mutually exclusive "stories."[2] But his comment also encourages an approach to *Twilight, a Symphony* as just that—a symphony. Joyce presents a story in variations where each variation enacts a repetition of an original melody.

Joyce resurrects Canadian pianist Glenn Gould and his work, the Goldberg Variations, to exploit theme-and-variation as both a formal and contextual device. "Gould or his ghost is, as you know, a character in—and something of an organizing principle of—*Twilight*," he writes in an email interview with the *Atlantic Online* (Lombreglia 1996). As we are told in "Our story so far," when Hugh and Magda sit talking, "they are listening to one of Glenn Gould's two recordings of the Goldberg Variations, recordings which link them in interesting ways. (Magdalena was born in June, 1955, the month and year of the first recording; they met at Pleasant Lake in the summer of 1981, just after Gould recorded the variations again in the same studio on East 30th Street in New York City.)" The music marks a return to their own memory of this first meeting, after they realize that they are both on the run. During the first meeting, Hugh surveys Magda's modest home and hears "the clatter of rain on the roof in the ceilingless room mixed with the hiss of noisy Bach from a terrible eight-track tape player with stained decals of Sesame Street figures on its grimy yellow plastic sides" ("twos"). Joyce's mention of an eight-track player suggests that the version of Bach Hugh hears is indeed the first predigital recording of Gould's Goldberg Variations. Although the detail appears trivial, it is one small piece of the vast fabric of interconnections that unite Hugh, Magda, and the music of Gould.[3]

As an "organizing principle" the story of the Goldberg Variations is itself a story of returns. Legend has it that Count Keyserling, Russian ambassador to the Saxon court in Dresden, had as his musician-in-service a young boy named Johann Gottlieb Goldberg. Keyserling is said to have had a terrible case of insomnia and, in an effort to find something to ease the long hours of the night, he commissioned a work from the reputable composer Johann Sebastian Bach. Bach was to compose music that the young Goldberg, also a Bach protégé, could perform during the count's hours of sleeplessness—perhaps even lull him to sleep. The result was the Goldberg Variations, though the origin of the aria on which they were based remains another source of debate. The only certainty is that sometime in the year 1725 the score was recorded in a notebook belonging to Bach's second wife, Anna Magdalena (who shares her name with the female protagonist of *Twilight*).

Furthermore, at the time of the composition the young performer was roughly twelve years old, and there is some dispute that the boy could have handled the technical complexities of the work. Hofstadter (1979) explains what is complex and unusual about the piece in a dialogue between Achilles and the Tortoise, characters he borrowed from Lewis Carroll, who borrowed them from the ancient Greek philosopher Zeno. In the dialogue—which is itself reflexive in that the Tortoise resolves to bore an insomniac Achilles to sleep with number theory—the Tortoise explains that the Goldberg Variations are held together not by a common melody but by "a common harmonic ground." Moreover, he describes how "every third variation is a canon" (a theme played against itself in different "voices"), a process that continues until "the final canon has entries just exactly one ninth apart" (Hofstadter 1979, 392).[4] The complexity of the composition heightens its legend.

Like Goldberg, Glenn Gould was a musical prodigy. He was said to have read music before he read words, and when Gould first recorded the Variations on piano in 1955, the event marked his musical debut at age twenty-two.[5] The recording not only brought instant fame to Gould but also popularized the Variations themselves. Before Gould the music was used primarily for performance, typically by harpsichord, and few earlier recordings exist. Gould is known for his eccentricities; among these were his disdain for concert halls and live performances (he once expressed the desire to do away with what he considered the reprehensible ritual of applause). Nevertheless, his decision to withdraw from live performance in 1964, not ten years after his debut, came as a shock and disappointment to those devoted to his music. Gould continued to compose, record, and even write essays on a wide range of topics but never returned to public performance. He did, however, return to the Goldberg Variations, compounding the mystery of a man who rerecorded the work that made him famous more than thirty years before. Though he completed the project, Gould died after suffering a stroke less than a year later, which not only kept his mystery intact but also conferred on that last recording an ethereal, even mythical, status.

Gould's second recording of the Variations marks the most definitive return of his artistic career. In his own "return to Gould" in an essay of the same name, Bruce Powe (1989) writes of the 1981 recording: "There is serenity and ecstasy, introspection and grandiosity in the last interpretation of the Goldberg Variations. Gould's return to this piece was poignant and ambiguous—a piece transformed by the spectre-visionary of the recording studio. His version is both a farewell and a rethinking."[6] The romantic assumption follows that Gould foresaw his own death, which heightens the "haunting" feeling commonly ascribed to the 1981 work. Powe himself only goes so far as to say that the assumption is "tempting," but in his introduction he, too, refers to the "haunting, darkened second version" and writes, "It is the aria, the autumnal air he offers, that makes him seem death-haunted, neurotically charged, even ill" (Powe 1989).[7] Gould's return to the Variations serves as the backdrop for Joyce's narrative, the source of the story's haunting tone. But Gould provides more than the background music for *Twilight*. His ghost underscores the ominous reason for Magda's return to Hugh, for she too seems to sense death approaching.

There were also more mundane motivations for Gould's return to the Variations. The development of digital recording technologies, though still primitive at the time, inspired him to undertake the 1981 recording. Gould saw the technologies as encouraging a more active role for the listener and a more collaborative atmosphere for composers and producers, both of which anticipate the creative ethos embraced by many hypertextualists. As Gould wrote more than two decades ago, "Electronic transmission has already inspired a new concept of multiple authorship responsibility in which the specific functions of the composer, the performer, and indeed the consumer overlap" (quoted in Powe 1989).[8]

Whereas Gould influences Joyce as an artist, the ghostly influence of both Gould and Goldberg affects Joyce's characters as mythical personae. For example, Hugh's son, Obie, shows signs of early musical genius: "We return home last night to find that Obie has composed a song, an ornate and visually beautiful child scrawl scoring a twelve bar sonata of two contrasting sections, replete with dotted notes, crescendi e dimuendi, tonics, and a haunting minor feeling" ("(son)ata"). The same "minor feeling" that haunts Obie's sonata haunts all of *Twilight*, for it refers to the G-minor that opens the aria of the Goldberg Variations. Through the assimilation of sound into his text (and images and video), Joyce attempts to show how media can merge to enhance, rather than obscure, a narrative object. The intent is to weave together not only different media but also different modes of perception, as Magda's musing on the porch suggests: "the birds wove the twilight into a tent, all their night music becoming an actual fabric of caring" ("birds weave"). The textures of music, images, and words thus converge not only in Joyce's *Twilight* but in Magda's twilight as well.

Readers hear the G-minor as a sound bite when they open two of the narrative's nodes. In "songs" readers hear the note as a single piano stroke as they begin to read of Hugh and Magda searching for any sign of the Twilight Doctor from the shore of the small Canadian town of Marathon. Toward the end of the node it is clear that a distinct sound has also reached the two characters: "We search the seam of the water and sky for any light, whether an oar boat's running lamps or an evening star. There is no light, and yet we think we hear something" ("songs"). If readers default to the next node, they hear a different note; unlike that of a piano, the sound is that of a "distant klaxon" from a ship. The text begins with a direct address that suggests a metafictional acknowledgment of the sound: "There. Hear that? Somewhere far on the water, bleating metallic G-sharp modulating to A-flat, its dull echo lingering on the silent edge of twilight" ("Calliope at Marathon"). Hugh reads the ship's horn as music, and the reader assumes that the ghost of Gould is again present, especially given Joyce's allusion to Calliope in the node title, which evokes the Greek muse of poetry, as well as the keyboard instrument of the same name.

The G-minor not only opens the aria of the Goldberg Variations but also concludes it. Hence, Joyce uses the same sound bite to open his pseudo-ending at "the end." As Magda slips into unconsciousness, shrouded in her "death masque," Hugh sees her, ironically, as a chrysalis. After Hugh phones the police and realizes Magda has not actually died, he removes the shroud in a moment of symbolic rebirth. At this moment the mythical identification of Hugh with Goldberg is most explicit: "Her eyes said why didn't you let me die. Yet it wasn't so bitter as it sounds. Not so sad. She knew he loved her. . . . Your name is Johann Gottlieb and I am the Countess Chrysalis" ("the end"). The passage reflects a confused, shifting, and at times indeterminate point of view, perhaps a result of the mythical personae intruding, appropriately, at the borders of life and death. But the irony, and indeed the *variation*, is that Hugh has failed to lull his countess to sleep.[9]

Sight, Sound, and Refrain

In addition to its thematic and mythical returns *Twilight* is replete with linguistic repetitions that tether narrative moments. Mark Bernstein (1998a) reminds us that the repetition "need not be complete and literal, for a writer may gain the effect of repetition by repeating some aspects—position, typography, color—while varying others." Joyce's textual refrains, which appear in several different nodes and often in slightly different ways, demonstrate this form of narrative return.

Joyce composes a series of five nodes he titles "ekphrastics," which refers to a form of descriptive poetry designed to evoke acute visual images.[10] The segments are numbered, but, much like memories, they do not link accordingly or in any given order. The text of each differs, but all five include the same concluding refrain: "This is how it will be to die." The "first ekphrastic" details a memory of "crossing in fog . . . the Hudson from Beacon to Newburgh, the bridge lights are feathery halos" ("first ekphrastic"). Along with the visual image of the bridge lights seen through the fog, the node includes a sound bite that is identical to the "metallic G-sharp" that opens "Calliope at Marathon." It enacts an audible return, and readers associate the "dull echo" heard by Hugh and Magda with the same sound Hugh hears while crossing the Hudson as a child. The memory, however, belongs to Hugh; that is, the text dramatizes a return at the level of his consciousness. The node concludes with the refrain: "Surrender: this is how it will be to die" ("first ekphrastic").

The remaining ekphrastics amend the opening word of the refrain in such a way as to reflect the sentiment of the memory evoked. The third ekphrastic, for example, tells of Magda's suffering, her "marrow dulled with morphine yet bone raw and in pain beyond pain." Its refrain follows: "Sweetly screaming: this is how it will be to die" ("third ekphrastic"). Joyce uses the refrain to unite different memories, allowing the reader to enact a return to the theme of death in varying contexts. Linguistic refrains work in concert with the nodes recurring at the level of the interface. Thus, *Twilight* not only enacts material returns instead of closure, but it also renders closure as a theme to which the reader repeatedly returns in a changed and ever-changing context.

In *A Thousand Plateaus* (1987) Deleuze and Guattari establish that the concept of "refrain" in music is inextricable from the delineation and organization of *territory* (their term is *ritournelle,* or "little return," and "refrain" is Brian Massumi's 1987 translation). Their refrain is a spatiotemporal phenomenon that "territorializes"; it is "a rhythmic pattern that serves to mark a point of stability in a field of chaos, like the tune a child hums in the dark to comfort him- or herself" (Murphy and Smith 2001, sec. 4). Deleuze and Guattari suggest that a process of deterritorialization and reterritorialization is necessary for the subject to continually enact an escape from the constraints of territorialization, often brought about by the "State," which itself can serve as a metaphor for any analogous oppressor.

In appropriations of their philosophical system—a system in which tropes appear at times to assume an agency unto themselves—it is difficult to determine whether the refrain needs to be "deterritorialized" (which would make it a negatively freighted concept) or whether the refrain already functions as the agent of deterritorializing and reterritorializing (which makes it more positive). For example, in Ian Buchanan's (1997) formulation the refrain "is essentially territorial, territorializing, or reterritorializing, and it quickly reclaims music for itself should [music] ever become self-indulgent, which is to say repetitive merely for the sake of hearing an enchanting little phrase over again." Here the refrain is always staking out and claiming territory—and it functions as the agent of this process. But the refrain is somewhat different in Murphy and Smith's appropriation:

> As a concrete example of the deterritorializing potential of the refrain, Deleuze and Guattari cite the analyses of LeRoi Jones (Amiri Baraka), who shows in *Blues People* how black slaves in America, in the conditions of forced labor, took their old African work songs, which were originally territorial refrains, and made use of them in a "deterritorialized" manner, in the process producing an "intensive" and plaintive use of the English language by blending it with their own African languages; these songs were in turn "reterritorialized" by whites in minstrel shows, and the use of "blackface" (Al Jolson); and then taken back

by blacks in another movement of deterritorialization and translated into a whole series of new musical forms (blues, hootchie-koochie, etc.) (Murphy and Smith 2001, sec. 8)[11]

In this example the refrain is something that is employed by slaves, then by white musicians, and finally by black musicians to both deterritorialize and reterritorialize; the refrain itself does not hold agency (as something that perpetually territorializes) but rather is employed by different groups of people with different or even competing agendas.

How does Deleuze and Guattari's refrain apply to network environments? The space of the digital network has been described in hypertext theory as the epitome of deterritorialized space—an unencumbered plain able to be traversed at speed by a fluid, nomadic subject. Common to the discourse was the portrayal of hypertext technology as the instrumentalization of Deleuze and Guattari's "smooth space," which stands in opposition to their "striated space" that is, by definition, territorialized.[12] But there are two problems with this understanding. First, "hypertext" fills the vacuum of agency and fulfills the operation of deterritorialization independently of a given user's application of the technology; that is, the hypothetical plain is always already deterritorialized by default. Furthermore, the very notion of a "plain" or even a fixed "territory" misconstrues the topological form of hypertext systems, which might be more accurately described as "aterritorial" given that the "landscape" itself is in flux and unmappable, at least in a static cartographical mode.

With regard to networked narrative environments, the (linguistic) refrain can be said to both deterritorialize and reterritorialize in relation to patterns formed by the text (rather than its dynamic structural topology). Because *narrative* returns are necessarily tied to the logic of semantic progression, they transcend a simply degenerative form of repetition—what Buchanan (1997) describes as "repetitive merely for the sake of hearing an enchanting little phrase over again." Narrative returns are inevitably performed in a different context, amid new surroundings, even when readers encounter a refrain that is itself unchanged. Joyce's *Twilight,* moreover, demonstrates how subtle changes to formulaic refrains can recast their meaning as the narrative progresses, regresses, and repeats.

More generally, the process of linking itself implies a rhetoric of repeated disorientation and reorientation. That is, a reader departs from a familiar node and arrives, in an instant, at an unfamiliar one without any immediate understanding of its relationship to what came before or its bearing on what comes next. For example, the node "see see" begins with a narrator who is not introduced, speaking of a boy who is named but unfamiliar: "A lost gesture. We are the last race of the carbon copy, the generation before the migration into light. 'Why do they call it a tab?' Jeremiah asks. (We call him electronic boy)." There is a text link present at the boy's question, which links to a node that frames a father's memory: "I will never forget . . . once in the city walking down Fifth Avenue at dusk with Obie, we were coming from a birthday trip to see the armor at the Metropolitan and then look for toys at FAO Schwartz. He was eleven then. I'm certain of that, one year into double digits, lost in the twilight between childhood and pre-teen; there wasn't one thing in the toy store which really caught his eye" ("towers in air").

The speaker is Hugh, who is sharing his memory with Magda in the narrative present. But the transition from the previous node is a difficult one. Not only does the reader arrive at a time and place different from the passage in the previous node (which is also populated by indeterminate and unfamiliar characters), but the text link also takes readers to the *middle* of "towers in air."[13] That is, when the text window opens, readers must scroll up if they wish to read the node from the beginning. In addition to the temporal and spatial disjunctions at the story level, the link thus involves a form of disorientation that arises directly from an engagement with the interface.

In the passage, Hugh further recalls pointing out the Empire State building to Obie:

[H]e kept insisting, maddeningly, that he didn't see why they ever thought it was the tallest building in the world. . . . I tried to explain that it was a matter of perspective, an optical illusion, feeling myself get more and more annoyed at a boy on his birthday. It was a litany, the way kids do: "That one over there is bigger," he replied to each explanation. The truth was, like your blue sky, I had no satisfactory explanation, even for me. . . . The truth, of course, is that he was right. It was bigger in any way that counts. It still is. ("towers in air")

When Hugh mentions "your blue sky," he refers to a memory Magda has shared with him earlier in the conversation—and a reader who scrolls up to the beginning of the passage finds that the detail appears earlier in the same node. Specifically, Magda recounts the time she overheard a child in a 7-11 convenience store ask her mother why the sky was blue. These reflections— on children asking parents to explain complexities of the world that they have long taken for granted—establish an interpretive ground for the previous node, "see see." In that scene the boy, presumably watching his father at a computer, asks him the reason for the name of a certain computer key. The father either does not answer or does not recount his answer; quite possibly, like the mother in the 7-11, and Hugh on Fifth Avenue, he does not have one. Instead, he muses that he belongs to the last generation of people for whom computers were not always a fact of life ("the last race of the carbon copy, the generation before the migration into light"). Even though the characters remain unfamiliar, the discrete moments are tied together by a recurrent pattern (any number of biographical blurbs will reveal that "Jeremiah" is the name of one of Joyce's own sons, which suggests we are reoriented in an entirely different ontological frame). Like Joyce's refrains, these recurrences routinely disorient and reorient the reader at the level of node-link-node.

Finding the Way in Twilight

If the reader of Joyce's *afternoon* wanders through an inscrutable and seemingly endless landscape, then the reader of *Twilight, a Symphony* embarks on a path more clearly signposted, entering the space of the text equipped with a detailed map. *Twilight* gestures away from *afternoon* with the inclusion of digital map overviews, an indication, some critics believe, of the author's desire to increase the reader's sense of orientation. Scott Carpenter (2000, 141), for example, finds that *Twilight* "provides a map of the textual sites visited during a reading session" in order to "alleviate the sense of disorientation experienced by readers in *afternoon*." Although this is not entirely accurate— the map provides a view of *all* sites, not necessarily just the ones "visited"— Carpenter is correct when he points out that "it is not certain that the map always provides a clearer sense of direction" (141).

But other factors contribute to what amounts to the elaborate but also problematic navigational apparatus of *Twilight*. A movement toward "spatial hypertext" in informational and educational software design influenced conceptions of hypertext systems in theory and practice. Spatial hypertext referred initially to any hypertext system represented in the form of a map (Marshall 1999, 1) and has its origins in systems developed from the late 1980s, such as Xerox's NoteCards. As interest in spatial hypertext grew, research began to focus more specifically on the ability of graphical representations of structure to suggest relationships through spatial proximity and visual attributes. Cathy Marshall, in collaboration with Frank Shipman and Russell Rogers, developed several software systems that rely on spatial hypertext, in addition to writing extensively on the concept (see Marshall 1999; Marshall and Rogers 1992; and Marshall and Shipman 1993). Marshall and Shipman (1993, 219) gloss spatial hypertext as a system where a reader/author can perceive the intended structures in space, just by noticing their geometrical relationships ("if this text is close to that text, then the two must be related"), visual characteristics ("if this text is in a twelve-point italicized serif font, it must fill an annotative role similar to the other twelve-point italicized text that's an annotation"), and recurrence ("this segment of text means something completely different when I read it over here"). If this structure is perceived by heuristic algorithms, it can then fill the same function as explicitly represented structure.

Thus, another factor that helped shape Joyce's navigational schema was the extension of graphical capabilities of the Storyspace interface itself, which allowed users to view and manipulate multiple overviews of the link-node structure, a function initially available only to the composer (and the user who installed a separate Storyspace authoring application). This added capability effectively made Storyspace a spatial interface at both the level of composition and reception. With *Twilight* Joyce wanted to depart from the perceived inscrutability of *afternoon,* but his desire to employ the new tools of a software system he helped to create likely played a part in the design of the work. After all, the operational features of spatial hypertext went hand in hand with the topographical rhetoric that dominated the poetics of much first-wave digital literature, Joyce's included.

To a large degree, then, many of the noticeable changes between *afternoon* and *Twilight* reflect changes made to the Storyspace software, and some are exclusive to Storyspace II, in which Joyce published *Twilight.*[14] For instance, there are always two windows open in the interface of *Twilight;* one is textual, the other graphical. The text window contains the text (and/or images) of the current node: this is where the narrative text is found. As the instructions to *Twilight* explain, the second window is a map window, which shows "the current space and its neighbors." As in earlier Storyspace applications, there are several map overview options, and *Twilight* includes the same outline, chart, and Storyspace map (which presents nodes in the notation of a directed graph). The Storyspace map, however, is clearly the privileged view, and it functions as the default map that readers encounter when they begin a reading. Joyce, in fact, does not even mention the other overviews in his accompanying instructional pamphlet, focusing instead on the qualities germane to the Storyspace map when describing the map window: "This [window] lets you see which are related spaces, which spaces a space contains or is contained in, and some of the links between spaces" ("Instructions").

The toolbar, or tool palette—the most basic way readers move between nodes—has also undergone an evolution of sorts. The toolbar of Storyspace II combines popular functions of earlier Storyspace reading applications. The palette includes a "compass tool," and, as the instructions note, readers "Click on the arrows of the Compass tool to move around in *Twilight* according to the placement of spaces (not their links)." Here Joyce describes a mode of "spatial navigation" that is in opposition to navigating via the network of interlinked text. Readers can use the arrows on the Compass or the arrow keys on the keyboard to move from one to the other (much as one moves between files and folders on a computer desktop). As Joyce writes in the instructional node in *Twilight*, "In the Storyspace Reader (as in the program) you can move around directly in the topography of the text" ("Reading Story-spaces"). Hence, readers can inhabit a fixed landscape, moving from one node to another by virtue of their adjacent location in space.[15]

There are logical disjunctions, however, between the topography of the interface and the topography of a physical landscape. The left and right arrows move readers to what "precedes and what follows" each node in its given spatial arrangement; they allow readers to move along "the same level" of the narrative structure ("Instructions"). This corresponds intuitively to an east-west axis suggested by the compass tool. But the up and down arrows do not move readers north and south on the plane of the computer screen. The up and down arrows move readers instead to structural levels "above" and "below." Specifically, "the up arrow moves you to the space that contains the space you were reading" (as in moving out from an egg yolk to its egg white). Conversely, the "down arrow moves to the (first) space contained within the space you were reading" (from an egg white to its yolk) ("Instructions").[16] The material embeddedness of the hypertextual structure complicates a strict cartographical rhetoric, since the compass does not represent movement north, south, east, and west as we perceive these directions on a two-dimensional plane; in effect, it does not actually work like a compass.

The movement up and down through the levels of a stacked hierarchy might be said to approximate movement along a north-south axis. This movement is not constrained by the height and width of the screen—what designers refer to as "screen real estate." But this assumption leaves readers without any corresponding conception of an east-west axis, which is constrained by dimensions of the screen. Collections of nodes pictured in a single map view are numbered and arranged from left to right in rows and, when the width of the screen is reached, a new row begins underneath. The default path moves readers according to the numbered boxes; that is, the right arrow follows the nodes from left to right and from top to bottom, much like the spatial arrangement of text on a page. The topography of the screen, then, includes another north-south axis in the space of each map view. A compass placed on this topography points intuitively to the north and south of the plane of the screen, not the "above" and "below" of the embedded nodes. The "topography of the interface" amounts to a stacked hierarchy of planes rather than a singular, mappable plain.

A Topography of Themes

Twilight's navigational apparatus goes beyond changes to the interface and software. Joyce creates a thematic topography—a conceptual landscape to which he assigns bearings that arise from his multilayered story. The thematic topography both organizes and motivates the narrative:

> The stories, insofar as there are stories here, move in two central arcs, east toward life (though in the past) and west toward death (though in the future). Above these is something like a dream or mind, a set of sometimes fragmentary, sometimes speculative linkages (with their own arcs). Below, in something approximating the present moment of the shifting text, is the beginning of a story. This story begins toward its end, yet well after the end of one of the histories (Pleasant Lake) and a bit beyond the song sequence (which takes place on the shores of another lake, Superior, in a small Canadian town called Marathon). ("Our story so far")[17]

East and west arcs move both temporally, in the past and the future, and thematically toward "life" and "death." Dreams circulate in the arc above, and below readers find the story in the present moment—a "beginning."

Joyce links the narrative's themes to the metastructural arcs. For example, after reuniting with Magda, Hugh contemplates the prospect of helping her die: "This night, not more than a year after learning again to love her, if I find the courage I will help her die. Like great birds, herons or swans, we have come north and westward in a wide orbit seeking the twilight doctor" ("4.Anna M."). At the level of the story, Hugh and Magda have traveled geographically north and westward around the shore of Lake Superior. The narrative moves also according to the thematic arcs: north, in a dreamlike state, and westward, toward death. The thematic arcs cue the reader at other moments, such as when Magda and Hugh walk anxiously along the lakeshore:

"We are looking west and southward. From here the water has the color of dull stone and seems to extend without margin. . . . Frightened by the bleakness of the cold, great lake stretching from Marathon to Duluth before us, we hold hands. For the last hour at least, as if by instinct we have sought whatever warmth is left us to store against the long night. . . . We search the seam of water and sky for any light, whether an oar boat's running lamps or evening star" ("Songs"). Still intent on their search for the Twilight Doctor, they are looking westward, which suggests not only the direction of their gaze but also the direction of their thoughts—toward their future and Magda's desired death. They are also looking southward, which evokes the thematic arc that moves toward the "present moment of the shifting text." The scene on its own suggests that Hugh and Magda temper their contemplation of the future by joining hands and sharing the warmth of the present moment.

In its broader context the node is part of the "song sequence" that comprises many of their experiences during the futile odyssey around the shores of Lake Superior, which Joyce places directly before "the present moment of the shifting text." Readers recall that "the story begins toward its end, yet well after the end of one of the histories (Pleasant Lake) and *a bit beyond the song sequence* (which takes place on the shores of another lake, Superior, in a small Canadian town called Marathon) [my emphasis]." Their southward gaze, then, anticipates the "story that begins toward its end," which will place Hugh and Magda together once more on "a screen porch in Spring," listening to the music of Glenn Gould. In addition to readers orienting themselves with the navigational maps of *Twilight*, they can also feel their way along any of the thematic arcs that both support and inform the narrative.

Polydirectional

Joyce's four-part structure recalls the "aria" that opens Richard Powers's *The Gold Bug Variations* (1992):

> What could be simpler? Four
> scale-steps descend from Do.
> Four such measures carry over
> the course of four phrases, then home.
>
> . . . the theme swells
> to four seasons, four compass points, four winds,
> forcing forth the four corners of the world
> perfect for getting lost in . . . (I)

The passage reminds us that "getting lost" is not necessarily a bad thing, especially when it involves being lost in the movements of musicality. But in *Twilight* such movement might not be as *simple* as the rhetorical question of the aria implies.

Some of the ways that the text orients the reader are conventional and familiar. "Our story so far," for example, provides a detailed catalog of people and places. Readers are told that Hugh accompanies Magda "on a fruitless quest around the shore of Lake Superior and across toward Hibbing, Minnesota where she hopes to enlist the aid of the Twilight Doctor, an increasingly notorious small town doctor committed to assisting dying patients who wish to commit suicide." They learn little else of the Doctor throughout the story, for he appears only in passing—literally passing Hugh and Magda on a lake freighter "as they sit by the frigid shore near Sault Saint Marie" ("Our story so far"). Nonetheless, the near miss orients readers by immediately establishing familiar conventions of character and plot, in addition to its detailed exposition of people, time, and place. Even though *Twilight* is by no means a conventional narrative, these narrative conventions contribute to Joyce's repertoire of orientational methods and tools.

But despite—or perhaps because of—its emphasis on orienting the reader, *Twilight* ultimately complicates the notion of "navigation." Two problems arise as a result of the narrative's navigational apparatus. First, the two topographies described in the narrative, one thematic and the other operational, do not cohere; rather, they complicate the reader's perception of movement through the text. Readers find that the conceptual topography of the story's thematic arcs has an unclear and at times contradictory relationship to the topography of the interface. The nodes in the Storyspace map are not arranged in a way that will necessarily reflect the thematic movement of the narrative. For example, if readers use the compass tool to move west (left) on the Storyspace map, the text they read indicates that they are not necessarily moving "west toward death and the future" along the central arc of that description. If they do attempt to use the left or right arrows to move in a continuous path east or west, the course of travel is limited to the nodes contained within any given Storyspace map view. Reaching the eastern- or westernmost node of a particular map view results in a computer beep telling readers that there are no more nodes located to the right or the left—they have reached an entirely operational dead end.

There are times when readers find coherences between operational and thematic movement along a given trajectory. For example, the node titled "modern man and baby" describes Hugh's experience of childnapping his son, Obie, from his estranged wife. Given that this scene occurs during the history at Pleasant Lake, it is easily locatable on the eastward arc—in the past, "toward life." Hugh, the narrator at this point, refers to "the crisis now a week and a day past." If the reader's next operational move is west, using the left compass arrow, she or he will in fact move west, thematically, toward the future. The node located to the left of "modern man and baby" is "Les Heurs," in which Hugh mentions that it is "ten days since my independence with Obie"—two days later in a temporal sequence. But these continuities are too rare to give readers a reliable bearing. Readers are unable to map with any consistency the movement (1) right, left, above, and below in the fixed landscape of the interface to the movement (2) above and below or east and west along Joyce's narrative arcs.

At the same time, Joyce describes the topography of the interface and his thematic topography in such a way as to suggest there should be a correspondence. When Joyce writes, "In the Storyspace Reader (as in the program) you can move around directly in the topography of the text" ("Reading Storyspaces"), he refers to the spatial arrangement of nodes, not the thematic arcs. It is not clear that readers can actively follow the thematic arcs when they *want* to move with them, even though this topography is the one that exists in a more explicitly meaningful relationship to the story. The fact that readers find no reliable way to follow storylines is not in itself problematic, especially for those accustomed to reading for emergent narrative structure in network environments. But the prospect of reconciling the two topographies in *Twilight* proves misleading.

Another problem with the navigational apparatus of *Twilight* arises when a reliance on "spatial navigation" threatens to eclipse the reader's experience of the semantic network. When readers navigate according to an interface map, they bypass the text links that constitute the text topology of the network fiction; in turn, they bypass any rhetorical linking strategy the narrative may accommodate. Since the links themselves require an interpretive engagement from the reader (signifying through recombination, juxtaposition, enjambment), they must be conceived as part of the mutable totality of the network fiction.

Discussing a spatial hypertext interface as "problematic" is not meant to suggest that some hypertext systems are ill-suited for artistic applications or that some are better suited than others, only that some systems lend themselves more readily to the reinscription of conventions associated primarily with a paradigm of print. In this case the desire to map the text and overview its totality informs the use of spatial hypertext to create a work of narrative fiction. That said, it is possible to argue that the unique potential for onscreen narratives resides in creating dynamic text-topologies rather than using the screen, in a diminished capacity, as a static map. Aesthetic techniques peculiar to network narratives are obscured in spatial navigation.

Furthermore, in placing too much emphasis on reading a hypertext narrative according to a static overview, readers not only pass over text-link semantics but also run the risk of adopting a solely "exhaustive" model of reading. The impetus of exhaustive reading practice is to visit every node, often by proceeding systematically through the text using some form of overview (either graphical or textual, as in an outline view). Since the links themselves constitute an integral part of a network narrative's structure, any systematic reading that seeks only to exhaust a complete catalog of nodes is inevitably a deficient reading of the work. Furthermore, since the exhaustive mode of reading grows out of the "panoptical impulse" for a totalizing viewpoint, it seeks to map the text with the utmost efficiency. In the attempt to discover new places, one must endeavor to avoid ground already covered. The map preempts the play of repetition.

In "Hypertext Gardens" Mark Bernstein (1998a) warns of the pitfalls of "rigid" hypertext structure: "By repeatedly inviting readers to leave the hypertext, by concentrating attention and traffic on navigational centers, and by pushing away from key pages, . . . rigid structure can hide a hypertext's message and distort its voice." *Twilight* certainly focuses attention on its "navigational centers." But Bernstein's statement begs a broader question with regard to hypertextual structure. When he discourages repeated invitations for readers "to *leave* the hypertext," what exactly does he mean by "leaving"? What constitutes a hypertext proper? With regard to tools of orientation, do these maps and overviews remain "external" to the text—as a table of contents or preface are commonly thought to be in a print text? Or should we consider them simply another node (or system of nodes) linked essentially to the text?

Gérard Genette (1997) has analyzed the form and function of what he calls the "paratext" of works of print. For Genette paratexts are liminal devices or conventions, both inside and outside the book, that participate in the interplay between book, author, publisher, and reader. Paratexts include titles, forewords, epigraphs, and dust jackets. He distinguishes between two types of paratexts, depending on *proximity* to the text: the *peritext* is in direct contact with the text (such as footnotes, typography, illustrations, titles, subtitles, and blurbs), whereas the *epitext* resides outside the text, and includes reviews, press releases, or correspondence written to or by the author (1997, 1–15). Genette's distinction, however, relies on the assumption that textual borders are self-evident, when, in digitally networked narratives, they clearly are not. It is possible to distinguish between inbound or outbound links for works on the Web. For example, works such as *The Unknown* (Gillespie et al. 1998–2001) and *253* (Ryman 1996) link to the press, criticism, and reviews on their work. But does the "direct contact" with these secondary texts mean that they now qualify as the *peritext*? And does this mean that any press, criticism, or reviews in print must still qualify as the *epitext*, residing outside the text? Linking clearly renders Genette's notion of *proximity* problematic, since all nodes are experientially equidistant.

For Koskimaa (1998) *Twilight* answers the question of paratext for itself given his contention that "[t]he switching between nodes, dialogue box, and map is nearly fatal for the reading experience." Koskimaa's comment suggests that "navigation," at least when it refers to the use of maps and overviews, can have a detrimental effect on "reading." Even the subheading of his essay, "Lost in the Story Space," signals a departure from early hypertextualists who might have used the same title to connote a positive—even celebratory—attitude toward disorientation. Similarly, Lombreglia (1996) finds the maps of *Twilight* "too complex and inscrutable to be of any real help." He adds, "I finally felt that . . . Joyce had made the wiser choice in presenting *afternoon, a story* simply and austerely." For these critics *Twilight* becomes the more disorienting work not despite its navigational aids but because of them; one might say that the text demonstrates the possibility of *over*viewing hypertextual structure.[18]

If *Twilight* implies a double logic of navigation, according to both a spatial topography and a semantic topology, then Joyce's instructions suggest that this may be a driving motivation for the work. He cites a passage from Mireille Rosello's "Screener's Maps" (1994, 151) in the epigraph to his instructional node "Reading Storyspaces": "The delay in the emergence of new knowledge may also be the condition of its future growth. Rather than imagining our period of transition to hypertext as a point when something old is replaced by something new, I would be content to see it as a time when two ways of reading or writing, *two ways of using maps,* are plausible at the same time" (my emphasis). Joyce envisions the map of a hypertextual "storyspace" as a tool that readers can understand in two ways simultaneously: topographically and topologically. Later on in these instructions, he tells readers, "You read in the way you always have, with touch and look, in a stream or in bursts, in a ritual, a rhythm or a reverie as you like it. Even so everything has changed, but for long enough now that many are used to the change and so it disappears (while others claim it has merely reverted to how it was before and thus never happened; and a few, happily, are content with what is plausible)." Joyce's reference to plausibility echoes Rosello's passage and suggests that he sees the practice of using the same map in two different ways as plausible in *Twilight,* and perhaps it is—though perhaps not both ways at once.

Contours of Otherendedness

Just as twilight marks a moment of transition in the course of the day, *Twilight* marks a transitional period in Joyce's own conception of network space, for his later theoretical narratives suggest a shift away from his own preoccupation with mapping: "Previously I have talked about the qualitative transformations in electronic texts in terms of contours, borrowing a geometric term for what I now think I have always really understood topologically, sensually (as a caress) and outside the linear" (Joyce 2000, 22). The notion of contour, introduced as early as 1992 in the collaborative essay "Contours of Constructive Hypertext" (Bernstein, Joyce, and Levine 1992), has undergone many transformations of its own in Joyce's critical writing.

Joyce writes extensively about contour in *Of Two Minds* (1995), and the subtitle of the book's third and final section, "Contours: Hypertext Poetics," is a clear indication of its significance for him. His definitions are fluid: "Contours are the shape of what we think we see as we see it but that we know we have seen only after we move over them, and new contours of our own shape themselves over what they have left us. They are, in short, what happens as we go" (Joyce 1995, 207). Later on in the same essay other definitions coalesce: "Contour is one expression of the perceptible form of a constantly changing text, made by any of its readers or writers at a given point in its reading or writing" (214). (Joyce would later call this simultaneously his "most discrete formulation" and one that "suffers from its fixity" [2000, 167].) He goes on to break the concept into a potentiality of component parts: "Its constituent elements include the current state of the text at hand, the perceived intentions and interactions of previous writers and readers that led to the text at hand, and those interactions with the text that the current reader or writer sees as leading from it" (1995, 214).[19] His repetition of the "text *at hand*" anticipates the concept's next semantic accretion: the contour as caress.[20] But it took Joyce's next book of theoretical narratives, *Othermindedness*, for him to elaborate on what he meant: "I meant how the thing (the other) for a long time (under, let's say, an outstretched hand) feels the same and yet changes, the shift of surface to surface within one surface that enacts the perception of flesh or the replacement of electronic text" (2000, 22). In his introduction Joyce resolves to continue "grounding our experience of the emergence of network culture in the body" (4), and his project runs parallel in this regard to that of Hayles (2002b), who asks what it would mean "to have a theoretical discourse that can talk about materiality and meaning together ... [t]hat connects the embodiment of readers/users who respond kinesthetically and proprioceptively as well as intellectually."

Much of "what is plausible" in reading network narratives depends on

how readers conceptualize their own embodied movement within and in relation to network environments—whether they continue to read with maps
or, instead, grow accustomed to understanding hypertextual structure in
terms of experiential contours (or some other "measure" of space). Either
way, it will take time for readers to explore without maps and, likewise, for
critics to eschew a cartographic paradigm.

The "here now" of *Twilight*

The changes to the narrative interface of *Twilight* reflect an attempt to endow the reader with greater navigational powers and at the same time preserve the allure of an uncharted narrative world. If Joyce "delights in potentially disorientating structures" of hypertext in *afternoon,* as Landow (1997,
117) suggests, then he delights in the possibilities of mapping an ultimately
comprehensible space in *Twilight.* The text, however, forces us to consider
how navigation can not only enhance but also impede our notion of reading
digital literature, where the process of disorientation and reorientation is integral to network aesthetics.

    If sudden dislocation and relocation at the level of node-link-node is a
constant in network fiction, Espen Aarseth describes an analogous experience on a macrocosmic scale with his distinction of *aporia* and *epiphany*:
"[T]he hypertext aporia prevents us from making sense of the whole because
we may not have access to a particular part. . . . Complementary to this trope
stands another: the epiphany. This is the sudden revelation that replaces the
aporia, a seeming detail with an unexpected, salvaging effect: the link out. . . .
Together, this pair constitutes the dynamic of hypertext discourse" (Aarseth
1997, 91).[21] The epiphany of *Twilight* involves—or rather is contingent upon—
a return to the porch where Hugh and Magda are reunited. The node "here"
marks one such return, though not strictly in Aarseth's sense of a "link *out*"
that satisfies a desire for closure. The phrase, "Having been here once here
now once again," which opens the node, refers to Magdalena's return to Hugh.
The scene occurs immediately after the introductory node of "Our story so
far," and, as we are told in that introductory node, "a lot has happened before
you got here." But after reading the text for a period of time, long enough
to feel that "a lot has happened" *after* our arrival, the experience of finding
our way back to the porch sets the stage for a potentially epiphanous understanding of Joyce's work. Having returned "here now once again," the reader
has effectively linked out of the narrative past and reached what is, experientially, a stationary vantage point from which to reflect on all that has happened. As Magda and Hugh look out on their world through the screen of the

porch, we look into theirs through a screen as well, one that likewise distorts what it frames. At the same time, the scene "here" does not mark any kind of comprehensive closure, since the node contains several links back in—both to the network structure and to Magda's predicament.

Despite its linguistic simplicity, "here now" is an elusive spatiotemporal construction, especially when it is embedded in narrative discourse. There is the time and place of the story, of narration, and of reading; there is also the time and place of writing, which seems to interpenetrate Joyce's narrative in a number of ways—in the scene, for example, where a son looks over his father's shoulder and inquires about the computer keys ("see see"), and in the several nodes interpolated by the rhetoric of computer code command lines, which reflexively evoke the process of composing *Twilight* onscreen (such as the "End Of File" that concludes the node titled "-30-," or the solitary phrase "out of memory," which appears in one of the many nodes titled "command"). But for the reader, arriving "here now" is also an arrival at another scene of writing: the movement of the literary arts into digital environments—what Joyce would call "the migration into light."

Together, *afternoon* and *Twilight* are two major works that constitute Joyce's own medial migration. But unlike *afternoon* (an excerpt of which was included in the Norton anthology *Postmodern American Fiction*), *Twilight* remains something of a relic. As Joyce notes, there were several "accidents of history" that prevented the work from gaining a wider audience, which included its publication as a CD when CD publication for hypertexts was coming to an end; the ascendancy of the Web, which turned many away from stand-alone applications such as Storyspace; and the fact that it was published only for Mac operating systems and not for Windows.[22] (The Eastgate catalog has noted for several years that a Windows version is "coming soon".)[23] The complexity and difficulty of the text's navigational apparatus has contributed to its marginalization both in the Storyspace line of hypertext fiction and in the broader field of digital literature. Nevertheless, along with retracing some of the steps (and missteps) of early hypertextualists regarding questions of navigation and orientation, *Twilight, a Symphony* marks a full-blown development of the concept of narrative return and establishes its role in an emerging network aesthetic.

4
Tending the Garden Plot

Moulthrop's *Victory Garden*

[T]he great Return was left unfinished, and so at the start of that fateful year
of the mirror, 1991, America set out once again on the torturous path of war-
fare. Once again, an Expedition was sent around the world, this time swift
and resolute and unconstrained.

—Stuart Moulthrop, *Victory Garden*

As more and more readers grew accustomed to unfamiliar literary interfaces
and, more generally, to an unfamiliar literary medium, critics moved beyond
questions of orientation and navigation and began to focus on other theoretical challenges posed by narratives in network environments. The question of *immersion* arose—often in an oversimplified opposition to the "interaction" required by hypertext technology. Despite the problematic reduction
of "interaction" to the physical engagement with the computer interface (e.g.,
choosing a hyperlink) common in the discourse, it was clear that the computer medium would have dramatic—even antithetical—implications for
narrative fiction, a literary form that traditionally derives its force by im-
mersing the reader in a fictional world and establishing points of identification between reader and character. In what ways do network fictions distance or alienate the reader? In what ways do they accommodate immersive
reading? Further, is such immersion necessarily *desirable?* These questions
of immersion, identification, and the materiality of digital literature arise in
any exploration of Stuart Moulthrop's *Victory Garden.*

Multipurpose Gardens

"Oboyoboy just when we'd wrung the last nostalgia from that Desert Storm,
by golly *WE GET TO DO IT AGAIN!*"[1] The narrator of *Victory Garden* comments derisively here on the "media men" who are "just about falling over
themselves with crisis-lust," unsated by the fact that they have just broadcast
a war with the highest quality production values in history. The speaker refers to the dual crises of Hurricane Bob and the Moscow coup in August of
1991, but the reference may just as well be to something that was yet to happen. Written and published in the months following the United States' 1991
war with Iraq (Operation Desert Storm), Moulthrop's *Victory Garden* is again

timely in the aftermath of Operation Enduring Freedom, the U.S.-led invasion of Iraq that began in 2003.

The narrative's political critique offers an overt and immediate point of contact for the reader, especially in light of the contemporaneous conflict in the Middle East. At the same time, it is a critique that does not lack objective subtlety. Although some early critics were quick to see *Victory Garden* as rooted in a leftist political ideology,[2] Moulthrop's narrative is not unequivocally leftist. Its political orientation in a sense mirrors its material structure, for neither sits on a stable axis. In fact, Moulthrop is more interested in revealing how a palette of information technologies contributes to and potentially *determines* the formation of political ideologies. In addition to popular forms of information dissemination, this palette would include hypertext technology, which reflexively questions its own role in disseminating information as the narrative of *Victory Garden* progresses.

Citing Sven Birkerts's observation that attitudes toward information technologies do not map neatly onto the familiar liberal/conservative axis, Moulthrop writes, "Newt Gingrich and Timothy Leary have both been advocates of the Internet. . . . I am interested less in old ideological positions than in those now emerging, which may be defined more by attitudes toward information and interpretive authority than by traditional political concerns" (Moulthrop 1997a, 674n4). The politics of *Victory Garden,* much like its plot, do not harbor foregone conclusions. In a 1994 interview Moulthrop says it "is a story about war and the futility of war, and about its nobility at the same time" (Dunn 1994). The formulation is perhaps nowhere more clear than in the work's title. Previous discussions of the title, such as in Koskimaa (2000), focus on its indebtedness to Borges's short fiction, "The Garden of the Forking Paths," which is well known to have planted the seeds of Moulthrop's *Garden.* But a victory garden refers specifically to World War II and the widespread practice, initially proposed by the U.S. Department of Agriculture in 1941, of planting gardens on residential or community property so that precious resources could be diverted to soldiers stationed overseas. While commercial farmers supplied the army, victory gardens supplemented dinner tables on the home front. By 1943, more than twenty million residential gardens were producing an estimated eight million tons of food, which amounted to nearly half of all the fresh vegetables consumed nationwide.[3] Cultivating vegetables also cultivated morale, and the victory garden stands as a symbol of the tremendous civilian support for the war effort. Thus, not only are the gardens credited with helping to win the war, but they also cap one of the most romantic periods in U.S. military history. A more sardonic reading, however, might equate Moulthrop's title with the many "gardens of remembrance" marking the places of human sacrifice that act as prelude to victory. The Normandy American Cemetery, where more than nine thousand soldiers were laid to rest, is one such reminder of great victory and great loss. There, inscribed on memorial walls, a "Garden of the Missing" lists names of more than fifteen hundred soldiers whose remains were not located or identified.

In discussing the map of *Victory Garden,* Raine Koskimaa (2000) follows Robert Coover in equating the graphic to either a garden or a graveyard—"the garden referring to Borges' story, the graveyard to Gulf War casualties." The overview map includes a North Garden, South Garden, and Mid Garden, and by clicking on any one of these three sections, readers can zoom in to see a more detailed version of each, where titles of nodes offer multiple points of entry to the story's narrative paths.

The graveyard interpretation rightly gestures toward a darkly ironic understanding of "victory," perhaps necessarily so in an age where irony comes easily for the postmodernist or, indeed, the postnationalist, who is simply unable to romanticize war. It is a gruesome irony that played itself out yet again in the coalition's occupation of Iraq during the second Gulf war. In May 2004 reports emerged from Fallujah of local volunteers having difficulty burying civilian casualties amid the ongoing fighting. According to one report the end of a month-long siege means that a woman who was killed while she attempted to flee the city can be moved to the municipal football stadium for burial; her husband has already been buried "in the garden of the house next door" (Glantz 2004). At once romantic and horrific, Moulthrop's title makes an ambivalent—and highly emotive—comment on the audience of war.

The names of Moulthrop's characters are equally suggestive. Both Emily Runbird and Victor Gardner have names derived from Viktor Runeberg, a minor character in Borges's "The Garden of the Forking Paths." Runeberg is mentioned in the opening of the document drafted by Dr. Yu Tsun, the narrator of Borges's story. We are told by an anonymous editor that the first two pages are missing. The document begins as follows: "and I hung up the phone. Immediately I recollected the voice that had spoken in German. It was that of Captain Richard Madden. Madden, in Viktor Runeberg's office, meant the end of all our work and—though this seemed a secondary matter, *or should have seemed so to me*—of our lives also. His being there meant that Runeberg had been arrested or murdered" (Borges 1993, 67). The short story continues and concludes within the narrative subframe of this document, with Yu Tsun as a second-degree narrator. But the initial passage carries a footnote after "murdered," in which the editor disputes the given account: "A malicious and outlandish statement. In point of fact, Captain Richard Madden had been attacked by the Prussian spy Hans Rabener, alias Viktor Runeberg, who drew

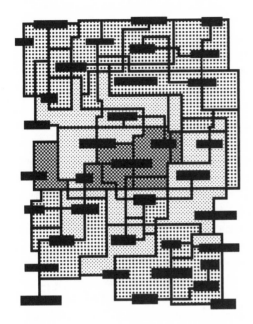

Figure 1. Map Overview. © East-gate Systems. Reproduced with permission.

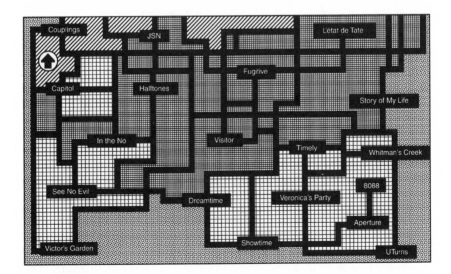

Figure 2. South Garden. © Eastgate Systems. Reproduced with permission.

an automatic pistol when Madden appeared with orders for the spy's arrest. Madden, in self-defense, had inflicted wounds of which the spy later died" (67). In Borges's story, agent Madden is in the service of the Allied forces, pursuing Yu, who is working as a spy for the Germans. In *Victory Garden* another agent Madden, formerly of the FBI, is pursuing another "U," which is the nickname of professor Boris Urquhart, who it would seem is fleeing from just about everyone, though his reasons are not entirely clear.

Like Viktor in Borges's "Garden," Victor Gardner plays nothing more than a passing role, even though his name suggests otherwise. When he does play a role, he is often at the mercy of more dominant female characters. For example, Emily Runbird, who is stationed in Riyadh sorting mail for the army, sends him several letters from the Gulf asking that he accept that their brief but deeply intimate relationship has ended: she has chosen Professor Boris Urquhart, who is also Victor's thesis adviser, as her lover ("Dear Victor"). Later, Victor is the object of a sexual seduction in which Jude Busch dresses up as Emily in a strange ritualistic attempt to unite all three of them (Emily may have been killed at this point in one's reading) ("Strange Love").[4] He is, however, the most outspoken detractor in a graduate seminar at the university, which on that day happens to be covering Borges's "The Garden of the Forking Paths" and its relationship to virtual reality and hypertext. The instructor—who is standing in for an absent (or rather missing) Professor Urquhart—introduces the text as a "tale of murder and communication, coincidence and crossed identities . . . [a] narrative essay on necessity and the nature of time" ("The Text"). Victor replies: "Garbage . . . Drivel. The Garden of Forking Bullshit. More like totally unnecessary and a huge *waste* of time. I think Urquhart is afraid to show up because he might have to hear how stupid his reading list is" ("The Text"). Emily credits his caustic wit and chronic complaining as part of what attracts her to him; she finally has someone to sit around and complain with ("Dangerous"). But the same qualities have led to Victor's self-imposed alienation, an alienation reflected on a metatextual level by his absence in the story's structural whole. Silvio Gaggi (1997, 134), in his poststructuralist critique, sees Victor as a hero appropriately decentered in a decentered novel: "[I]f we fully identify Victor with the novel as a whole, it might be argued that the decentered structure of the novel itself represents or is analogous to Victor himself. If the novel is the portrait of a person—as the correspondence between the title and the name of the character imply—then we have an image of the individual as multiple, ambiguous, and decentered." Victor's significance as "title character," however, is more than cryptic, especially when read in the context of his intertextual relationship to Borges's Viktor Runeberg. The corrective footnote in "The

Garden of the Forking Paths" foregrounds the relationship between fact and fiction, truth and history—a perennial preoccupation for Borges. "As Pierre Menard teaches us," writes Timothy McGrath (n.d.), "history serves better as the mother of truth, rather than a truth unto itself." In the Borges story Viktor Runeberg shifts from ally to spy, victim to provocateur, as a result of single editorial interpolation. Readers do not even know for certain his true name. Victor Gardner also evokes ambiguity, even though his own role suggests neither the victory gardens made by those more passive American participants in war nor the burial grounds for those lost in active duty; in fact, this Victor does nothing to cultivate morale, either for or against the war. He simply notes its imminence during a seminar where the other students are trying to come to terms with what is meant by the "real world": " 'A world that's about to have another war,' Victor put in" ("Plain Enough"). To paraphrase Moulthrop's narrator, while many others had their "ass on the line," Victor is one of those who had his "on the couch" ("War Zone"). Ironically, none of this makes him any less of a symbol as an American audience of an American war: Victor will stand for victim and protector, provocateur and imperialist, and all before he can take a stand of his own.

The names of the characters in *Victory Garden* have other political and historical significance beyond Borges, a significance that also gestures toward a particularly U.S. context. For instance, in a narrative of prismatic possibility Emily Runbird falls victim (in some readings) to what must be seen as an incredibly unlikely fate. An Iraqi Scud missile manages to breach the reputedly unassailable U.S. Patriot missile defense system and strike her barracks in Riyadh. It is a turn of events Emily herself would never have imagined. In a letter to Thea Agnew (a professor at the university and a close friend of both Emily and her sister, Veronica), she writes,

> Do I feel any anxiety about my own ass out here? No more than I do when we forget and let Boris do the driving. On second thought, I'm a lot *less* worried than when Boris is driving.

> You never know. We've got a lieutenant here who's an astrophysicist back in the real world. Lieutenant says if your in a rear posting like ours your more likely to get clobbered by a sizeable meteor . . . ("I'm OK")[5]

"Emily" is a testament to military improbability. During World War II the Japanese planned covert operations to attack the West Coast of the United States by launching a seaplane from a submarine. The plane was to fly inland and drop incendiary bombs on the heavily forested regions of Oregon, which, it was hoped, would cause massive forest fires that would spread to the cities. There were two raids in 1942, but neither succeeded in starting fires or causing collateral damage (Woodbury 1990). The mountain on which the first bomb landed on the mainland United States is named Mt. Emily—located ten miles northeast of Brookings, Oregon. Thus, if the chance of a Scud missile hitting a mail sorter stationed in Riyadh seems unlikely, so too would the chance of the Japanese bombing Oregon.

In a scene that follows one year from Emily's presumed death, Thea's new partner (who is, in a convolution of plot that can easily go unnoticed, also Moulthrop's narrator)[6] helps her pack for a trip to London:

> I pick up the big calendar we salvaged from the bottom of the heap and square it up neatly on Thea's desk, thinking, now you're ready to face the future. Only then do I realize that it's last year's calendar, untouched since February 1991. I start to say something but then my eyes catch another detail. Using a razorblade, someone has sliced the square for February 26 out of the page. The cut was deep, taking several other days with it.
>
> I say nothing. ("And Then Again")

The passage establishes a historical parallel. According to a U.S. Department of Defense paper, in the early evening of February 25, 1991, Iraq launched one Scud missile toward Dhahran, Saudi Arabia (U.S. Department of Defense 2000). The Scud broke up on reentry and showered a U.S. housing compound with debris. The warhead, however, struck a warehouse serving as an army barracks in the Dhahran suburb of Al Khobar. The explosion and resulting fire killed twenty-eight soldiers and injured one hundred, half of them seriously. This single incident caused more combat casualties than any other in Operation Desert Storm. February 26, then, marks the day Thea would have received news of Emily's death.

More than a matter of referential synchronicity in a work of historical fiction, the connection is crucial to *Victory Garden* as political critique. The same Department of Defense paper, citing a report by the MIT Center of International Studies,[7] faults the Patriot defense system for failing to intercept the missile: "One Patriot battery on Dhahran airfield was not operational and another nearby did not track the Scud, apparently because of a software problem" (United States Department of Defense 2000). Much controversy has surrounded the efficacy of the Patriot missile systems since their popular introduction in the first Gulf War. Ironically, often the problem lies not with their own advanced software but with the relative simplicity and crudeness of their target. Scuds are unpredictable; they often tumble or break up mid-flight. In short, they are difficult to track because they are so "low-tech." An independent report by the House Government Operations Subcommittee on National Security led by Professor Theodore Postol of MIT determined that the Patriot "kill rate" was in fact lower than 10 percent and possibly zero percent, a dramatic decrease from the 80 percent (in Saudi Arabia) and 50 percent (in Israel) initially reported by the U.S. Army (St. Clair 2003). The "software problem" appears to be chronic and, indeed, deadly. In the second war in the Gulf a Patriot missile engaged and brought down an RAF plane returning from an air raid on Basra, killing the two pilots. The media widely reported the event, but the tragedy was by no means an isolated instance of the technology—a defense system no less—unintentionally turned against its users (St. Clair 2003). The implication of *Victory Garden* is clear: if technology is to determine our greatest military victories, it will also determine our greatest failures.

U and Emily

If *Victory Garden* encourages an engagement in the politics and polemic of military conflict, Moulthrop's characters personalize this engagement. The reader's desire to return to the text is in part predicated on the desire to find out if Emily Runbird will return home safely from the war. Both Emily's return and her death offer possible narrative outcomes or closures and compel readers to read on. In Brooks's (1984, 37) model these possibilities *arouse* desire while the narrative *tells* of Boris Urquhart's desire for his lover and his desire for her safe return. The psychological dynamics at work thus position the reader in such a way as to establish a point of identification with Boris. Furthermore, Boris, like the reader, can connect with Emily only through textual means:

> All the letters from home. It's important what you're doing. Keeping the links together, reminding them that it all connects. . . .

> But what message can I send? What do I say to you Emily? Emily my love my future. Emily my lost sanity.

> Emily my only hope against time.

> Come back. ("What Do I Say")

At times the identity of Boris, or "U," is bound up explicitly with the identity of "you" the narratee, so that effectively *you* and *U* are addressed simultaneously as audience. An exchange between Boris and Provost Tate at the observatory, which consists of a chronological sequence of three nodes on a default path, demonstrates this compound address:

> Tate shrugged and pushed himself off the railing. "Well as long as you've dropped by, I've got something here I'd like to show you. Something you might find interesting . . .
>
> This is the prison journal of Ishibashi Taro, better known to the world of letters as Master Johdan." ("Relic")
>
> "Who?" U wondered.
>
> "Such ignorance," Tate scolded him. "Master Johdan was one of the greatest Japanese intellectuals of the wartime period. . . ."
>
> "Never heard of him."
>
> Tate shook his head. "Such a shame. He died young and at the wrong time, and his work's been badly neglected. It was November 1945. Johdan was awaiting trial for war crimes, though there's little doubt he would have been cleared and rehabilitated. But such bad luck. A week before he suffered a fatal seizure, likely a stroke. He was only 43. Very sad." ("Very Sad")
>
> "A stroke," U repeated.
>
> Tate snapped his fingers. "Like that, really."
>
> "Unfortunate," U said.
>
> "Oh yes," Tate assured him. . . . "What you see there are the last words that he wrote. . . . If you'll pardon my somewhat halting translation, I'll read it to you. . . ."
>
> U said nothing, so he began. ("Last Words")

At other times the narrative addresses "you" the reader directly, step-ping out of its ontological frame in a manner reminiscent of Calvino's representation of "you" in *If on a Winter's Night a Traveler*. The reader of Calvino's book "is an individual reading the novel (and presumably his or her self) as well as a character in the novel (over which he or she has no control)" (Gaggi 1997, 50). The novel opens: "You are about to begin reading Italo Calvino's new novel, *If on a winter's night a traveler*. Relax. Concentrate. Dispel every other thought" (Calvino 1981, 3).[8] But while Calvino is bound to the print medium, Moulthrop's narrative exploits the materiality of the screen to further destabilize the ontological boundary between reader and character.

In perhaps the most compelling instance, Tate is overseeing Boris's experiment that is meant to allow the entry of (textual) data into a dreamer's unconsciousness and thereby affect the outcome of the dream. The experiment relies on the SuperChaotic Analog Matrix Device (SCAMD), a machine designed by Boris as an "interface to the Unconscious" ("Controversial")—although the acronym, a homophone for *scammed*, is a possible comment on its efficacy. The two hope to demonstrate the media-hyped machine to a group of professionals. Meanwhile Boris's colleague, Macarthur, is wired and ready in a room down the hall, the subject of the "the world's first Interactive Dream" ("I.D."). Tate proudly introduces the machine, and the narrative switches abruptly to direct address:

It sits there paradoxically, the ultimate black box.
You see a metal enclosure approximately fifteen centimeters by ten by three. There are no visible power leads. There are no connection points, junctions, sockets, or terminals. The casing shows no vents or openings of any kind. It doesn't even appear to have seams. There are no lights, no switches, no keyboards, monitors or cables.

—Ingenious, you say, but uh, what does one do about input. To say nothing of output?

Tate grins his mischievous grin and claps you cheerily on the shoulder.—Oh not to worry, he says, we'll think of something.

Besides, you only have to connect with it once. ("The LaST Machine")

From this node the default leads the reader to an image of a black box (".").

Figure 3. The SCAMD, among other things. © Eastgate Systems. Reproduced with permission.

Metaphorically, the black screen is to the computer medium what the white page is to print: both evoke the blankness and indeterminacy of an uninscribed space. Laurence Sterne exploits the blank white page famously in *Tristram Shandy*, when he asks that the reader literally draw his own picture of the character Widow Wadman instead of Sterne's providing a textual description: "To conceive this right,—call for pen and ink—here's paper ready to your hand.—Sit down, Sir, paint her to your own mind—as like your mistress as you can—as unlike your wife as your conscience will let you—'tis all one to me—please but your own fancy" (1759–67/1978, 388–89).[9] (Sterne also includes an entirely *black* page in his novel following the death of the semi-autobiographical vicar, Yorick, which is intended to signify an effusive inscription of mourning [29–30]. The appearance of the black screen in *Victory Garden* following the missile strike on Emily's barracks could also be an echo of this mode of mourning.) The title of the node, a simple full stop, is similarly indeterminate and recalls the isolated full stop that concludes the Ithaca chapter of James Joyce's *Ulysses*, which has been said to represent anything from the collapsing of the cosmos to Molly Bloom's anus. As the concluding punctuation mark in a grammatical sentence, it marks the concluding node on several of Moulthrop's orchestrated paths; at the same time, it always symbolizes another "point" of departure in a network fiction.

When considered as an indeterminate *object,* the black box is reminiscent of the "machine" that appears several times in Donald Barthelme's short fiction "The Explanation" (the image, a simple black square, also appears once in the piece that follows in the *City Life* collection, "Kierkegaard Unfair to Schlegel") (Barthelme 1968). Much like Moulthrop's narrative, "The Explanation" puts forth a form of political consciousness, if only a disingenuous or satirical one. It opens, in the question and answer format that structures the entire text, with a consideration of the black box's utilitarian potential:

Q: Do you believe that this machine could be helpful in changing the government?
A: Changing the government . . .
Q: Making it more responsive to the needs of the people?
A: I don't know what it is. What does it do?
Q: Well, look at it.
[black box pictured again]
A: It offers no clues.
Q: It has a certain reticence.
A: I don't know what it does. (69–70)

The black box in *Victory Garden* raises similar questions and even gives us reason to question its figurative status. Closer inspection reveals that it fits the narrative's description of "fifteen centimeters by ten by three" (with depth an unknown variable on the screen). When you attempt to continue reading, you find there is no default node, nor are there any links made visible via the Control key function, which highlights linked text in the Storyspace program. You are compelled to click both inside and outside the box. Nothing happens. The box stares back at you. You are confounded, with no idea how to input, to "say nothing of output."[10] While both *you* the observer of the SCAMD and *you* the reader each sit baffled before a different machine, the reader/machine interaction is literalized on yet another level if one assumes that the reader is in some way implicated in Boris's bizarre experiment—already part of a collective, interactive dream. If, as Tate says, "you only have to connect with it once," then it would seem that you have already connected.

The reader's position is underscored by other intertextual relationships. "U" recalls Yu Tsun, the narrator of Borges's "Garden of the Forking Paths." Yu is the descendant of the great Chinese author Ts'ui Pên, whose labyrinthine garden and unfinished novel turn out to be one and the same. Both Yu and "U" feel the "swarming sensation" brought on by the overwhelming vertigo of seeing everything and everyone connected in some way and the realization that, despite the infinite number of permutations these connections evoke, ultimately the future already exists. (As Boris says in "Story of My Life": "Various things, some of them dark and some perhaps terrible, are about to happen in a place called Tara.")

At the same time, there is a crucial difference between the two characters insofar as they implicate the reader. For Yu Tsun there is only one plot, as is the case for the reader of Borges's story. At one point Stephen Albert, the keeper of Ts'ui Pên's great novel, reads aloud excerpts from the "heap of contradictory drafts." The passages concern the movement of Chinese armies and, in one "epic chapter," tell of their march to victory in the same battle but by dramatically different means. While contemplating the dizzying multiplicity of the battle scene, Yu Tsun explains, "From that moment on, I felt about me and within my dark body an invisible, intangible swarming. Not the swarming of the divergent, parallel and finally coalescent armies, but a more inaccessible, more intimate agitation that they in some manner prefigured" (Borges 1993, 76).[11] He then realizes that he will have to murder the man before him; the reader, in turn, realizes that there is only one possible outcome in the "Garden of the Forking Paths." But in *Victory Garden,* with every plot assembled comes the realization that there are other plots nested in the same system of links and nodes. Just as readers can share Boris's concern for Emily, they can also share his inexplicable and inescapable "swarming sensation." Indeed, if the narrative is a model for a hypertextual reality, Boris himself seems close to understanding it; however, his awareness of various other futures, all existing simultaneously, can manifest itself only in the form of failed mind experiments or his own irrational paranoia.

Dead Again, Home Again

Despite the varied ways of drawing readers in, the literary machinery of *Victory Garden* can also effectively shut readers out, alienating them from the fictional world. In the network, readers encounter mutually exclusive outcomes in what they might assume to be a self-contained representational system. Much debate has focused on the existence of mutually exclusive plotlines in first-wave network fictions, not least in two of the "classical" contributions to the field, Joyce's *afternoon* and Moulthrop's *Victory Garden.* For many early practitioners, the idea that digital networks could accommodate a multiplicity of plotlines became integral to an ethos of hypertextuality.

Joyce's own embrace of this ethos, however, is often misconstrued. He writes of *afternoon,* "I wanted, quite simply, to write a novel that would change in successive readings and to make those changing versions according to the connections that I had for some time naturally discovered in the process of writing and that I wanted my readers to share" (1995, 31). The passage, usually cited partially, appeared often in early criticism as a support for interactive fiction written in the mode of arborescent hypertext, but it is not clear from the passage itself whether the "change" refers to a variability of narration and expression of textual material or to a variability of outcomes at the level of the represented story. Joyce's subsequent explanation suggests that he is primarily interested in variability of expression: "In my eyes, paragraphs on many different pages could just as well go with paragraphs on many other pages, although with different effects and for different purposes. All that kept me from doing so was the fact that, in print at least, one paragraph inevitably follows another" (1995, 31). Joyce makes his stance even more clear years later in *Othermindedness* (2000, 133), when he describes hypertext writing workshops where he engaged writers with "aesthetic and readerly questions about linking rather than encouraging a choose-your-own adventure sort of drearily branching fiction."

Moulthrop, by contrast, is explicit about his intent to experiment with divergent, convergent, and conflicting plotlines, and he describes *Victory Garden* as an attempt to rationalize the seemingly irrational copresence of multiple plots: "In many versions of the story [Emily] is killed, and in some versions she is not. . . . The idea is to make it rational. When you reach a point at which she doesn't die, I am hoping the reader asks, 'What was different about this reading that got me here? How was the world different to produce this outcome?' That's my agenda in hypertext. I try to rationalize the differences" (Dunn 1994). His agenda bears the stamp of another novelist, Ts'ui Pên, who was not content to accept the notion of "absolute and uniform" time (Borges 1993, 77). Nonetheless, the contradictions in *Victory Garden*'s plot have confounded critics, perhaps in large part because they arise unexpectedly and unannounced, often late in one's reading, after an otherwise cohesive narrative has emerged. Reader-response critics, in particular, have a tendency to exhibit their own "swarming sensation" in critical discussions of the text. Robert Selig's review of *Victory Garden* in *Contemporary Literature* offers one such example: "As I continued my search through the narrative maze, this sense of Emily's importance to the story kept me from foreseeing a shocking event that suddenly darkened the antiwar theme. Emily finds herself under attack by rumbling Iraqi missiles, one hits her barracks, and the screen goes dark. My later trips down many different pathways seemed to confirm beyond any doubt that a missile has killed her. But just when I thought I had grasped a central turn of the plot, it all slipped away from me. As I kept looking, I found a discordant sequence in which a still-alive Emily comes back unharmed from the war" (2000, 648).

Emily has a major role in the story; she is one of the poles of the story's epistolary counterpoint, which transpires amid the tension of the narrative present. But perhaps more than any of the other plotlines, which remain largely unresolved rather than contradictory (such as Boris's wild flight from Madden in Harley's Porsche), Emily's safe return/death/resurrection finds itself at the center of literary criticism. Even in Gaggi's poststructuralist critique, which hinges on the notion of a decentered human subject as constructed by a decentered hypertextual narrative, "the death of Emily Runbird" is somewhat oddly "the central event in the novel" (Gaggi 1997, 127).

The distinction of arborescent and network structure resolves the critical aporia in *Victory Garden*, which does not aspire to an endless number of versions and is, ultimately, a relatively controlled experiment in narrative discord.[12] Marie-Laure Ryan (2001a) uses the notion of the "aleph" to demonstrate that the practice of creating "a new story with each reading becomes untenable." A reference to the Borges story of the same name, the aleph is a cabbalistic object that allows its viewer to behold the entirety of history and humanity. The alephic text, then, is in theory a narrative that contains all narratives and, in actuality, one that entertains the utopian fantasy of the computer as inexhaustible literary machine. But the paucity of texts that actually pursue an "alephic idealism" speaks for itself; they are not only untenable but also arguably undesirable. Theoretically, alephic texts constitute an attempt to realize infinitude; aesthetically, they embrace excess.[13] Regardless of the medium, the pursuit of endlessness and infinitude in a literary work usually has a fatal outcome—analogous to a flawed system that is unable to select only what it needs from its surrounding environment. As Niklas Luhmann (2000, 29) writes, "A work of art must distinguish itself externally from other objects or events, or it will lose itself in the world." At worst, the work of art will fail to distinguish itself from its environment and cease to function as a work of art. At the very least, whether in a biological system or a literary one, the result of indiscriminate selection is some form of obesity.

Selig fails to take constraint into account in the conclusion of his otherwise incisive review: "Far from wanting closure in hypertext fiction, I offer its authors a friendly challenge. Create with more and more pathways, lexias, link points, guard fields, changing combinations, and above all, subtleties and nuances of narrative that will not let us stop. Do not just try to make it new. Make it endlessly new, endlessly renewable, a perpetual pleasure to read, the ultimate expression of where hypertext can take us" (Selig 2000, 658). Here Selig's call for excess does nothing more than rehearse the same brand of utopianism that made early hypertext theory so unpopular more than a decade earlier. Ryan's model, by contrast, recognizes the role of constraint in an aesthetic of emergence: she likens "hypertexts" to "the narrative equivalent of a jig-saw puzzle [whereby] the reader tries to construct a narrative image from fragments that come to her in a more or less random order, by fitting each lexia into a global pattern that slowly takes shape in the mind" (Ryan 2001a). But while the analogy amounts more or less to a description of a network narrative, it does not account for arborescent narratives with a finite number of possible outcomes. Furthermore, her analogy does not account for hybridized examples of network, arborescent, and axial narratives. In turn, it gestures toward a misguided suggestion that the hypertext–as–jigsaw puzzle represents a normative form of hypertext narrative.

Victory Garden employs both network and arborescent structure simultaneously, which is, not surprisingly, a source of some confusion given that it is considered one of the most representative works of the field. The work, in fact, represents two forms of hypertextual writing that have diverged in the years since its publication—it is itself a fork in the road of digital literature. More specifically, *Victory Garden* can be described as a network narrative with a nested arborescent structure. The arborescent structure occupies a comparably small part of the entire narrative framework. There are at least six nodes that suggest Emily's death or suggest a future where she has died (including but not limited to "and," "and" [different nodes that carry the same name], "And Now," "Anima," "The Love You Take," and "Ghost"). There are at least twelve nodes that depict a future in which she has returned from the war (including but not limited to "All You Need," "greenback," "West End," "Happy Warrior," "All right," "Four O'Clock," "-Victor-," "-Emily-," "Future Tense," "Reality-based," and "Because Because Because").[14] The group of fewer than twenty nodes that contains mutually exclusive outcomes is dramatically smaller than nearly one thousand nodes that make up the network. The comparison demonstrates a small structure of mutually exclusive scenes in relation to a much larger structure of scenes that can intersect unproblematically. In their own narratological study of *Victory Garden*, James Phelan and Edward Maloney support this understanding. They consider the consequence of variable expression of the narrative discourse for the overall comprehension of the story's characters and events: "[D]oes one set of paths through the whole of the narrative create a substantially different reading experience from another set of paths? Our answer is no. In our view, Moulthrop writes the narrative in such a way that the temporal order of our experience of [nodes] is not finally crucial to the experience of the whole" (1999–2000, 273). Phelan and Maloney describe a reading experience in which the emergence of recombinant elements, more than a fixed or linear progression, contributes to textual coherence. They also observe that aside from "a few strands of the overall narrative" (273), there is, in fact, an *overall* coherence to be found. In essence, they are describing the form of network fiction.

The distinction of *Victory Garden* as a hybrid structure resolves convolutions evident in some critiques of the text, which attempt to describe a text in which arborescent "branches" also "intersect" in the network topology. Koskimaa's critique gestures, albeit parenthetically, toward the same distinction when discussing Moulthrop's map: "[The map] made explicit the spatial structure behind the text (which, not too surprisingly, can be described as 'a garden of forking paths,' or better yet, 'a garden of intersecting paths')" (Koskimaa 2000). *Victory Garden* is less a garden of forking paths—or, in the most errant sense, a *realization* of Borges's "Garden of Forking Paths"—and more an "experiment in the network novel," to borrow the subtitle of Scott Rettberg's 2003 dissertation. At the same time, it reminds us that in order to accept the mutual exclusions of an arborescent structure in the same narrative (while acknowledging the problematic notion of "sameness"), we also have to accept the possibility of going *back in time*. Of course, one can always follow Ts'ui Pên's belief in "an infinite series of times, in a dizzily growing, ever-spreading network of diverging, converging, and parallel times" (Borges 1993, 77).

The distinction, furthermore, speaks to the theoretical question of "immersion versus interactivity." *Immersion* is generally framed in literary discourse as a reader's engagement—potentially to the point of physiological trance (Nell 1988)—with the representational elements of a text: its characters, setting, and the action and outcomes of the overall storyworld. *Interactivity*, by contrast, refers to a physical engagement with the material carrier of the representational elements, a bodily interaction with a medium. Both network and arborescent fiction require that the reader make choices at the level of the interface that affect the production of the text's meaning. This decision making constitutes Ryan's (1994, sec. 33) "weak" form of interactivity in digital texts, which involves "a deliberate play with signs leading to a production of meaning," as opposed to "the strong form of producing these signs."[15] But if both network and arborescent fictions are interactive in this regard, it is difficult to align one mode or the other with a greater or lesser degree of immersion without further qualification of the specific context. Despite their deliberate foregrounding of medial interactivity, arborescent fictions that cast the reader in a first-person role "in" the story, for instance, still might seem more immersive than other forms of fiction where the reader maintains a position as an observer "outside" of the story.

Nevertheless, arborescent fictions tend to work explicitly against a reader's immersion in a *singular* fictional world given that they always contain multiple outcomes and, by extension, multiple worlds. In *Victory Garden* the plot bifurcations disrupt the integrity of the otherwise ontologically discrete world of Tara, located somewhere in the southern United States. There is a threat not only to the perceived bodily integrity of Emily but also to the integrity of this intelligible "world." Even though this threat is a metafictional one, the force of any local disruption depends to a degree on the attainment of a global immersion. Put simply, an overall textual integrity must first be established if it is to be disrupted in any significant way.

The Art of War Stories

There are other factors, however, that complicate a reader's immersion in network fiction—not least of which is the repetition of textual elements. It follows from narratology that repetition complicates immersion in print narratives by destabilizing temporality and signaling textual artifice. But do the dynamics of repetition necessarily work against immersion in network fiction? In *Victory Garden,* as in *Twilight,* repetition is not simply foregrounded as a function of the network environment but rather suffuses the text as a thematic and formal device. Indeed, the story of Emily's return, which can be conceptualized as either a loop or a broken loop, is only one among many narrative returns, recurrences, and repetitions that range from the historically grand to the typographically minute.

Some of *Victory Garden*'s repetitions function in much the same way as formal repetitions in print. For example, readers can begin the story at a point when Thea is awakened middream by a knocking on her door: "Thea started up out of sleep, her dream turned suddenly inside out. A dream of her grandmother's house on the Nebraska prairie, Thea pacing the straw mat in the front room as the sky fell dark, the candleflames blown horizontal by the wind shrilling through the keyholes. A storm was coming down, a storm whose cold snap she could already feel inside her breast. A terrible storm" ("Hi Mom"). A text link—"A dream of her grandmother's house on the Nebraska prairie"—allows readers to "enter" the dream. It opens a node titled "Om," which renders Thea's dream state:

∧∧

The land beneath your hurtling body is undeniably Nebraska. Look over there, see, it say [*sic*] "LINCOLN" in big block letters. So over there, yeah, this thing looks like a bulls-eye you're dropping toward, why that must be the "O" in O—O—

Omygod what's that—

Flash of matte black skin cleaves the cloudy firmament, now you see it, now you don't, now you do: here she is, bird, Beast, great wings spread V-for-Veritas, turbine scream clearly audible as you fall closer closer clearly on track to intercept . . . ("Om")

The node is part of a longer dream sequence of nodes that each carry the same striped, horizontal bar running halfway across the top of the screen. The typographical repetition signals the sequence, which includes nodes representing not only Thea's dream but also the unconscious point of view of a number of characters—and, at times, no particular character at all, for "you" might be the dreamer. Although such sudden shifts of perspective can prove disorienting, especially when that perspective entails an alternate state of consciousness, the typographical repetition always announces the reader's entry into the collective dream.

In addition to typographical repetitions such as those marking the dream state, other linguistic repetitions achieve similar effects as they would in print texts. For example, the title of the node, the common meditative mantra "Om," further introduces an alternate state of consciousness—one that is interrupted at once by Leroy's knocking and, metatextually, by the reader's own intervention in the dream. The mantra is invoked again: since Thea dreams of her childhood home in Nebraska, the text plays on *Om*, implicitly, as a near homonym for *home*. But instead of acting as a peaceful mantra, the "Om" becomes a cry of disbelief as the dream subject begins to drop toward the ground below. Readers "hear" the "O" first as the subject falls toward that same block letter in "LINCOLN," and next when "Om" is absorbed by "Omygod," her reaction to a flying object that swoops down to intercept her. (The phrase stands for an interruption of a quite different variety when it is repeated in a node titled "Tender," when the soldiers in the Riyadh mailroom are talking about sex. A soldier named Yvonne says to Emily, "you know how it is, girl, they get it in there for a minute or two then it's O-O-Omygod and they let their fat ass fall asleep on you.") The "bird, Beast [with] great wings spread V-for-Veritas," is the flying object in question, its "black matte skin" and "turbine scream" typical of the sleek B-2 fighter planes used by the military in Desert Storm.

If these repetitions carry over from literary techniques found in print fiction, some of the effects arising from recurring nodes are peculiar to the network environment. By following the dream sequence in a slightly different way, for instance, the black object recurs but this time as a flying van driven by John Wayne and James Earl Jones. We can think of this object, which sustains no single interpretation, in the same way we think of any given hypertextual node: our interpretation often depends on how we approach it—where *approach* refers to our traversal of network space. The example of objects morphing from one reading to the next illustrates a hypertextual maxim, that nothing is ever quite the same on a return visit, but only in the most extreme sense. More commonly, a reader returns to a node and finds that information accumulated since a first reading endows it with new meaning. In both cases the network environment prompts the reader's act of repeating and recombining semantic elements.

Thematically, the same crucial questions underpin the narrative: Why do we return to war, and to what exactly are we trying to return? Some of Moulthrop's characters are quick to draw their own conclusions. Madden, who is a Vietnam veteran, shares a drink with his friend Snyder as the two consider the Gulf War as a possible corrective for the U.S. military failure in Vietnam:

> "Is that what this is about?" Madden wondered, working at his scotch. "They didn't get the plan down back in those jungle days, so now we get a second chance?"
>
> Snyder smiled. "Well ain't just that the American way these days?" Then he turned on him a look that went back over darker ground. "But you know what we're talking about. You were there."
>
> Madden thought about it. "I guess I was. But what kind of fool would ever want to go back?" ("Even Up")

Madden wonders if, more than a simple failure of the world's decision makers to peer back over the same "darker ground," an even greater problem is a persistent belief that the best way to erase a military failure is to repeat a military success. His musing recalls an actual speech made by President H. W. Bush following the first Gulf War, in which the president proclaims that the "specter of Vietnam has been buried forever in the desert sands of the Arabian peninsula" (Bush 1991). In *Victory Garden* the narrator's description of a June homecoming parade in Washington, DC, puts forth a more nuanced possibility—that we return to war so that we can return from it:

> It's a long way yet to the Fourth of July but the parades have already begun. Veterans come marching down the Mall and up from the Battery. The Fleet is in and stealth jets overfly the Capitol. Schwarzkopf and Powell get their keys to the city.
>
> What can you say about it?
>
> In elder days this was called a Triumph, with captives led in chains behind the hero's car. But there are no chains and no prisoners here. This is America and everyone is free.
>
> We are not celebrating a victory but a homecoming and safe passage. It is another chapter in our grand obsession with Return. ("6/10/91")

Elsewhere the narrator describes the legacy of Richard Nixon, destined never to return to glory in his nation's history: "In some cases Return is simply impossible; this too is part of the American story" ("National Dick"). The digression is a comment on the metaphysical nature of historical repetition: often attempts to return to a *former glory* amount to a perverted—in this case even deadly—form of nostalgia.

Moments of formal and discursive interplay ultimately destabilize whatever comment the narrative puts forth on the philosophical nature of repetition. The Nixon node concludes with "Simply this: the possibility of No Return" ("National Dick"), and it does not allow the reader to default (the function of the Storyspace software that advances readers to the next node on a predetermined path). There is, however, a text link at "No Return," which plays on the fact that the Return key on the computer keyboard activates the default. Even though the default is not an option here, the presence of the text link reminds us that we can return to the text but only with a certain activism. For readers who have been lulled by the repeated keystroke of the navigational default, perhaps found themselves immersed in the storyworld, the "possibility of No Return" breaks the spell. Readers must pause to take stock of where they have been and where they might be going, both in terms of their place in the story and their place amid the expansive topology of nodes. The moment foregrounds not the traversals of a storyworld by its characters but the traversals of a medium by a reader; the artifice of the text is reflexively and self-consciously exposed.

The creation of art that persists in continually and unapologetically questioning its own medium is a project Moulthrop has come to fully embrace. In his essay "From Work to Play" (2003a) he considers the political implications of immersion in art and the correlated condition of media transparency.[16] For him, when it comes to real-world conflict, it may be imperative that a medium insist on calling attention to itself and, conversely, that a reader insist on calling attention to the medium. He writes, "It may happen that in refusing the transparency of media we make ourselves better able to interrogate the nature of the conflict, perhaps even to understand more clearly what we mean when we talk about war and other deadly games" (Moulthrop 2003a). From this point of view a reflexive medium enables us to better interrogate and better understand what it carries; that is, the view of the "screener" (to borrow Mireille Rosello's [1994] term for the hypertext user) becomes more complete and comprehensive than that of the reader who is completely immersed.

The practice of politicizing art by way of revealing its artifice has familiar precedents in poetry and theater: Language poetry and Brecht's epic theater both employ techniques to detach and alienate audiences from whatever reality is represented. The proximity to and full awareness of a creative artifact instead becomes more important and, in fact, essential for a critical and reasoned response. As Benjamin (1999, 366) has said of Brecht's works, they must be "first noticed, and then understood," and they must have "first a pedagogical effect, then a political one, and last a poetic one." A consideration of digital fiction in light of such precedents is instructive in identifying not only resonances but also ruptures in how we understand the devices used to this effect. The technique of direct address in theater, for example, is intended to break the immersive trance of the spectator by transcending the "fourth wall," which separates audience from actor. The same can be said of an overly self-conscious novel in print, such as *Tristram Shandy,* which continually reminds readers that their reality is not that of eighteenth-century England but rather that of *reading.* In a work of digital fiction, however, where the reader is already implicated, implicitly or explicitly, in the diegetic progression of events, already complicit in the drama unfolding, direct address can potentially heighten an immersive effect (as is the case with "you" in *Victory Garden*).

In an essay that in many ways anticipates the discourse on immersion and interactivity, Charles Bernstein (1992) articulates an analogous tension between *absorption* and *artifice* (or *impermeability*) that arises in the context of poetry. The essay, titled "Artifice of Absorption," includes extended meditations on its terminology:

> By *absorption* I mean engrossing, engulfing completely, engaging, arresting attention, reverie, attention intensification, rhapsodic, spellbinding, mesmerizing, hypnotic, total, riveting, enthralling: belief, conviction, silence.

> *Impermeability* suggests artifice, boredom, exaggeration, attention scattering, distraction, digression, interruptive, transgressive, undecorous, anticonventional, unintegrated, fractured, fragmented, fanciful, ornately stylized, rococo, baroque, structural, mannered, fanciful, ironic, iconic, schtick, camp, diffuse, decorative, repellent, inchoate, programmatic, didactic, theatrical, background muzak, amusing: scepticism, doubt, noise, resistance. (30)

The comparative length of these two lists is a reflexive comment on their respective qualities: *impermeability,* the more critically laden of the two terms, yields a much longer list. Significantly, Bernstein (1992, 22) also recognizes the permeability of the categories themselves, describing them as "colorations more than dichotomies," both present during the acts of reading and writing. Much like Moulthrop's understanding of narrative fiction in "From Work to Play," he recognizes that "[i]n order for a sociohistorical reading to be possible, absorption of the poem's own ideological imaginary must be blocked; the refusal of immersion is a prerequisite to understanding (in the literal sense of standing *under* rather than inside)" (1992, 21). In fact, Bernstein's later advocation of "impermeable" verse reads like a paraphrase of Moulthrop's stated position: "For many readers and writers, the limits on what can be conveyed absorptively are too great, & the products of such approaches are too misleading. For such writers, the project is to wake us from the hypnosis of absorption" (1992, 54).

Predating the particular brand of political aesthetics of "From Work to Play" by more than a decade, *Victory Garden* does not put its model into practice. Perhaps for the same reason, the text offers a more ambivalent commentary on the art—and artifice—of war stories. The thematic framework of *Victory Garden* speaks to the concept of immersion at the level of the story. Emily, for example, is the only character situated in the military establishment and, geographically, in the Middle East—the only character, it would seem, who is literally immersed in a "deadly game." But the narrative foregrounds her perspective in another way: even though her letters to her friends back home suggest a firsthand account of war, she appears well aware of her own limited view: "spose you have to say what that reporter said about the Vietnam I the only position you can have ON the thing is your position IN it" ("Opinion"). Emily does not see herself as "in" the war but rather as removed from it. Furthermore, as a mail clerk she is an arm of print media's apparatus, processing information that is much slower, much heavier, and arguably much easier to regulate and censor than electronic mail. She is oddly detached and isolated not only from her friends at home but also from the war to which she was sent, neither "IN" war's reality nor inundated, like her psychologically unstable lover, Boris Urquhart, by its mediation.

The text, however, goes beyond this thematic commentary when the medium is brought into the play of signification. Emily's "view" takes an ironic turn when the lights go out in her Riyadh mailroom following the likely missile attack ("Blackout," "."). In some readings a black screen suggests the darkness that befalls Emily and the members of her company in the mailroom; in others the blackness is followed by a node that displays a shattered screen, suggesting that Emily and her company have been hit and likely killed by the strike ("and"). Readers do not know for sure what happens to Emily at this point. Instead, one is left with Moulthrop's distinctive "breakdown"—the crash that reminds us what we are actually looking at, and reminds us of the fragility of our own point of view, in both the physical and ideological sense. With the fracturing of this window, our immersion is blocked in a manner that recalls the Bob Perelman poem, "Binary," in which another glass division is called to our attention with more subtlety but to much the same effect:

Finally the I writing
and the you reading (breath still misting the glass)
examples of the body partitioned by the word.[17]

More can be said about the reader's sense of immersion and the screen that both allows and prevents it. In a way the reader's position parallels that of Emily's friends back home, who are caught in a continual twenty-four-hour news cycle replete with facts, opinions, and images of the war; that is, we too are passive recipients, and the best we can hope for, so to speak, is good reception. But as a hypertext, *Victory Garden* brings the war to our personal screens in a different way, one that beckons a movement from consumption to participation. It asks that we make use of the network form to resist the passivity more commonly associated with an allegiance to the screen; it ensures that the process of shaping the story, any story, is no longer invisible.

Here Moulthrop's intent to use hypertext technology reflexively, to question its role in disseminating information as it does so, becomes clear.[18]

The medium and, more specifically, the hypertextuality of *Victory Garden* tend to disrupt a wholly immersive depiction of war. But the narrative, somewhat paradoxically, also relies on strategies of immersion to convey its implicit message of interrogating the medium. After all, if the reader's position mirrors the position of Emily's friends, then the narrative is designed to evoke a genuine concern for Emily's welfare. The political critique in *Victory Garden* thus arises both from an instrumental engagement with an unfamiliar reading/writing technology and an empathetic identification with the characters and events of the story.

Garden Care

When so much of critical discourse is painting *immersion* as a lack of critical distance, passive consumption, or even naïveté, while at the same time the entertainment industry is dreaming up and creating ever more immersive digital simulations, works of digital fiction occupy a rather unique place in the ecology of creative media. *Victory Garden,* for one, prompts a closer consideration of immersion, not only in relation to digital narratives but also in relation to narrative fiction in general.

For those who refuse to accept that a successful storytelling technology is an invisible storytelling technology, the movement away from narrative forms goes hand in hand with a resistance to medial transparency. Moulthrop (2003a) quotes Janet Murray, who claims in *Hamlet on the Holodeck* (1997) that "[e]ventually all successful storytelling technologies become 'transparent': we lose consciousness of the medium and see neither print nor film but only the power of the story itself." The same potential loss of consciousness of the medium, for Moulthrop, is all the more reason to consider "turn[ing] away from storytelling as the prime agenda of art" (2003a).[19]

It is by no means apparent that medial transparency is or should be the measure of a successful narrative (*successful* being a relative and subjective measure), and the canon of twentieth-century literature, which is replete with works designed to disrupt or subvert common expectations with regard to temporality, spatiality, and causality, would suggest that this is often not the case. Furthermore, as countless theorists of the postmodern have pointed out, we live in a society in which artifacts both cultural and commercial insist on calling attention to themselves, to their artifice, whether it is a work of digital fiction online or a billboard on the side of the road. In both scenarios, often a message is conveyed only through the interplay between a story and the story-producing mechanism.[20]

What is apparent, however, is the extent to which the case against immersion in narrative is overstated. The argument is in large part reactionary, attributable to the emergence of technologies that promise (or *threaten*, depending on your stance) to realize medial transparency not in an "eventual" process of cultural acclimation but rather in one immediate stroke of technological innovation, be it via glove and goggles or an as yet uncreated "holodeck" (Murray 1997). But immersion theories themselves also tend toward extremes; they are often too negative or too broad. Of the negative conception, Marie-Laure Ryan (1994, sec. 20) writes, "[I]mmersion in a virtual world is viewed by most theorists of postmodernism as a passive subjection to the authority of the world-designer—a subjection exemplified by the entrapment of tourists in the self-enclosed virtual realities of theme parks or vacation resorts (where the visitor's only freedom is the freedom to use his credit card)." Clearly, the opposite of self-consciousness is not always naïveté; rather, readers can indulge in something akin to a "self-conscious immersion"—a *willing* suspension of disbelief. Often critics simply need to be more realistic about what it means to be immersed in synthetic realities.

Any theory of immersion, abstracted from a given context, moreover, suffers in its breadth. Common to the discourse of immersion theory is the notion that the realist novelist and the virtual reality environment designer pursue the same goal—the disappearance of the medium. But a historicizing continuum of transparent media is suspect when it conflates immersion in representation (as in a Victorian novel), which is largely a cognitive phenomenon, with immersion in simulation (as in a VR environment), which employs variables—visual, auditory, haptic—that encourage a corporeal immersion. Lev Manovich makes the same distinction based on one's bodily position in relation to the medium: a representational form, such as a painting, exists in a physical location separate from the embodied viewer, whereas "in the simulation tradition, the spectator exists in a single coherent space—the physical space and the virtual space that continues it" (Manovich 2001, 113).

Digital narratives such as *Victory Garden* sit somewhere in the middle of this continuum. On the one hand, they betray their historical contingency in their heavy reliance on (an arguably conservative) narrative poetics. On the other hand, they signal a moment in literary history when an age-old cultural form opens itself to the possibilities of digital aesthetics. Clearly, those who tell stories with computers do not need to call attention to the techniques and conventions of their medium; digital fictions impede transparency by virtue of their unfamiliarity—their literary machinery is already strange enough.[21] For the same reason a focus on interactivity and materiality has meant that the relationship between immersion and a hypertextual reading experience has yet to be established with a great deal of clarity.

In their essay "The Pleasures of Immersion and Interaction" (2004) Andrew Hargadon and J. Yellowlees Douglas discuss the role of schemata in shaping the affective experience of the hypertext reader.[22] They suggest that the predictability afforded by schemata contributes to an immersive reading experience, while a disruption of a schema, which they describe as characteristic of hypertext fictions, requires the reader's engagement. The notion of genre and schema is of course crucial in shaping any reading experience. And Hargadon and Douglas's essay addresses more complex (and also more common) scenarios where a combination and subversion of schemata elicits an affective response from a reader or viewer; that is, often stories are compelling precisely because they are unpredictable, and they proceed under the guise of one schema for the sole purpose of destabilizing it with the intrusion of another. With regard to digital literature, however, the end-claim that hypertextual reading (ordering narrative elements and choosing from a multiplicity of active links) works against immersion simply restates an understanding put forth in early hypertext criticism.[23] There are simply other possibilities to consider regarding immersive or absorptive reading experiences and digital environments.

In a footnote to their essay Hargadon and Douglas (2004) do, in fact, gesture toward the ways in which immersive experience can arise in network environments. They state that "when hypertext episodes . . . represent causally linked lexias that generate narrative tension, readers may become immersed in the narrative." They are furthermore correct in noting that, inevitably, any critical response to the question of immersion in network environments will depend on time—and not just in the sense of *familiarization* acquired over time to which Murray refers. For example, where immersion is possible, it is not likely to be possible for long in "high-maintenance" digital texts—those that require a constant material engagement. But this point does little more than extend the current discourse on immersion; as Hargadon and Douglas point out, the same statement holds true for both print and digital texts: "since engagement tends to focus our attention on the frame and materials themselves, texts such as *Ulysses* or *afternoon* tend to immerse us only for short periods before demanding our engagement" (2004).

Rather than simply attempting to locate immersive experience in network fictions, it might be necessary to first redefine it. Immersion in network fiction may indeed be more a function of what Joyce calls "successive attendings" as opposed to the sustained attention span that a book demands. But in comparing networks and books as reading environments, it is easy to break down a binary of successive vs. sustained when considering pragmatic situations of reading. It is conceivable, for instance, that a reader seated before the glow of an LCD screen and repeatedly defaulting through a seemingly endless text would become entranced just like—if not somehow more than—the reader who is, in Viktor Nell's (1988) terms, "lost in a book." Conversely, a continuous, uninterrupted immersion is an ideal state that is, in practice, likely to be disrupted by a wide array of extratextual intrusions.

One possible and productive approach is to cast immersion in network fiction in terms of *affect* rather than *trance*, which—contrary to the suggestions of some critics lamenting a perceived demise of book culture (Birkerts 1994)—is not necessarily the normative state of reading fiction anyway.[24] After all, a sustained state of trance is not a prerequisite for an affective response. That is, an affective response is not a direct function of a "steady, unbroken rhythm of reading ... that fully occupies our cognitive capacities" (Hargadon and Douglas 2004). In *Narrative as Virtual Reality: Immersion and Interactivity in Literature and Electronic Media* Ryan identifies three forms that fall under a "poetics of immersion": *spatial,* where the reader develops a sense of being at the scene of narrated events; *temporal,* where the reader is caught up in narrative suspense; and *emotional,* where the reader develops a personal investment in the experience of the characters (Ryan 2001b). Ryan's form of emotional immersion accommodates the affective force of Emily's character (as a symbol of those who incur the heaviest costs of war) without necessarily having to satisfy a sanctified, holistic trance privileged in some modes of literary criticism. The distinction can apply equally to print and digital texts, but it is especially useful in understanding that an engagement with the text's form and medium is integral—and not disruptive—to the experience of reading digital literature.

But if an *emotional* immersion is possible in network fiction, so too is a *temporal* immersion. In fact, temporal immersion in network fiction can occur not despite but because of the presence of narrative returns. For example, at one point in the story Boris, dressed in military fatigues and sporting a custom-grown moustache that gives him the semblance of Saddam Hussein,[25] realizes that he is being followed by agent Madden. After firing off a few rounds from his sidearm at a party at Thea's house, he drives away in his friend Harley's Porsche, without Harley's knowledge. As he drives, he repeats aloud to himself: "*U must flee*" ("Take Off"). Boris finds Harley outside of the campus café while attempting to elude Madden, and Harley joins him, showing concern for his friend and his car in equal parts. They manage to lose Madden but attract the attention of a police patrol car, and then several of them. The Porsche runs out of fuel just before it encounters a police barricade that has been set up ahead of them ("Gas?"). A display of racially motivated police brutality reminiscent of the Rodney King affair ensues and ends abruptly when the officers realize that Harley, their target, is in fact a CNN reporter. Boris, meanwhile, reverse head-butts the officer who is about to handcuff him and flees again, this time on foot. As he makes his way to a nearby ditch, he catches a glimpse of Madden's sedan arriving at the scene.

There are three nodes that describe Boris's escape: "Ring," "Ring Cycle," and "Ring About." Each begins in a nearly identical way:

U ran through the dark field . . . ("Ring")

Once more U ran through the dark field . . . ("Ring Cycle")

U is once again still always running through that dark field . . . ("Ring Around")

As Koskimaa (2000) points out, the three nodes can be read as if they are related causally, since they appear in sequence along the default path titled "Ring," albeit with several nodes interspersed between them.[26] But this is one among many possible readings. For the reader who has encountered the node "Ring" several times, for instance, the node "Ring Cycle" and "Ring Around" will have a dramatically different and, in particular, a more comical impact than it will for the reader who has only encountered it once or not at all. The possible permutations and recombinations of these nodes on a material level depend also on the formal repetitions and variations they contain, which allows readers to make chronological distinctions independent of their order (for instance, "Once more" and "Once again" denote some prior occurrence). But even this device does not yield a stable interpretation at the level of the discourse. Does the phrase "Once more" in the node "Ring Cycle" refer to Boris *still* running or running *again* (having stopped then resumed)? Or does it refer specifically to the material repetition of the node itself? Do the temporal gaps in between these running scenes mimic the effect of filmic cuts, where readers assume Boris continues to run even when he is out of frame? Or does the temporal progression of Boris's escape resume from wherever readers last left it?

The text of "Ring About" suggests that this scene repeats itself on yet another level: "U is once again still always running through that dark field, slipping scrambling through his own footprints on the dry ground. He knows

Madden is behind him somewhere but he doesn't dare look. You've had this dream before, you know." The familiar direct address is ambiguous. Boris may be simply talking to himself (as he is known to do) or this scene—and, for that matter, all three of the escape scenes—may be an actual dream that occurs (or recurs) while he is hooked up to the SCAMD dream machine. But in a metatextual sense the comment can allude to the reader's own narrative returns and may also suggest that "you" the reader are likely to have experienced a dream of being chased, which in the Freudian lexicon is one of the most common of dream archetypes. The effect of these cycles is similar for Boris's friends as it is for the reader, as we are continually asking: Where exactly (physically and mentally) is Boris? Either way, when Boris is "running through that dark field," the narrative tension remains unresolved, and returning to the scene serves to heighten that tension. Repetition, through establishing rhythm, can set up and sustain expectation.[27] Rather than simply signaling artifice, the nodal repetitions in *Victory Garden* can function in this way, drawing readers, again and again, into the represented world of the narrative—a world in which they are strangely implicated. Thus, it is possible to suggest that while the plot progression can engage the reader in events of the storyworld, so too can a plot *regression*.

The example suggests more generally that the process of calling attention to textual artifice can itself encourage or enhance a reader's sense of immersion; or, as Bernstein puts it, "impermeable textual elements may actually contribute toward absorptive effects" (1992, 29).[28] In his own example Bernstein discusses a dramatization of narrative return—or perhaps *rewind*—arising from Beckett's *Krapp's Last Tape*. In that play the sole character sits hunched over a tape recording he made thirty years prior, an old and broken artist desperate to recover something of his younger, idealist self: "What *Krapp* seems to show is that the constant interruptions created by turning the tape off & on, sometimes fastforwarding in between, make the experience all the more intense: . . . an antiabsorptive technique is used for absorptive ends" (Bernstein 1992, 82). Here interruption and repetition, albeit played out as a theme, create an analogous form of tension.

The narrative returns that are foregrounded in *Victory Garden* bridge the material, the formal, and the semantic elements of the text; in turn, they prompt a dialogue between the materiality and fictionality of the text that carries more meaning than would reading these elements in isolation. *Victory Garden,* moreover, demonstrates that narrative returns not only force a self-conscious engagement with the digital medium but also can act as a vehicle for immersive experience—at least, that is, until a crack in our screen suggests otherwise.

5
Fluid or Overflowing

The Unknown and *water writes always in *plural*

As Robert Coover (1999) has said, *Victory Garden* remains one of the "early classics" of digital literature. But it has solidified its place in the short history of network fiction at least in part through the flexibility of its "classical" form. In the mid-1990s more and more artists began taking their experiments to the World Wide Web, and more and more readers were finding them—most often at no cost. The publishers of *Victory Garden* responded to this shift in 2003 with the release of the *Victory Garden* World Wide Web Sampler, which contains 105 nodes and "about 500 links" designed to encourage further interest in the full version of the work.[1] By then, Moulthrop himself had already taken his artistic practice to the Web with the release of several acclaimed works, including *The Color of Television* with Sean Cohen (1996), *Hegirascope* (1995/1997), and *Pax, an Instrument* (2003).

The World Wide Web has dramatically changed and expanded the field of digital literature. But while greater ease of publication and distribution stand out as highly visible phenomena, other qualities of the Web environment have had a less-immediate but equally profound impact on the aesthetics of digital narratives. For many, a move to the Web meant freedom from material limits and boundaries, though such a move, in actuality, amounts to freedom only from the material limits of print. Nonetheless, in opening up seemingly limitless possibilities for the creation of endless and endlessly linked texts, the Web further polarized the relationship between selectivity and restraint on one hand, excess on the other.

The notion of textual excess is evoked in the very term *hyper*text, and early critics clearly established that hypertext technology "brings with it an excess of narrative possibilities" (Harpold 2003). But the significance of the concept does not arise from digital textuality and is not exclusive to it. The quality of excess can be understood as a privileged stylistic trait across many literary genres and periods, from the heroic epic to literature of the Baroque and, more recently, modernism's encyclopedic novel. In these contexts excess can be understood either in terms of an abundance of textual material or as a lavish and overly adorned writing style. Whether it describes the multitude of a Walt Whitman poem or the infinitude of a David Foster Wallace novel, it is also clear that excess is not necessarily a negative quality. Tom LeClair (1989, 1) even equates excess with mastery in his study of late-twentieth-century American novelists, among them Pynchon, Coover, and Barth: "In a culture that seems to exceed any power that art might impose on it [these authors] . . . gather, represent, and reform the time's excesses into fictions that exceed the time's literary conventions and thereby master the time, the methods of fictions, and the reader." As LeClair suggests, the "art of excess" involves much more than page count or stylistic flourish. The notion of excess, furthermore, applies beyond narrative prose. It can refer to a multiplicity or surplus of meaning in language, and poetic language is often governed by this expectation. In the poststructuralist sense an excess of discursive meaning is an inevitable outcome of the play of signifiers.

While all of these forms of textual excess remain relevant to writing in digital environments, the digital medium also endows the term with new significance; "hypertextual excess" takes on a meaning that is media-specific. An overabundance of links can constitute an excess of choice—an example in which the apparent freedom afforded by hypertext technology can also be a source of its difficulty. This form of excess is a function of a dynamic graphical interface that has no immediate parallel in print.[2] In addition, hypertexts can generate a surplus of meaning in a way that is uniquely hypertextual. Through the recombination of nodes in a network text, a significance or meaning can arise that exists not in one node or the other but only as a result of their association—what Adrian Miles (2002, sec. 8) calls a "nonlinguistic excess." Drawing parallels to film theory and the work of Eisenstein, he describes how the juxtaposition of two nodes, much like a cut between two cinematic shots, can "generate an idea that neither contained" by itself.

As Terry Harpold (2003) suggests, excess is not an inherent flaw of the form: "The accidents of reading a hypertext (changing your destination, forgetting your point of departure, or getting lost along the way) are not *a priori* the effects of inappropriate cues, misinterpreted reference or poor design, but the general condition of the hypertext as *text* (a fabric of iterable marks), amplified by the narrative turns of the link (the trace of the marks' iterability)." There is, however, a downside to hypertextual excess. Poorly designed or flawed hypertexts do exist, and what they often have in common is a failure to recognize the aesthetic value of selectivity and restraint. As the writers of the Oulipo demonstrated decades ago, the idea of "constraint" can, in fact, be quite liberating.[3] This recognition takes on even greater urgency for narrative fiction in digital environments. For instance, when Harpold refers to the "iterability" of the text and the role of the hyperlink in ensuring that the text is indeed stable and repeatable, it is possible to build on his observation with regard to a hypertextual *narrative*. To ensure narrative coherence, network fictions rely not only on the iterability of the textual trace but also on the hypertextual node. The themes and structure of a network fiction become visible through narrative returns. Such recurrences are elemental in network fiction in that they constitute shared and stable components of an otherwise mutable text. As Rita Raley (2002) explains, "Without a repeatable and shared element, we could only have an absolutely singular work, which means that a digital text needs a degree of repeatability in order for it to function as a text. The loop serves as just such a repeatable element." Scripting cycles and orchestrating loops in network narratives is thus a fundamental challenge of the form. *The Unknown* and *water writes always in *plural* are two Web-based works that have responded to this challenge in different ways and with dramatically different approaches to the problem of excess.

About the Unknown

> Holy the unknown buggered and suffering beggars . . .
> —Allen Ginsberg, "Footnote to *Howl*"

It is not uncommon for an unfinished work of literature to generate criticism and garner acclaim. Fitzgerald's *The Last Tycoon* and Melville's *Billy Budd* are just two examples of works by canonized literary figures who, at the time of their death, left works incomplete. The unfinished novel by Scott Rettberg, William Gillespie, Dirk Stratton, and Frank Marquardt differs markedly from these examples, and not only by virtue of its network form. Rettberg, Gillespie, Stratton, and Marquardt are not canonized literary figures, nor are they dead. They are the Unknown, a title that names both the group of authors and their Web-based narrative—"we are the creature, the creature is us," as they say ("hard_code.htm").[4] Katie Gilligan, who contributed artwork to the novel by creating one painting a day for three months, is also included in the Unknown collective, but as the authors point out ("default.html"), she customarily appears in brackets, parentheses, or in footnoted form.

The Unknown chronicles an expansive book tour by four authors, named Scott Rettberg, William Gillespie, Dirk Stratton, and Frank Marquardt, who are promoting a work of print fiction called *The Unknown Anthology*. When the collaborative project began in 1998, the authors intended to promote and publish an actual work of fiction called *The Unknown Anthology* (and eventually did so in 2002), but the confusion between real and imaginary literature, between authors who are characters and characters who are authors, simply sets the stage for the Unknown's complete disregard for an ordered portrayal of reality. Worlds collide in the text, and boundaries of past and present, real and fictional, are transgressed, that is, when and if such boundaries are distinguishable at all.

One node that demonstrates the confusion—or what might be better described, from an authorial perspective, as the conflation—of ontological levels also offers an uncharacteristically brief summation of the Unknown's mission. The node consists entirely of an email from Scott Rettberg to Laura Miller, a name widely known in the hypertext community as belonging to the critic who wrote dismissive reviews[5] of hypertext fiction for the *New York Times Book Review:*

Date: Sat, 21 Nov 1998 13:57:18 -0600
Subject: The Unknown
From: Scott Rettberg
To: Laura Miller, Salon <u>Magazine</u>
CC: The Unknown

Hi Laura,

When's the last time you reviewed a decent hypertext novel? Wait don't stop reading. We're the Unknown, a group of hypertext novelists who have written a hypertext novel, *The Unknown,* as a publicity stunt for an anthology of our own best writing we're publishing called *The Unknown.* The hypertext novel is the story of <u>our book tour</u> that we haven't gone on yet. Now I know you've had some bad experiences with hypertext novels in the past. Read your piece in the *New York Times* and, for the most part, agreed with you wholeheartedly. But this is different. This is a hypertext novel that has a <u>story, er, several, storylines.</u> It's no *Grammatron.* It's a satire of the contemporary <u>American Publishing Industry.</u> It's a <u>documentary.</u> It's an <u>art gallery.</u> It's encyclopedic [*sic*]. Three of the four authors of the novel portion of *The Unknown* learned how to write encyclopedic novels from Krass-Mueller, in his fiction-writing workshop at prestigious Illinois State University. But after we had graduated with our M.A.s we discovered very quickly that none of us were geniuses. It was only after getting together, and hatching this project, that we were finally able to come up with a book that was almost as big and almost as funny as *In Cold Jest*. And then we put it on the World Wide Web, vastly undercutting our competition by making it free for everyone to read.

So anyway, enough prattle:
http://www.spinelessbooks.com/unknown/tomorrow.htm

Best,
Scott Rettberg ("112198.htm")

From the outset, then, the project was primarily a project about a project, with a regression of self-conscious commentaries in tow. In addition to *The Unknown Anthology* in print and *The Unknown* hypertext novel there are several other works that generate lengthy commentary, though it is not necessarily clear in what stage of real or imaginative development they exist. These include the *Criticism of the Unknown* (and its criticism), the *Unknown* film (they choose Terry Gilliam over Francis Ford Coppola as director), the *Unknownpalooza* (Unknown's outdoor rock concert, where they give live readings in between performing rock bands), and *The Unknown Time Machine*, the sequel to the hypertext novel in which the authors go back in time. The last is a work conceived but not yet written—though one scene from this sequel appears interpolated in the hypertext novel, in which they make use of a modified Palm Pilot to travel back to the eighteenth century and meet with Christopher Wren, only to be brought back to the present by the editor of the *electronic book review*, Joseph Tabbi ("endconstruction.htm"). The Unknown also comment on the comments of others, and their online press kit provides external links to everything from newspaper reviews in the Chicago press, where the writers are primarily based, to an MA thesis written by a student in Copenhagen.[6] Add to this list any number of critiques of each other's own work—short stories and poems (some included in full), presumably fodder for *Criticism of the Unknown*. All of the versions and spin-offs of *The Unknown* are subsumed by the network fiction; and the protracted temporal frame of composition (predominantly 1998 to 2001) makes such criticism of criticism possible.

Three of the Unknown, Scott, William, and Dirk, enjoy an ongoing interaction with their audience, though whether they do so more as real-life authors or fictional author/characters is a matter of debate. Much of the later material, for example, is derived from self-interviews and self-reviews of the many (real-life) live readings performed in several U.S. cities. Nevertheless, the narrative is replete with characters based on real-life personalities who commiserate with those who are apparently products of the fictional world, and a list of Unknown "People" includes roughly three hundred names (not in alphabetical order) ("somanypeople.htm"). "Laura Miller," "Joseph Tabbi," and "Christopher Wren," for instance, have (or had) real-life counterparts. "Krass-Mueller" does not, though a description of his novel *In Cold Jest* bears a resemblance to the encyclopedic *Infinite Jest* by David Foster Wallace.

Rettberg's letter to Laura Miller discloses the Unknown's desire to create an encyclopedic novel in a network environment, and elsewhere the authors speak of evoking "nothing less than an entire world, a world with details and nuances and layers and cross-references in and out of itself" ("aesthetic.htm"). Believing this to be the aspiration of all "great art," they acknowledge that the notion implies nothing short of an "arrogant thesis" ("aesthetic.htm"). Nonetheless, the evocation of *worlds*—worlds that never quite attain or even aspire to a coherent "entirety" by any measure of verisimilitude or referentiality—would better describe the result. The worlds of *The Unknown* leak, and the authors revel in the mess. Audacious, interminable, hyperreflexive, *The Unknown* knowingly inhabits a precarious position for a work that, in light of its form, already questions commonplace understandings of "literature." The fictionalized critic George Will even calls it "dangerous," which, obviously, amounts to another self-commentary ("papertopics.htm"). *The Unknown* grants itself something akin to critical immunity, preempting criticism with self-criticism, and absorbing, contextualizing, and in essence fictionalizing everything else. The authors welcome any danger but only after they have located an escape route.

Any critic of *The Unknown* accepts a certain vulnerability by doing something the authors themselves (at least ostensibly) have refused to do: take the work seriously. But the precedent to do just that came in 1998 when the work was coawarded first prize (along with Geniwate's *Rice*) in the international trAce/Alt-X Hypertext Competition. Robert Coover judged the event and, in addition to lauding *The Unknown*'s allegiance to text-based narrative in the digital medium, he writes that "[o]ne of its more impressive achievements is to locate a frame (the endless tour) that allows for a great range of wildly variant stories without need of a linear chronology, always naggingly troublesome to a hyperfiction" (Coover 1998). The same frame prescribes an ideal space for narrative recurrence.[7]

Unknown Recurrences

For a work celebrated by some as a triumph of popular literature on the Web, and one of the first digital fictions accessible to nonacademics (see "dac2001. htm"), *The Unknown* foregrounds repetition in complex ways. It is a promotional tour for a book that does not yet exist, but it is also a documentary of sorts for a group of unknown authors. Without the book they, too, are yet to exist as authors; at least they are yet to be recognized as such—that is, known authors of *The Unknown Anthology*. So the Unknown author-characters precede the unknown authors of the same name. For the uninitiated reader especially, with no prior knowledge of the preexisting authors, the simulacra of Scott, William, Dirk, and Frank quite literally precede their original embodied versions. The phenomenon plays directly into postmodernist articulations of subjectivity.

It would seem that the precession of the fictional Scott, William, Dirk, and Frank recalls Baudrillard's hyperreal, whereby the simulacrum not only precedes its original but, further, threatens to assume primacy. Just as the simulation *loses dependence* on its original in Baudrillard's model, the "original Unknown" loses dependence on the "original unknown," with the magnitude and ubiquity of its digitized identity denying any vestige of the real. The Unknown collective seems to epitomize Baudrillard's "artificial resurrection" of signs, which follows the "liquidation of all referentials," the effective severance of language from reality (Baudrillard 1988, 167). It is a resurrection that seems redoubled in the narrative, if self-mockingly, with Dirk Stratton. After his rapid ascendancy as a contemporary messiah and cult leader, Dirk is unceremoniously murdered, stabbed two thousand times by the mob at the Los Angeles millennium celebration ("ladirkdeath.htm"), only to be brought back to his friends with the help of aliens who possess a variation of cloning technology ("inthehospital3.htm"). Dirk is thus repeatedly divorced from his referent, each time in more dramatic and also more artificial and contrived fashion.

But an application of Baudrillard's model yields only a superficial reading; indeed, there are only surfaces in the hyperreal. Partly inspired by what appears to have been a rather unnerving trip to Disneyland, his hyperreal, at least in its early 1980s articulations, grows out of a classically alarmist reaction to media technologies. It puts forth one-dimensional portrayals of television and, later, virtual reality, as powerful factors hastening a nefarious culture of simulation. Like many poststructuralist accounts, Baudrillard's model moves beyond the strictly binary logic of original and copy, but for him this culture of simulation is cause for grave concern. For him an effacement of origins is an effacement of objective causes or truths, the ethical and political implications of which are dangerously clear:

Is any given bombing in Italy the work of leftist extremists; or of extreme right-wing provocation; or staged by centrists to bring every terrorist extreme into disrepute and to shore up its own failing power; or again, is it a police-inspired scenario in order to appeal to calls for public security? All this is equally true, and the search for proof—indeed the objectivity of the fact—does not check this vertigo of interpretation. We are in a logic of simulation which has nothing to do with a logic of facts and an order of reasons. (1988, 174)

Baudrillard's critique rests on the assumption that the origin[al] was, at one time, stable and knowable rather than unanchored, in a state of metaphysical or at least linguistic flux. The same assumption makes his critique vulnerable, as it denies (and fears) the phenomenological force of cycles: "The Gordian knot can at least be cut. As for the Moebius strip, if it is split in two, it results in an additional spiral without there being any possibility of resolving its surfaces (here the reversible continuity of hypotheses)" (1988, 176). Moreover, he writes, "if the entire cycle of any act or event is envisaged in a system where linear continuity and dialectical polarity no longer exist, in a field unhinged by simulation, then all determination evaporates, every act terminates at the end of the cycle having benefited everyone and been scattered in all directions" (1988, 175). Baudrillard's abstract claim invites an abstract rejoinder: rather than render events and problems indecipherable and interminably relative, the mere recognition of complex cyclical factors can open interpretations and multiply possibilities that might otherwise be excluded by a more restrictive cause-and-effect model. His foreboding renders his own model an expression of a directed and definitive closure, the "end of a cycle" in the broadest possible sense, whereby the metaphorical world of simulation moves ever closer to the hyperreal world that will ultimately consume it. But what then? What happens after that?

With regard to literature, LeClair (1987) likens the cultural despair explicit in Baudrillard's comments to the preoccupation with exhaustion. He looks to systems theory to circumvent the endgames of postmodernist fiction and extend valuable poststructuralist methodologies: "[I]n an open system, such as literature or language . . . [r]elativity could become saving mutation, and deconstruction might become reconstruction" (LeClair 1987, 10). Baudrillard's movement toward the hyperreal ultimately and somewhat ironically relies on a linear continuity he deems to be absent. As Mark Poster (1999, 46) points out, Baudrillard's theory of simulation culminates, not surprisingly, when it *becomes* the principle of reality. According to Poster Baudrillard writes *The Perfect Crime* (1996) to declare that his idea of the simulacrum has been "stolen" by reality itself; it has become the dominant form of culture; it can no longer function as a concept because it has been realized as truth (Poster 1999, 46). Poster himself accepts the declaration with a heavy dose of cynicism: "Baudrillard is too competent a social theorist not to see the problem he is raising in its general significance. If the concept of simulation is now reduced to mimetic description, critical theory (and Enlightenment discourse more generally) is nullified" (46). Needless to say, what is a triumph for a theorist becomes the effective demise of a culture, or at least culture's claim to truth values. In Baudrillard's own words, "The simulacrum now hides, not the truth, but the fact that there is none, that is to say, the continuation of Nothingness" (Baudrillard 1996, 146). The narrative of *The Unknown* marks a departure from this view. For the Unknown authors, hope abounds, as does truth, even if it remains unknown:

> When you get right down to it, it's all <u>sublime.</u> That is, indescribable. You don't stop though. You keep trying to <u>describe</u> it. . . .
>
> What you <u>don't know</u> can and will hurt you, but not as much as will what you already know which already has and will continue to bring you <u>pain.</u>
>
> This is also the ultimate cause of <u>joy.</u> ("unknown.htm")

For the authors "the Unknown" exists, it is deep, and it is indeed quite full.

Derrida developed his theoretical ideas on repetition at about the same time Baudrillard theorized the simulacrum and still before the wide proliferation of digital media, but he puts forth an affirmative and playful articulation that more closely informs the ethos that emerges in *The Unknown*. (At one point Frank even obsesses over Derrida, wildly bellowing out his name during one of their hotel room binges—just before Dirk shoots the television set. William is there to reassure him: "It's cool, Frank, it's cool. Derrida isn't here, man, there's no <u>theory</u> here man" ["boshotel.htm"].) Derrida, too, moves beyond a constricting polarity of original and copy, but he differs from Baudrillard in his emphasis on their reciprocating interdependence: the echo is not simply subordinate and secondary to its source but also defines and confirms it. In *Writing and Difference* (1978, 246) Derrida notes that "there is no word, nor in general a sign, which is not constituted by the possibility of repeating itself." The Derridean critique affirms the play of repetition, for there is no stable identity or origin to be lost and lamented. The "original" author is always already in question or, to indulge the relevant trope, always in some sense unknown.

The significance lies not in how one orders the sequence of Unknown and unknown but rather in the dynamic play between the two, a process that refashions both poles as a result. The narrative emphasizes—even sensationalizes—the play between the two Scotts, Williams, Dirks, and Franks—while each "unknown" ensures that the other is not elided or replaced. But the narrative goes further in exploiting the play between signifier and signified when it attempts to literalize the play between the "Unknown" and the "unknown" authors. The two in fact meet in a bar in Indianapolis, a moment that proves disorienting for everyone involved, including the reader, especially since the node is written from the point of view of the "real" authors, who, "[o]n the whole . . . were kind of put off" by their "fictional characters" ("indianapolis.htm"). After drinks, during which time the "real" Scott and William fall in love with the fictional Dirk, they are joined by their (fictional) colleague Kilgore Trout. (An "unknown" and unsuccessful science fiction writer who figures prominently in Kurt Vonnegut's canon, Trout similarly meets his creator in an awkward encounter in *Breakfast of Champions* [1973].) They all decide to share a limousine back to their hotel, where the characters readily accept each other's ontological status, though with some degree of discomfort: "The ride to our hotel was crowded. Fictional characters, it turns out, take up just as much room in a limo as real people. And with Kilgore Trout along for the ride, fiction outnumbered reality 4 to 3. William, Scott, and Dirk were used to this by now, of course, having watched their, what could only be charitably described as, 'lives' be completely overwhelmed by their own hypertext fiction" ("indianapolis3.htm"). The author/characters find that their namesakes are uncomfortably real; meanwhile, the "real" authors, Scott, William, Dirk, and Frank, have been textualized yet again. During the ride the "real" Dirk tries desperately to gain some perspective: " 'Before The Unknown, I never would have imagined touching a limo, much less riding in them as often as we do,' Dirk muttered, to no one in particular. 'Not that I'm complaining, but what good is a limo if you have to sit with your knees caressing your cheeks!' " ("indianapolis3.htm"). The comic quality of the scene, and of the narrative in general, forestalls any sense of cultural dread amid the unconstrained doublings. For the Unknown it is immaterial whether the original has been effaced and replaced, or whether it simply never existed in any stable and certain way. The response to both—reckless and unconstrained celebration—remains the same.

The author/character collective of the Unknown is a most unconventional commodity, and one of the wonders of the work is its incredible capacity for self-promotion, albeit for a "product" that is, in fact, free.[8] As they self-promote the Unknown, they also create or, rather, continually recreate its authorial consciousness, a process that occurs *over the course* of narrative since the narrative itself is published in progress. It is thus not only about the process of its making but also occurring (or "set") in the process of its own making. The fact that the individual authors do not necessarily compose their corresponding character adds yet another layer of complexity to the process, as the entity of the Unknown continually remakes itself in a highly integrated way.

A description of *The Unknown* as "self-making" gestures toward a systems-theoretical understanding of autopoietic textuality. *Autopoiesis,* a term introduced by biologists Francisco Varela and Humberto Maturana in the 1970s, refers to any system in which an organized structure fundamentally complements the way that it functions. For example, a biological cell is self-making and self-organizing in that it produces (and is produced by) the same components that constitute it.[9] *The Unknown* behaves as a self-making (and self-marketing) system by using its own constitution to continually reconstitute itself. But a qualification is necessary, perhaps even more so in a work that claims to be simultaneously author and text incarnate. That is, the narrative is not necessarily a system in and of itself. The "systems novel" emerged in critical discourse as an experimentalist (print) narrative that *refers to* discourse systems and *evokes* recursive constructs. The mechanisms of systems theory become themes of the text. LeClair, who popularized the notion of the "systems novel" with his work on DeLillo's fiction, speaks of "communication loops ranging from the biological to the technological, environmental to personal, linguistic, prelinguistic, and postlinguistic, loops that are both saving and destroying, evolutionary spirals and vicious circles, feedback variation and mechanistic repetition, elegant ellipses and snarling complications" (LeClair 1987, xi). The enumeration points to the "fundamental subjects" of DeLillo's fiction; which is also to say that beyond formal linguistic constructions that can be said to "bend back on themselves," these fictions do not instantiate material loops. They are all conventionally bound books. More generally, recent debates on systems theory and literature have led to the claim that narratives are not systems in and of themselves; in critic Bruce Clarke's (2003, 1) terms any narrative is only ever an "element" that enters and is processed by a social system.[10] LeClair at one point compares the novel to a system: "The novel, *like* a character or any living system, could be a store of shifting, self-regulating information about man and his environment" (1987, 11; my emphasis). But here the shifting and self-regulating is rhetorical. The "systems novel" is not the *novel as system*.

Network narratives, however, challenge this assumption because they involve material recursions—digitally mediated feedback loops initiated by the reader. Their systematic machinery is both literary and literal since they rely on cybernetic circuitry. For the reader the material network remains distinct from the discursive one. Furthermore, both behave like "operationally closed" subsystems in the larger literary system implied by the network fiction. Different systems theories deal with the issue of open and closed systems in different ways, some contending that closed systems can *only* exist in theory. General Systems Theory, initiated in 1949 by biologist Ludwig von Bertalanffy with a book of the same name, adheres to the view that all living systems are open. Specifically, open systems "communicate, have a metabolism, and exchange their components in order to compensate entropy" (Cramer 2001). Through its overtly holistic philosophy, General Systems Theory maintains a heavy environmentalist agenda.

The systems theory of Niklas Luhmann differs from General Systems Theory with regard to closed systems. Borrowing from Humberto Maturana and Francisco Varela's description of natural systems, Luhmann breaks down the dialectic of open and closed by referring to systems that are closed operationally but remain open environmentally. Clarke (2003) refers to this elaboration as a *double positivity*. Appropriating this double positivity for literary theory means that a writing system can remain open structurally (environmentally) while remaining closed organizationally (operationally). Just as two systems in the same environment can exchange energy and heat, it is possible to suggest that subsystems nested in the network environment participate in an analogous form of exchange—that is, as long as any such analogy is anchored by the interpretive act of a reader materially engaging with a text.

A generalized example might involve the process of the observer's "jumping" systemic levels. In a work of fiction these jumps can refer to the cognitive process of drawing distinctions, but they can also correspond to hypertextual jumps from node to node. As Barth's "Frame-tale" succinctly demonstrates, the notion of an exchange or dialogue across semantic, formal, and material levels is not unique to the digital medium, but it does function as a powerful attribute of its literature. Scott Rettberg (the embodied version) suggests a similar understanding when he writes that "electronic literature functions best . . . when the reader's interaction with the machine is part of the metaphor of the work itself" (Rettberg 2003, 5).

Tabbi (2002) similarly focuses on print texts that trace the moment-by-moment shifts of consciousness, a potential (re)production in the reader's mind of the *cognitive* recursions that transpire in the mind of the writer. Tabbi's critique places emphasis not on the *representation* of consciousness per se but on the capacity of text, of "literary notation," to record cognitive phenomena. Arriving well after the saturation of digital writing technologies, Tabbi's critique can and does apply systems theory to hypertext. He sees hypertexts as a "textual analogue for distributed cognition," continually mapping "an ever-shifting boundary between system and environment by filtering signal from noise" (2002, 83).

The collaborative *Unknown* builds on the notion of distributed cognition. When observing their own text, the individual authors must consider—or better, *entertain*—a collective identity. In systems-theoretical terms the "Unknown" continually observes itself in order to reorganize itself on a higher level. The act of reading *The Unknown*, however, and to some degree the act of reading any network text, complicates part of this equation. It is true that the authors' own self-awareness may constitute a *higher* conceptual level, which would in turn reflect a distinction drawn during the act of composition. But in a network novel, which is divorced from the fixity of a hierarchical progression, this does not necessarily translate as a jump UP for the reader reading. In this sense many of the loops in *The Unknown* are indeed "strange," in Hofstadter's (1979) use of the term. The reader moves through a dense tangle of the Unknown's self-observations, a reflexive exercise that has as its goal the obliteration of a singularly coherent narrative voice.

Like a systems novelist, the Unknown is determined to test the capacity of literary notation to record its thought processes, though no single system of notation will suit its needs. While the protagonists share the same reality as dozens of well-known authors, they, too, inhabit their well-known writing styles. Using a literary technique they call "ripping off" (Unknown 1999), they emulate the voice of DeLillo, Vonnegut, Kerouac, Beckett, and Poe to name only a few, thus encouraging the dynamic play between another two poles: the "known" and the Unknown. These styles and modes of discourse contribute to the continual recreation of the Unknown, which contains enough multitudes to accommodate them all, at once. Indeed, if the Unknown is an autopoietic system, it is not a very selective nor, in turn, a very efficient one. In incorporating everything from its environment it deems useful or relevant, it has opted for an exhaustive approach. One of the authors' own definitions would suggest as much: "The Unknown = any two words that haven't been <u>put together yet</u>" ("unknown2.htm").

In addition to its engagement with theoretical and metaphysical repetitions, *The Unknown*, like other network fictions, instantiates returns in an expressly narratological mode. The narrative returns arise from the discrete formal repetitions that are products of the graphical interface. Most obvious to the reader are the color-coded borders appearing on each node, which relate to the six colored buttons that run horizontally along the bottom. The buttons correspond to the color-coded lines of the Chicago Transit Authority's rail system (known as the "L" for its long section of elevated track in and around the city). The rail system provides the organizing metaphor of the novel. Moving from left to right on the navigational buttons, readers find "the sickening decadent hypertext novel" on the Red Line; the Purple Line provides the "metafictional bullshit"; the Blue Line a "sort of documentary"; the Orange Line "correspondence"; the Brown Line "cool art" that includes Katie Gilligan's paintings; and the Green Line accommodates all of the Unknown's "Live Readings," with reports, reviews, reflections, and audio links to some of the live recordings. The six "lines" offer an overt and immediate point of reference, what the embodied Rettberg (2003, 82) calls an "ontological" mode of orientation rather than one based on plot, theme, or character. The "lines" also reinforce the trope of multilinearity that informs the story web itself. The text is, as LeClair (2000) has described it, a "monstrosity," but it is nonetheless a highly structured one.

A (lengthy) debate transpires among the Unknown in *The Unknown* regarding the inclusion of a home page that would effectively represent an authoritative starting point for the narrative (Dirk adamantly believes it would "violate the essence of our hypertextuality" and fly in the face of what he sees as "pure" hypertext). A home page is eventually included, partly at the behest of the programmer, at "default.html," and not surprisingly, it includes the discussion of whether or not to include the home page. Several other pages also function as hubs, in the mode of concentrating "transit." One of these hubs is "unknown.htm," which the Unknown authors claim to be the first node composed. It begins with a Pynchon quotation that tempers their "arrogant thesis": "Everybody gets told to write about what they know. The trouble with many of us is that at the earlier stages of life we think we know everything—or to put it more usefully, we are often unaware of the scope and structure of our ignorance. Ignorance is not just a blank space on a person's mental map. It has contours and coherence, and for all I know rules of operation as well" Thomas Pynchon ("unknown.htm"). Framed by the narrative, the passage suggests an oblique claim of ignorance: the authors ostensibly make writing about the Unknown a facile and mind-numbing chore (as their line of "metafictional bullshit" suggests). But here they announce and underscore the genuine challenge of writing "about the unknown." In addition, the passage evokes the lyrical ambiguity of the "unknown" as a concept. It becomes not only knowledge that is yet to be but also knowledge gained at one time, then (perhaps intentionally) lost, un-known in the way something that is done is then undone, or something constructed (perhaps Pynchon's "structure of ignorance") is deconstructed. The notion rehearses a cyclical repetition that destabilizes the more familiar, linear passage from the unknown to the known. In turn, the node itself becomes an appropriate place to begin reading.

The "unknown" plays a structural role, as well as a rhetorical one. Scattered throughout the narrative, the word <u>unknown</u> commonly anchors a hyperlink that returns the reader to one of the hubs. Furthermore, the term motivates three poems that exercise simple language constraints that repeat with each line of the poem's progression. For example, "mamadada.htm" begins with a metaphorical construction, "The Unknown is," whereas "like.htm" begins with the simile "the unknown is like." Both link from another poem that employs the constraint of a one-thousand-word limit ("1000words.htm"). A fourth poem (also reached from an <u>unknown</u> link in the one-thousand-word poem), incoherently called "I Have These Unknown Go Mad," carries a trace of the opening of Ginsberg's *Howl* in its comment on madness. The Unknown's one-thousand-word poem, in fact, nearly alludes to Ginsberg's "Footnote to *Howl*" by way of numerical constraint. But where Ginsberg repeats the word *holy* seventy-seven times throughout the body of his poem, *unknown* appears in their poem eighty times (not including the title and banner). Not surprisingly, the Unknown poets manage to overdo it.[11]

More generally, the structural organization of *The Unknown* can give rise to narrative recursions. As Dirk points out in one of the Unknown's self-interviews, the story is designed so that "frequently hypertext links will take you back to a page that you've already read before" (Unknown 1999). Furthermore, the authors add PREVIOUS and NEXT links on a number of nodes. These are separate from the Back and Forward buttons on Web browsers, and they also serve a different purpose. Choosing PREVIOUS on a given node will take readers to a node that has been designated by the authors to be previous in the linking topology rather than the node visited previously by the reader and recorded by the browser. This feature predominantly caters to the chronology of the story's progression (which does exist), and it allows readers to string together a succession of events. But since a reader often arrives at a node late in or at the end of one of these successions, the feature also enacts a temporal return to prior events in the storyworld. A reader who arrives at a node that details the beginning of the investigation of Dirk's death in Los Angeles, for instance, can move back through at least ten nodes describing scenes building up to and including the "murder bloody and sad" ("invesigation.htm"). In this hypothetical microreading the sequence culminates with the node "fame.htm," but with regard to the causal order of narrative progression, the same node *begins* the descent of a decadent and indulgent Unknown: "At some point it had simply <u>gone too far</u>" ("fame.htm"). Significantly, it is a process of reading mirrored in the Unknown's process of composition. As Rettberg (2003, 56–57) writes: "An 'ending,' such as Dirk's death in Los Angeles, didn't bring the writing, or the narrative, to a halt, but instead served as an occasion for the generation of new material, which either contextualized or reversed that 'ending.' If Dirk had been slaughtered as a cult leader and messiah figure, shouldn't he have written some gospels prior to his assassination? What might the conversion of one of his disciples [have] been like? . . . Why not add a resurrection?"

One feature that foregrounds narrative returns in *The Unknown* is a product of its greater network environment of the World Wide Web. On the Web the default status of hyperlinks is text underlined and in blue; purple text indicates a link already visited. This visual cueing allows users to locate links and to register which ones have been visited and which have not. The Unknown authors make use of the same default, changing the colors of the linked and unlinked text according to their own color-coded design. These markings prove crucial to the reader confronted by what is ultimately a surplus of choice. The hub of "unknown.htm," for instance, includes twenty-six linked words or phrases (what Bernstein [1998b] refers to as a "tangle"), not to mention the links to the six "Lines"; the links to the "Map," "Bookstores," "People," "Contact," "Press," and "Anthology" that also appear on each node; and the three audio links that appear in a frame off to the right. In addition to offering the reader some sense of the text's macrostructure, the experience of returning to a node and finding the traces of a past visit can be a most welcome one.

The surplus of links also encourages readers to consider the links' narrative function more generally. Many early contributors to the critical theory of hypertext fiction, such as Jeff Parker in "A Poetics of the Link" (2001) and Rettberg himself in "The Pleasure (and Pain) of Link Poetics" (2002), have emphasized the rhetorical role of links and the development of broader linking strategies that inform the mood, tone, and themes of the narrative. Links can create effects analogous to poetical enjambment and ironical juxtaposition. The links in *The Unknown* perform both but beyond that do not convey any cohesive rhetorical linking strategy to the reader. What the Unknown's links do offer is a way out—an escape from the daunting unknown. The title of an article by Julia Keller (1999), who reviews one of the Unknown's live performances, puts it best: "Hypertext Novel Offers Easily Accessible Exits." Or, as Rettberg (2003, 61) says, "The link is an entrance but also an exit." In this sense the novel is recast not as a text that is endless but rather as one that is "end-full." At the same time, one needs to question not the availability of exits but the persistent desire to use them.

Prone to Unknown Excess

The Unknown authors are not prone to excess; they make it an objective. Their objective is also their undoing, despite the fact that they fully acknowl-

edge the problem they have created. During one of their self-interviews conducted live on radio and transcribed for their text, Dirk discloses his senti-
ments with regard to the bloated state of their hypertext novel:

> I'd like to read this quotation from *The Conversation News,* January 15,
> 1975:
>> *Investigators for the Texas Highway Department claim that a cow burp
>> has valuable energy potential. For whatever reason, a department pub-
>> lication announced that the nation's cows belch an estimated 50 million
>> tons of hydrocarbons into the air each year. Reportedly, ten cows burp
>> enough gas in a year to satisfy the annual space heating, water heating,
>> and cooking requirements for a small house.*
>
> And to me that, I feel, is a fitting metaphor for The Unknown. It's ex-
> cessive, it's gaseous, it's waste product that we've turned into art. (Un-
> known 1999)

On a metafictional plane the novel comments reflexively on the propen-
sity for excess in the Web environment. Unconstrained by physical space,
a network text can accommodate an overwhelming number of links and
nodes, and each node can scroll on unforgivingly, as do some of the nodes in
The Unknown. The radio self-interview exceeds four thousand words, which
in itself is not remarkable but arguably excessive as a single node in a network. The observation is significant in light of a hypertextual ethos that origi-
nated with the privileging of short, self-contained "lexia." Extended bouts
of scrolling, in this sense, would also contradict Dirk's desire for "pure" hypertext.

In addition to their metafictional musings about the novel's undoing, the
path to excess results in a parallel undoing of the character/authors. Their
fame makes them reckless, destructive, overindulgent, and abusive, both to
each other and with regard to the substances they ingest. Thematically, repetition is again manifest but this time as a symptom. Scott develops a peculiar
speech impairment when he is under the heavy influence of alcohol and/or
drugs, which compels him to say everything twice. As William describes it,
"I've got a bottle of malt liquor in a brown paper bag and a pocketful of al-
falfa sprouts and I say to Scott, buddy, what can we cook up with this? He
says, cookbooks, cookbooks. He's not talking real straight at this point, has
been thinking he's the Oracle at Delphi or else the Oracle at Oracle, I couldn't
tell which, because he'd say one word and repeat it as if it meant more repeated" ("sanfranfrank.htm"). William exhibits the same symptom in a more
oblique way. Just before his amateur bungee jumping attempt, which leaves

him in a coma, he arrives sporting a tattoo of Gertrude Stein, who is well known and often parodied for her use of repetition as a transcendental technique in poetry ("bungie2.htm"). Meanwhile, Dirk, now a cult leader, immerses himself for bouts of time in "some kind of Ginsbergian chanting" (indianapolis2.htm).

In the end (to use the phrase loosely) their acknowledgment of excess does not redeem their novel.[12] Even the "encyclopedic novels" that the Unknown authors allude to and cite employ various constraints that they lack. For example, Joyce's *Ulysses* constricts itself to just over a *single* day in one city, whereas the bulk of *The Unknown* spans several years (not to mention the scenes in the distant past and distant future) and spreads to dozens of cities. Joyce's novel works from a schema he drew up beforehand, which involves specific structural connections to the *Odyssey*. *The Unknown* authors, by contrast, develop an ad hoc structure in the Chicago "L" system after observing that certain groups of nodes suggest distinct modes of expression.[13]

Ultimately repetition and excess are a fatal mix, if fatal can refer here to moments when the reading experience degenerates. Writing after the 1998 trAce/Alt-X Hypertext Competition, Michael Shumate, in his review, "Whatever Happened to Editors Anyhow?" laments the poor copyediting in many of the submitted works. His reaction to *The Unknown* involves a specific denotation of *edit;* that is, "to remove (a part) from a text":

The Unknown, while relatively clean at the level of basic grammar and mechanics—especially considering its surfeit of text—suffers greatly from the lack of a content editor. There is much good material in it— some of it funny, some of it insightful about writing in general and writing hypertext in particular—but it is hard to get to the berries for the thicket of briars around them. It calls to mind a reviewer's remark about the length of Norman Mailer's *The Executioner's Song* twenty odd years ago, that Mailer had apparently decided that if he couldn't get one any other way, he was going to shoot for a Nobel Prize in Typing. Here we have entire chat sessions included for our edification. Such transcriptions have their uses for archival and reference purposes certainly, but for any reader who was not there, reading a log of other people's chat is surely one of the more dispiriting experiences of modern life. The repetition, the confused references to the fourth exchange back, the self-described gestures and facial expressions that we were not present to experience in the moment—as my eye glazes over such text I begin to feel the moments of my life draining away and I have to wonder at how I spend my time. Although I recognize that over-the-topness is a goal here, the point is made long, long before one browses *The Unknown*'s ten hundred nodes. (Shumate 1998)

Shumate's call for editors bears relevance to the wider distribution of digital fiction both online and off, for the lack of clean editing puts an inevitably marginalized new field at an even greater disadvantage. With regard to digital text it is common to hear advocates speak triumphantly of the relative ease of amending, updating, and uploading, but rarely does one actually see such easily correctable errors corrected. And there *are* copyediting errors in *The Unknown;* in fact, the press kit misspells *Shumate* as "Schumate" (Unknown n.d.).

An excessive and unconstrained network fiction impedes the movement of narrative returns, for it is necessary to complete or close something in order to return to it. We cannot speak of a return until we speak of closure on some level. As Derrida (1978, 295) writes: "Once the circle turns, once the volume rolls itself up, once the book is repeated, its identification with itself gathers an imperceptible difference which permits us efficaciously, rigorously, that is, discreetly, to exit from closure." Derrida suggests that it is necessary to perceive a "whole," though this does not necessarily imply a whole book or even a whole novel. In a network text even a memorable succession of nodes can constitute a meaningful whole to which a reader can return in the context of some difference. Hypertextual excess, however, is not simply a measure of links and nodes, and the discourse of the Unknown is so dispersed that it too can render nodal recurrences ineffective and insignificant. True, any critique of a network text must acknowledge that meaning emerges differently in a multilinear fiction than it does in a linear one. Plot progression and character development cannot occur along a fixed temporal axis—some claim they cannot occur at all.[14] But in terms of reading network fiction, *The Unknown* builds toward a recombinant aesthetic pronounced in network fiction but then continues building and building until it can no longer sustain narrative emergence.

Surface Tension

> After waiting at home every morning for a fortnight, and inventing every evening a fresh excuse for her, the visitor did at last appear.
> —Jane Austen, *Pride and Prejudice*

Written at roughly the same time, and similarly published in progress on the Web, Linda Carroli and Josephine Wilson's *water writes always in *plural*

(1998) differs dramatically from *The Unknown* in its self-conscious exercise of selectivity and restraint. The network narrative is the product of a residency set up by the Australian Network for Art and Technology (ANAT), in cooperation with the Electronic Writing and Research Ensemble in Adelaide, to bring together Carroli, a Brisbane-based writer, and Wilson, a Perth-based writer, for a creative collaboration. The authors are brought together, however, only by a high-speed Internet connection and online "chat" software called Internet Relay Chat (IRC).[15] Unlike the Unknown authors, three of whom lived in the same area, the authors of *water,* though liberated in some sense from geographical barriers, did not have any physical contact. In fact, they did not physically meet until after the completion of the work.

The work itself was circumscribed. The residency lasted only eight weeks, providing a definitive commencement and culmination of the project, and the lack of any tangible and dimensional text proved a challenge, especially for Wilson, who struggled to conceptualize the work spatially. Given the way water behaves, constantly seeking form and containment, her struggle makes the eventual title of the work only more appropriate. Wilson recalls the difficulty she had when "it came time to map the space, (not having access to Software such as Story Space which enables you to do this graphically, and manipulate paths and sequences)" (Wilson 1998). In this regard, the Web environment itself constrained the work in a way that was not just media-specific; it was application-specific as well. For the authors in "virtual residence," the Web freed them from certain limitations as it introduced new ones: in effect, they had no physical contact with each other, or with their text.

The writers exercised their own form of selective restraint during the process of composition. Where the Unknown authors include conversational and dialogic material that transpires among them, in addition to an entire "Line" of correspondence (what Shumate refers to as the prodigious "chat sessions included for our edification"), Carroli and Wilson offer a much different treatment of "chat." They equate their online logs to textual noise, from which a literary work emerges according to a further process of selection. *Noise,* in systems-theoretical terms, is what remains outside after the boundaries of a system are established and its internal structure is configured; in a literary work noise might stand in opposition to *coherence* or *meaning.* Only a few IRC transcriptions actually appear as citations in the text: one involves an exchange in which "inky" (presumably Wilson) finds that she is writing—or "talking"—to herself in light of "linda's" (virtual) absence ("whereru.html");[16] another is a brief excerpt from an exchange that results from "linda's" decision to enter another chat room while waiting for a response from her coauthor. Once there, "linda" is subject to a sexual advance by "gamma" (reminiscent of the virtual harassment and eventual "rape in cyberspace" popularized by Julian Dibbell's 1993 essay), who subsequently issues obscene and vitriolic threats after "linda" rejects him ("kill.html").[17] The reader reaches this transcript excerpt from a text link in another node that, ironically, discusses the importance of relying on the "kindness of strangers" ("quiet.html").

By filtering, then contextually framing, the "chat" they incorporate into the narrative, Carroli and Wilson allow readers to identify the concept or concepts they are attempting to isolate: here the paradox of talking to oneself in an online chat room, and the (social, psychological, and legal) complexities of sexual harassment in a so-called virtual, albeit definitively textual, world. True, comparisons between *water and The Unknown are complicated somewhat by the fact that the Unknown authors are explicitly the protagonists of the text; their dialogue constitutes the live action of the narrative, and one must acknowledge that a "transcription" of correspondence is quite possibly a scripted exchange that parodies the Web environment it inhabits. But the significance of the comparison lies in *water's embrace of a different aesthetic, one that not only echoes Shumate's claim that "reading a log of other people's chat is surely one of the more dispiriting experiences of modern life," but one that also suggests a more restrictive form of "autopoietic textuality." Their systematic composition involves selection on a more refined scale. The fabric of Carroli and Wilson's correspondence becomes an environment of raw material that lies beyond the operational borders of their literary system, a source that is at once fixed in a digitized archive yet fluid in terms of accessibility and searchability. As Wilson writes, "By keeping logs, we find that we can refer back to our conversations and words to isolate particular ideas and trajectories. It is from these that much of the content for our texts has emerged, either directly or indirectly" (ANAT 1998).

If endings are problematic for The Unknown, *water writes always in *plural complicates beginnings. The first page displays only one sentence, broken up into four lines, four different colors, and four different fonts:

a woman
stands on a street corner
waiting
for a stranger. (Carroli and Wilson 1998)

Each of the four lines contains a text link into different sections of the narrative—into the "trajectories" described by Carroli and Wilson. After establishing a character (the woman) and a setting (a street corner), however, the fictional story barely progresses beyond this scene for the remainder of the work. The woman does little, says even less, and never really goes anywhere, unless of course one considers the perambulations of her thought. The theoretical implications of the woman waiting preoccupy the authors, who question everything from the suggestiveness of the situation from a gendered point of view to the impossibility of the statement itself from a logical point of view. The scene preoccupies the authors, as well as a narrator whom they create or at least hypothesize:

> A woman stands on a street corner waiting for a stranger. . . . This is of course, from the point of view of the woman, an impossible story.

> Can you wait for a completely empty signifier? There is something this woman is not telling us. Or there must be a third party who has told this woman "Wait on that corner and you will see a stranger." (And this then must be a town where there is only one stranger; this must be the day "the stranger came to town").

> Or else, to jump the frame, there must be a narrator, who is not waiting but is instead withholding—one for whom "waiting" is a ploy, a tactic, a way of making us hold our breath (Next Please!) ("woman.html")

Such authorial musings and meditations about the waiting woman, often in tandem with direct citations from philosophers and literary critics, constitute the majority of the text.

If each of the four phrases opens onto the text's thematic trajectories, then the reader senses the broadest contour with the motif of waiting. "Our narrator knows about waiting," the reader is told outright at one point ("woman. html"). But while the narrator knows about waiting, the woman does not seem at all sure about for whom or what she is waiting: "There she stands, our lady in waiting, attending the return of the husband she never had, the lover who did not phone back, alone on a corner, waiting for a way out . . ." ("woman.html"). The narrative explores waiting in the abstract so that the experience of waiting takes on a wider significance for author and reader. An array of metafictional delays transpires during the writing and reading of the text. As Wilson (1998) says, "On one level, it was a pragmatic issue for us— Waiting for machines to do their stuff, waiting for people to turn up. Waiting for images to download, waiting to get on a server, waiting to learn how to do things on the Net. Waiting for the phone to ring. Waiting to hear from

each other. Waiting for an automated answering system to direct your call."
All the while, the fictional woman, standing on a street corner, has no choice
but to continue to wait.

If *water uses hypertext to reflect on the ways machines make us wait, it
also uses hypertext to reflect on itself. The work is intensely reflexive, as are
many of the early contributions to the field. Many critics have closely aligned
the literature of hypertext with postmodernist aesthetics, which typically
makes reflexivity a master trope. But not all do so in a positive vein. "One
ultimately wonders," Parker (2003) writes, "in hypertext will we ever get
away from self-reflexivity and meta-fiction or will we just eventually drown
ourselves in the flood of our own references to what we are trying to do?"
Michael Joyce, moreover, has sought to curb the commonplace notion that
literary hypertext *must* occupy an exclusively postmodernist space. "Its insistence on the wholly formed multiple reading makes hyperfiction's connection with so-called postmodernist fiction seem to me unfortunate," he
writes, and goes on to say that "Postmodernist (fabulist, meta-fictional, etc.)
in that sense suggests flatness, lackluster bubbles from day-old champagne"
(2000, 127).

Whether or not it is a "postmodernist" trait, *water welcomes reflexivity.
At the same time, Carroli and Wilson's text departs from the plenitude of
works, both fiction and nonfiction, that position hypertext technology as the
embodiment and effective fulfillment of postmodernist and poststructuralist
literary theory. The authors view such embodiment theories with suspicion
given that they "elide the unavoidable context in which Hypertext is written" and fail to consider the "Computers, Software, Hardware" as just that—
material trappings of an already technological practice of writing (Wilson
1998). Wilson further rehearses one of the major complaints that followed Jay
David Bolter's *Writing Space* (1991): "Aside from the problematic relationship
of theory to practice . . . , there is the whole question of agency, which . . . is
displaced from the collaborators, to the computer" (Wilson 1998). In *water* the material properties of hypertext technology serve to illuminate semiotic instabilities that are already inherent in language. The hyperlink cannot
embody or confirm the potentially infinite deferral of the linguistic signifier, which requires that the reader cognitively process the meaning of signs.
Whether it is cast in light or cast in ink, "every word," to borrow a phrase
from Harry Mathews, "becomes a banana peel" (quoted in McHale 2000, 19).
Conversely, no matter how mutable or unstable a "virtual" text, hyperlinks
are manifest in a physical sense.

While a hypertext cannot embody semiotic instability simply by virtue
of its material properties, it can dramatize it in ways unavailable to print,

which is what *water does. As N. Katherine Hayles (2000) claims, the digital signifier is more complex than a print signifier because it always already exists as the assignment of some underlying code: "[T]he signifier in a digital environment has a complex internal structure quite unlike the flat mark of print. Moreover, this complexity requires for its implementation constant encoding and decoding, for example when the browser reads new Web pages or retrieves from memory previously cached copies. To recognize the layered dynamic interactions between text and code, I have elsewhere proposed the term 'flickering signifiers' for screenic text." She continues: "Is it fanciful to suppose that Linda Carrolli [sic] and Josephine Wilson allude to this phenomenon when they begin [*water writes always in *plural] with an image of a woman waiting on the road, like an empty signifier waiting to be filled with the reader's suppositions? Or does she rather serve as an anthropomorphic agent who both inscribes and is inscribed by the empty screen waiting to be written upon once the encoding/decoding operations have performed their operations?" Hayles recognizes the polysemantic implications of the woman waiting on the corner of a street, which is simultaneously the corner of a *screen*. Her comments, however, also underscore her broader agenda. For her the instability of electronic text is inherently manifest. Her intent to carry "the instabilities implicit in the Lacanian floating signifier one step further" with the notion of *flickering signifiers* and "their tendency toward unexpected metamorphoses, attenuations, and dispersions" (1999b, 29) marks a jump from linguistic theory and the movements of meaning to a material medium and the movements of a machine. In this regard she gestures toward an understanding where linguistic instability is "literalized" in the new medium. Nevertheless, what her commentary ultimately underscores is our desire to subject semiotic phenomena to some form of narration. In fact, it would seem here that the process of signification itself is deferred: without any sort of directed or causal relationship, the reader waits for the woman's signification, while the woman waits for the stranger to be signified, while the authors wait for their narrator to—in the words of Joyce's *afternoon* narrator—"signify one way or another," and so on.

The reflexivity of *water can be understood in a narratological context, specifically, as a comment on the arbitrary nature of story beginnings. For example, in a reflexive work an opening line or passage seems to come easily. As John Barth notes, when one has difficultly writing a novel, one simply begins by writing about one who has difficulty writing a novel.[18] Carroli and Wilson similarly decided to write about waiting while they waited to write, a decision no doubt motivated somewhat by the eight-week time constraint. In a node embedded later in the narrative an unnamed speaker reflects on the ease with which she "starts": "Were I to render my life in hypertext I would begin not at the beginning, wherever that might be, but with the words START NOW. I mean these two words not to command the narrative with my baton in hand, but to state the obvious: even in the infinite potentialities of hypertext, the reader must start, if they want to begin. The writer must begin, if they want to start" ("what.html"). What follows from a reflexive beginning, however, may not come quite as readily, for it is less likely to be enclosed in an originary paradox and thus is subject to the demands of metonymy (one can recall the simplicity of Barth's "Frame-tale," which does not transcend its recursive "beginnings"). An opening sentence always marks a point of departure but, even more so, a potential link to an overwhelming and inconceivable number of destinations. Here the *link* is present also in the form of a digitally mediated hyperlink. As the unnamed speaker points out, it therefore marks an intensely hypertextual moment.

Against the Current

In *water writes always in *plural* waiting implies vulnerability. Waiting is a submission to an "other," in this case a stranger: "What if the stranger can't, I mean doesn't, come? *This places us into the framework of waiting and expectation.* It is a fear that nothing will happen, or worse still, that something might" ("woman.html"). As their citation of Barthes' *A Lover's Discourse* elsewhere points out, she who waits submits because she desires whatever she waits for: "The stranger is no longer a source of pleasure, but residual desire. The boredom acknowledges the possibility of desire, boredom sets in because there is the possibility that something or someone is worth waiting for, that an object of desire will make its presence felt, for the longing to return."[19] If there were no desire, there would be no waiting.

But despite the vulnerability induced by waiting, waiting itself gradually becomes a nuanced form of affirmation as the narrative progresses. Waiting creates a contemplative or meditative space, or at least it provides the initial conditions that allow for its creation. The meditative space refers on the one hand to the space of the woman's thought (one might say that her thoughts accelerate as her body, inversely, tends toward stillness), but on the other hand it refers—again reflexively—to the network space inhabited by the reader. Indeed, for some, the idea of a contemplative network space (now effectively concomitant with the Web) is a potential; for others it remains an impossibility—a sentiment that reflects a broader view that there is no place for contemplative narrative fiction in any form in a culture inundated with the graphical, the animated, and the immediate.[20] For Carroli and Wilson the "water that writes" flows slowly and deliberately, resistant to the surge of immediacy. In recognizing that "the pace of waiting is slowness" ("Waiting. html"), the authors locate a certain virtue not in the *absence of* but rather the *alternative to* speed. For them, it is also a virtue endangered:

> We apologise for being late, for making others wait. This is bad manners—"good manners cost nothing" you know. The time spent waiting is an eternity. We languish in these small eternities.

> But I fear that waiting will be extinguished by the pursuit of pure speed, flat and undiscerning. ("Waiting.html")

Furthermore, the authors aim to revisit the commonplace understanding that "[a]ny moment spent waiting is idle, lost momentum, a sign of slowness. Poor service" ("Waiting.html"). Their project attempts to realize in the network environment a contemplative space for narrative forms. The meditations of and about the woman waiting anticipate Hélène Cixous, who, writing of Joyce's *Moral Tales and Meditations* (2001), speaks of the "viscosity of time" apparent in his narratives, which privileges contemplation over action, connection over resolution. The authors of *water* similarly write "*adagio . . .* languid, longing & lingering" ("Waiting.html").

In turn, they resist a commonplace conception of hypertext technology: that it is necessarily about speed. George Landow (1997, 82) set the stage for such a conception when he announced that the "speed with which one can move between passages and points [in hypertext] changes both the way we read and the way we write, just as the high-speed number-crunching computing changed various scientific fields by making possible investigations that before had required too much time or risk." Granted, Landow's primary interest here is the efficiency of pedagogical hypertext, and from its predigital origins in Vannevar Bush's (1945/2001) MEMEX, hypertext technology was intended to facilitate the gathering and retrieval of information. To this end speed is crucial. But the same virtue has potentially adverse implications for some forms of information "processing," which would include *reading*. Nicholas Burbules (1997, 104) suggests that the hyperlink has already assumed an "apparent naturalness" that needs to be counteracted: "[The] speed [of the hyperlink] in taking a user from one point to another makes the moment of transition too fleeting to be an object of reflection itself." Carried into an aesthetic domain, where there is no correspondence between "the

high-speed number-crunching" and the act of interpreting, say, the metaphorical relations in a text, the stakes are clearly even higher.

The Unknown addresses the problem of speed during a scene in which
one of the authors' live readings goes awry in the presence of (a fictionalized version of) the critic Larry McCaffery. In that instance "speed reading"
has harmful consequences for the audience but only after it becomes, literally, reading on speed:

> McCaffery, though, had in fact caused all the trouble by trying to buy
> speed off of his grad students, and then distributing it to Dirk (and
> the rest of us). Not that the idea of a speed-reading was a bad one al-
> together. By now we were getting fairly tired of these things, so the
> quicker the applause subsided and the volumes of The Unknown an-
> thology were moved off the shelves and autographed three times, the
> better.... But Dirk on speed caused some kind of hyper-reaction
> among the crowd members, to whom Dirk was manifesting his psy-
> chic powers as he read a series of sestinas. It was a mad rush and
> bodies were merely obstacles to be stepped on, even nearly crushed.
> ("sandiego.htm")[21]

In *water writes always in *plural, by contrast, "Pure speed is a measure, a fe-
tish, an excess" ("Waiting.html"), and its own narrative is overtly deliberate
and unhurried.

The theme of slowness in waiting and writing also informs a medial reflexivity. While Carroli and Wilson document their time on the Internet,
they also document the time *of* the Internet, which seems to protract even the
shortest spells of waiting precisely because we expect it to transcend time.
The theme makes a broad comment on its medium. In a review of Joyce's
Othermindedness (2000) Carroli (2001) writes of the notion of *nextness*:

> Nextness, as Joyce describes it, is a measure of the future. We live in a
> constant state of nextness, anticipation of the future and the promise
> of speed. In that waiting is the anticipation of "a true electronic form."
> In keeping with theories of remediation, he notes, "the new electronic
> literature will seem self-evident, as if we have always seen it and, para-
> doxically, as if we have never seen it before." In a constant state of
> nextness, the new electronic literature will bear a great burden: to be
> simultaneously new and old, unfamiliar and familiar, possible and im-
> possible. The new electronic literature will emerge from the other-
> mindedness of network culture.

In utilizing the medium to extend and "remediate" the literary arts, we are waiting not only for the Net—for what it does and how quickly it will do it—but also for what it will become. *water espouses this idea both explicitly in its story and implicitly in its texture and tone, and it insists that we exercise patience in practicing what is, in a historical continuum of writing technologies, a writing technology in its infancy.

Recirculative

In *water repetition is closely bound to the notion of waiting. On a social level there is the anticipation of a return predicated on some departure. The authors again cite Barthes' *A Lover's Discourse:*

> For Barthes, waiting is that
> "tumult of anxiety provoked by
> waiting for the loved being,
>
>   subject to trivial
>   delays
>
>   (rendezvous, letters,
>   telephone calls,
>   returns)."
>   ("Waiting.html")

The concept of repetition in waiting, and repetition *as* waiting, also arises in relation to the act of composition: "In writing about waiting, I feel that I am really writing about impatience. Wait. I repeat the word to convey its manifold applications; apprehension, wait, warning, wait, restraint, wait, expectation, wait, passivity, wait, yielding, wait, doubt, wait" ("Waiting.html").

The text as a whole is structured as a succession of returns to the opening page, marking both a return to a woman who waits and a sentence that waits, so to speak, for the reader to choose one of the four available links. The linked phrases, arranged one on top of the other, suggest a hierarchical reading order. All of them, however, offer a possible point of entry, and the reader does not have to read the nodes that follow in any particular order. Most of the subsequent nodes contain multiple text links that make a singularly prescribed reading impossible. In addition, the linking topology is constructed so that the four initial links do not constitute structurally separate paths that simply return to the home page when completed; that is, nodes reached from the link "a woman" may be reached also by entering the narrative at "waiting," reflecting the genuinely networked form of the text. The narrative's cyclical structure informs its thematic framework reciprocally. Each return to the opening page parallels the woman's own conscious rehearsals as she imagines innumerable scenarios of how her strange encounter will play out. These scenes "occur" only as hypotheses, and the woman must cognitively take herself back to the street corner and restate her predicament before constructing another one.

For the woman, these rehearsals suggest a generative form of repetition— "every iteration steels her" ("apple1.html"). Likewise, the authors have managed to generate an entire work through repeated encounters with the same sentence. In doing so, they dramatize the hermeneutic act of returning to any text, here on an expressly microstructural scale. For the reader the effect of repetition is more complex. At first, one is subject to an audio sampling of Beethoven's *Fur Elise*, which accompanies the opening page. Popularly recognized as one of the most overused and overplayed pieces of classical music in history, *Fur Elise*, as appropriated here, mimics the experience of the automated sound tracks that play while one is left on hold on the phone. Whenever the entire song (or song cycle) repeats, the caller on hold knows all too well that she or he has been waiting for a long time. Hence, when *Fur Elise* starts up with every link back to "a woman / stands on a street corner / waiting / for a stranger," the reader becomes acutely aware of the extended time of the wait or, as the authors put it, the "weight of time" ("weight. html").[22]

The piano sonata alludes to the waiting experienced by Carroli and Wilson during composition, but it also reflects their immediate acknowledgment of the unfamiliar and possibly uncomfortable demands they place on readers. They ask that readers entertain a cyclical text and, at the same time, one that barely progresses, at least according to more conventional measures of narrative. Arguably, the work does not qualify as a narrative at all; in fact, the Australian Network for Art and Technology describes it as "a work which investigates and deconstructs narrative in a series of departures and intersections" (ANAT 1998). Either way, the hope is that the reader, like the women whose waiting gradually engenders the text of *water*, comes to value connection over resolution. Still, even without a story resolution there is a certain closure with each cyclical return. Compared to *The Unknown*, recursive closures play a much more integral role in the reading experience of *water*.

Carroli and Wilson's *water* generates meaning not only in its effective implementation of cycles but also through a playful resistance to them. Amid the cyclical flow of the text there is one conspicuous snag, one choice that leads readers to an abrupt "dead end." At one point in the narrative the woman considers a postcard she received from "a man she barely knew, who left long ago . . . Postmarked Berlin" ("Berlin.html"). Her longing leads her to a contemplation of marriage:

> She puts her hand on her chest, thinks about the man. Blue-black hair.
> <u>She would like to get married.</u>
> Well wouldn't you? ("Berlin.html")

The text link in this passage takes readers to an image of a medieval knight, on a white horse, and, indeed, in "shining armour." Below the image are the instructions: "Go Back. This Is a Dead End" ("knight.html").

The message is obvious; but more than just an unenviable fate—"a dead end"—the authors equate the institution of marriage to a myth, one that takes on inevitably ironic overtones when invoked in a contemporary social context. For them, stereotypical stories of such "knights" delivering salvation tend to overwrite the agency—or, more specifically, the desire—of the woman, who can do nothing other than wait for her hero to arrive. They cite Cixous, whose own landmark essays in the 1970s underscore the connection between women's desire and women's language. Cixous likewise recognizes the problem of the superficially benign theme of the mythical knight in the context of literary history and, in turn, resists it: "Once upon again a time, . . . it is the same story repeating woman's destiny in love across the centuries with the cruel hoax of its plot. And each <u>story,</u> each myth says to her: 'There is no place for your desire in our affairs of State'" (Cixous 1986, 67; cited in "once.html"). Above the Cixous quotation sits an image of a notably bored Cinderella, sitting by her mop and bucket, clock overhead, waiting for her prince.

The authors of *water recycle patriarchal myths that have informed literature, politically and aesthetically, over time and use them as a basis for their feminist critique. It is a two-pronged critique, of method and subject matter. For example, they make several references to "Lucy Gray," the titular character of William Wordsworth's (1799) poem of the same name. Lucy Gray, like Beethoven's "Elise," contributes to the composite identity of the woman waiting. In Wordsworth's poem Lucy Gray is told by her father to take a lantern and lead her mother through a blizzard. They are separated; then Lucy becomes lost, falls into a crevice, and dies. She returns, ghostlike, as the song of the wind:

> [S]ome maintain that to this day
> She is a living child;

That you may see sweet Lucy Gray
Upon the lonesome wild.

O'er rough and smooth she trips along,
And never looks behind;
And sings a solitary song
That whistles in the wind. (Wordsworth 1891, 121–22)

Carroli and Wilson, however, endeavor to resurrect her in a more contemporary context, through their composition of "Lucy Gray's School Song," a simple children's song with rather complex themes. Its lyrics fault age-old epistemologies in light of new technology that offers radical tools of thought:

Times have changed in recent years, we learn a different way
with calculators and computers work is more like play
The children of so long ago would envy us our day
We still strive for wisdom in the same old way. ("lucygray.html")

Lucy Gray's ghostly voice returns but only on the authors' own terms: the song is performed by a contemporary version of "Lucy Gray," who appears along with a contemporary version of "Elise," the two of them as schoolchildren attending a lesson. Both girls are restless in class and are reluctant to wait for their turn to speak.

The authors take their critique further in redressing patriarchal writing methodologies. At one point their target takes on a specifically American context, when romantic-era pioneers were conquering and cultivating a vast frontier at the same time that they were cultivating a uniquely American literature:

Once upon a time in a far away land the word was thought to be akin to a spade, or a shovel—necessary, useful—as close to the Body as the arm that bound the working man to the handle of his simple honest Tool.

In this fertile world of long ago, a scribe once wrote—"A sentence should read as if its Author, had he held a plough instead of a pen, could have drawn a furrow Deep and Straight to the end." ("Knight2.html")

In this new myth the scribe, who is none other than Henry David Thoreau, ultimately dies "a slow and humiliating death after falling Head first into a hole of his own Digging" ("Knight2.html"). As he ploughs onward, Thoreau literally digs himself into a hole with his words. Whereas Thoreau falls, the presence of Lucy Gray at the lesson would imply that she escapes not only her father's instructions to go out into the storm but also the straight and deep furrows of Wordsworth's own poem.

In *water a contrast emerges between the straight and deep lines of male writing and the curves and surfaces of hypertextual contours. In turn, "hypertext" assumes an expressly feminine quality. For the authors, however, technology itself guarantees no quick comforts for women writing. In fact, Wilson notes that before the eight-week residency, she had only "a fragmented knowledge of the field; it was something I read about, remained outside of, slightly in awe" (Wilson 1998). She speaks of a number of "assumptions" that can deter creative participation in digital environments, namely, the idea that "there are these people called 'Experts' whose technical knowledge immediately qualifies them over and above other people with other sorts of knowledges"; she adds, "(No doubt issues of gender are unavoidable here too)" (1998). In this sense, if technology is itself strange to the authors of *water, then technology, obliquely cast in male terms, is the stranger for whom the woman waits.

The fact of a *woman* waiting is indeed essential to a work with strong feminist concerns. (Her stillness and silence are also an obvious contrast to *The Unknown,* which sets four men in motion on a quintessentially male road trip with the aim of seeking attention and displaying bravado.) Waiting, the authors insist, means something different for a woman: "As the man who licked his lips could tell you, there is a history to women who <u>wait</u> on corners" ("apple1.html"). At one point they ask, "Is this the feminine; to be the one left waiting?" ("Waiting.html"). Given a recent and much-debated statement issued by the Vatican, declaring "[l]istening, welcoming, humility, faithfulness, praise and *waiting* [my emphasis]" to be the characteristic traits of women, the authors' question can hardly be considered extreme.[23] Even though questions of gender are, as Wilson suggests, unavoidable, the authors do not grant a naive equivalency to technology and masculinity. At the same time, they avoid the opposing extreme: they do not adopt the strategy of some feminists who appropriate the multilinearity of hypertext writing technology as an empowering alternative to the putatively male linearity of print. For example, Carolyn Guyer, author of the network narrative *Quibbling,*[24] writes, "We know that being denied personal authority inclines us to prefer . . . decentered contexts, and we have learned, especially from our mothers, that the woven practice of women's intuitive attention and reasoned care is a fuller, more balanced process than simple rational linearity" (cited in Joyce 1995, 89). Guyer's comments move toward a brand of "hyperfeminism" that Diane Greco (1996, 88) counters:

> In this view, hypertext is an alternative to "simple rational linearity,"
> which itself opposes ostensibly female (or perhaps, feminine) charac-
> teristics of intuition, attentiveness, and care, all of which are transmit-
> ted from one woman to another via the universal experience of having
> a (certain kind of) mother. The opportunities for non-linear expres-
> sion which hypertext affords coalesce, in this view, to form a writing
> that is "female" in a very particular way: hypertext writing embraces
> an ethic of care that is essentially intuitive, complicated, detailed, but
> also "fuller" and "balanced." It is important to note that not all hyper-
> texts written by women exemplify this aesthetic.

Clearly, an understanding of hypertext technology as better suited to female writers simply reverses a form of technological determinism on feminist terms.

Although *water writes always in *plural has obvious feminist preoccupations, it also exhibits a *post*feminist sensibility. Emerging popularly in the
1980s and 1990s, postfeminism is often described as a response to the exclusions and prescriptions of feminism—a tempering of the antagonisms that
made feminism as matriarchal as any patriarchy is patriarchal (and, in this
regard, might suggest an opposing sense of restraint in relation to the excesses of feminism). Though there is probably more confusion than consensus regarding the term, *postfeminism* can be understood not necessarily
in terms of an abandonment of or movement beyond feminism but rather
as a more nuanced movement within it, and it might help in discussing what
water is and what it does.

As Lisa Joyce (1996) writes, "postfeminism remains an awkward yet laud-
able movement among younger women, one which embraces pluralism and
homosexuality, one that expects that women are just as involved in the electronic frontier of the web as men are." The *electronic book review,* through
its Weave interface, has followed this "thread" into the new millennium
with its continuing collection on feminist art theory and practice, "writing (post)feminism."[25] In her contribution to the *ebr* thread, " 'I'll be a postfeminist in a postpatriarchy,' or, Can We Really Imagine Life after Feminism?"
Lisa Yaszek (2005) credits Cris Mazza, fiction writer and editor of two an-
thologies of *Chick Lit* (1995, 1996), with moving beyond discussions of what
postfeminist writing responds to and toward a description of "what it actually looks like." For Mazza postfeminist fiction is

writing that says women are independent and confident but not lacking in their share of human weakness and not necessarily self-empowered; that they are dealing with who they've made themselves into rather than blaming the rest of the world; that women can use and abuse another human being as well as anyone; that women can be conflicted about what they want and therefore get nothing; that women can love until they hurt someone, turn their own hurt into love, refuse to love, or even ignore the notion of love completely as they confront the other 90 percent of life. Postfeminist writing says female characters don't have to be superhuman in order to be interesting. Just human. (Mazza 2000, 105)

For Yaszek feminist literature all too often succumbs to a polarity: either too many stories about superwomen, or too many stories about victims—a shortfall *water deftly avoids. Just like Mazza's hypothetical character, the woman waiting does not do anything heroic and is a victim only of her own passing insecurities. She is conflicted, vacillating with desire and boredom. But she blames no one for her predicament—for where she finds herself, literally and figuratively, at this time and place in her life. She evokes the quality of a postfeminist protagonist.

But *water reflects a postfeminist sensibility in another important way, one that further demonstrates an aesthetic of restraint. The text questions the stereotypical binary distinction of "male" and "female" writing. Aside from the biological differences of the embodied writer, there is yet to be any convincing evidence to suggest that there are stable stylistic or structural differences that constitute essentially "male" or "female" writing.[26] This viewpoint marks a departure from the feminism of Cixous and her articulation of *l'écriture féminine,* which implies an essentialist link between the body and writing, one in which the creative fluidity of the female is inextricably biological and artistic. Speaking from a postfeminist perspective, Lisa Joyce (2005) remains skeptical of such essentialism:

We have heard for years about . . . how the way a woman writes is different than the way a man writes. I have never understood how to take this. Is there a quantifiable difference between men's and women's writing? Something about the number of adjectives? The sentence structure? (my son says that it has something to do with lots and lots of capital letters and exclamation points). I hesitate to make this kind of judgment, that without the presence of the writing body, the writing itself could be different according to the writing body's gender.

Even though the authors of *water writes always in *plural cite Cixous liberally, they are cautious with regard to advocating an absolute notion of "women's writing" (their stance can also be tempered by humor, as in regard to Thoreau). Indeed, *water is a fluid work but not necessarily in opposition to the solid rationality of "male" writing—it is not "fluid" in the stereotypically feminine sense.

In this regard the work resists a poststructuralist feminism that privileges womanhood in terms of an *excess* of fluidity. For instance, the French feminist theorist Luce Irigaray, along with Cixous, sought to undo the phallocentric bias that portrayed female sexuality (after Freud and Lacan) as lack or absence. Noting that "fluid is always [in] a relation [to] excess or lack vis-à-vis unity" (1985, 115), Irigaray embraces the idea of excess as a means of opening up subject positions for women that patriarchy denies—not only politically, socially, or economically but also in thought and in language.[27] Although questioning the subjectivity of their protagonist is a vital part of the text, it is only one part of the broader project of weaving the narrative threads of feminism, technology, and the movement toward network culture and consciousness.

Carroli and Wilson are intent to explore streams and flows motivated by collaboration as much as by notions of gender: "Through our dialogues . . . distance between speech and writing, between reading and writing seemed somehow more fluid and formless" (Carroli 1998). The "plural water" of their title refers to the authors themselves, whose voices can be distinct at one moment and inseparable the next. Thus, even though they write "always" in plural, they retain a fluid singularity; *water* is, in grammatical terms, an *uncountable* noun—at once singular and plural.[28]

Conserving Media's Ecology

Carroli and Wilson recognize the importance of shaping and constricting the flow of their text. The narrative recirculates with restraint, and the title of their work gestures toward this idea. The fragment "*water writes always in *plural" appears in French artist Marcel Duchamp's text "*The.*"[29] In the text, his first in the English language, Duchamp systematically replaces the article *the* with an asterisk throughout.[30] The act is reductive, involving the omission of words; but, at the same time, the asterisk confirms the omission and calls attention to it. While Duchamp has admitted to reveling in an abstract exercise in his decision to shed the article, critics have issued varied interpretations on the substitution game (for example, since *asterisk*, from the Latin *astra*, connotes "star," many have read the work as documenting the artist's interest in stars and, quite possibly, in its concrete arrangement of thirteen stars on the page, suggestive of a constellation in itself).[31]

Nonetheless, the effect of the marked omission lends itself to further interpretation. Perhaps Duchamp thought of the article as superfluous, unnecessary, even excessive, especially as he was struggling to come to terms with the complexities of the English language. Whatever the reason, the abstract exercise results in a paradox: it demonstrates how a linguistic and grammatical reduction can result in a semantic accretion. For example, *the* is a definite article; it specifies. Remove it, and whatever noun it modifies assumes an indefinite plurality. The paradox inflects the plurality of Carroli and Wilson's text: the utterance anchoring the text, "*a* woman / stands on *a* street corner / waiting / for *a* stranger," exploits the indefinite article *a*, opening its narrative to the possibility of *any* woman, *any* street corner, and *any* stranger.[32]

As a fragment of Duchamp's text and the title of Carroli and Wilson's narrative, "*water writes always in *plural" illustrates linguistic complexity. But it also lends itself to lyrical simplicity. Language, like water, surrounds us; it is a resource, and as such, it is possible to overuse it—indeed, to "unknown" extremes. Both *The Unknown* and *water writes always in *plural* foreground repetition in the network environment of the Web. Both remind us that excess has pragmatic and aesthetic implications for network textuality. In opting for a more restrained approach to their network text, Carroli and Wilson are able to exploit the dynamics of repetition for narrative emergence.

6

Mythology Proceeding

Morrissey's *The Jew's Daughter*

Sing, Muse, of that man of many turns, the wanderer . . .
—Homer, *The Odyssey*

If Carroli and Wilson recycle meaning through narrative returns, Judd Morrissey, in *The Jew's Daughter* (2000), suggests how one might recycle the printed page when creating narrative fiction for the computer screen. With a text that simultaneously adopts the conventions of print and departs from the conventions of the Web, Morrissey mobilizes not only his vision of a fictional world on the page but also the page itself. *The Jew's Daughter* marks a conscious appropriation of the rhetorical and stylistic qualities of the printed page but also accommodates digitally mediated links that subvert the expectations of Web-based hyperlinks. These links allow for a process of replacement and repetition that occurs within a single transient frame. As the reading that follows will suggest, such medial mobility can have profound implications for the narrative discourse.

A Processual Page

The pages of *The Jew's Daughter* look everything like but act nothing like pages. Insofar as one can use a computer screen to replicate the look of a printed page, Morrissey endeavors to do so. The font, the margins, and most significant, the fact that the text breaks at the top left-hand corner and the bottom right-hand corner all gesture toward a conspicuously pagelike appearance. In this regard one begins with what seems to be more *page* than hypertextual *node*. In addition, the qualities that have come to characterize the face of Internet materiality, such as the tool bars, scroll bars, and navigational buttons of Web browsers, are either absent or deemphasized in the design and functioning of *The Jew's Daughter*.

There is, however, one element on the screen that appears to belong exclusively to the domain of digital text: a word highlighted in blue. Readers presume the word is the site of a hyperlink. It is. And it isn't. Morrissey, along with Lori Talley, uses a software program called Macromedia Flash to compose *The Jew's Daughter*.[1] Flash allows its users to animate text and images on the Web, and many works of online fiction and poetry exploit it for a wide array of kinetic and cinematic effects. In *The Jew's Daughter* Morrissey uses Flash to simulate and subvert one's engagement with the hyperlink. Rather than click on a word, the reader needs only to position the cursor over it and a "rollover" activates the link, bringing up new textual material without perceptually shifting the frame of reference of the "page."[2] There is no clicking involved; clicking, an act so familiarly iconic to the act of reading digital texts, is no longer an option. Readers can, however, click on a small box at the top of the screen that opens a navigational window. It details the number of the current page and allows readers to type in the number of a page they wish to "turn to"—an example of how the page paradigm is reinforced rhetorically.

Inevitably, *The Jew's Daughter* has extended the tired debate over what constitutes a *hypertext* or a *hyperlink* per se. While the term *hypertext* has been applied so widely that it has lost its utility as a description of a specific form of literature, the attempt to define a hyperlink arises on slightly different terms. Rather than asking questions concerning the media-dependency or media-specificity of hypertexts, the debate over the hyperlink would ask, "Must a hyperlink make use of some form of HyperText Markup Language to be thought of as such?" Or, "Is a rollover a form of *hyperlink*?" But whether or not this word in blue in Morrissey's text is a hyperlink is a moot point. What matters here is that the Flash-animated transition constitutes a digitally mediated poetical effect; it is an example of "electropoetics," to borrow the title of one of the thematic threads of the *electronic book review*.[3] The page is transformed subtly, almost imperceptibly; much of the text remains, but some of it is replaced, and the reader must reread the text to determine where and how it is different. Hence, the page not only behaves much differently than a page in print does, but it also departs from and comments on the node-link structure that has become the dominant form of network narrative both before and after the Web.

Much has been made of *The Jew's Daughter*'s departure from the dominant —or, to invoke a more problematic but still common adjective, the *classical*— mode of network fiction. But perhaps too much has been made of it. The extant criticism of Morrissey's narrative has confined itself almost exclusively to discussions of formal and technological innovation. The work is undoubtedly innovative, both for its subversion of the hyperlink and its peculiar return to the printed page. As Matthew Mirapaul (2000) writes in a (short-lived) arts and technology column in the *New York Times*, "At a time when hypertext authors are experimenting with video, 3-D environments and other multimedia elements in order to escape this link-chained cage, Morrissey has returned to the plain, white rectangular page." Implicit in Mirapaul's comment is the fact that a "text-only narrative" becomes, at the hand of some circuitous movement of history or, at the very least, the movement of a certain irony, a distinctly *radical* statement for an artist working in electronic forms.

With so much emphasis on technological advance, it is clear that a little narrative theory can go a long way toward a better understanding of the work. Consider this description by a curator for "Interactive Web Art": "Judd Morrissey's 'The Jew's Daughter' is an all-text piece of new digital literature, but unlike traditional hypertext literature, the links do not take the reader to a different location. Rather, clicking on the single hyperlink on each page changes significant chunks of the text on that same page. The page is now the same, only different. In this way, Morrissey has redefined narrative flow to be something other than the traditional linear march of words" (Fifield 2002). The description of "clicking" may suffice for a generic reference to network navigation, but the fact that Morrissey consciously moves away from the act of *clicking* as a necessity of *reading* in network environments should be emphasized. In even greater need of qualification, however, is the description of Morrissey's "redefinition" of narrative flow as something other than a "traditional linear march of words" (Fifield 2002). More than most narratives, *The Jew's Daughter* insists on its own rereading, and its innovation lies precisely in its use of the digital medium to do so. But unlike other works of network fiction (here, "hypertext literature"), in which the narrative emerges differently for different readers, *The Jew's Daughter* will always present a text that is ordered in the same way. Thus, the fixity of its telling makes the work in fact *more linear* compared to its hypertext literature counterparts, where "linearity" is a measure of the mobility of textual elements rather than a temporal or chronological progression of story events.[4] There are no bifurcations; each page contains only one link. As Scott Rettberg (2002) observes, "the story proceeds in a shifting, fragmentary but ultimately linear way." It is therefore not strictly a networked, arborescent, or axial hypertext structure, but it is emergent, recombinatory, and replete with narrative returns.

To balance the technical virtuosity of *The Jew's Daughter* with its patent literary qualities, it is necessary to distinguish between material and discursive complexity—not with the purpose of partitioning the two (they are, as this study demonstrates, in constant dialogue) but rather to reiterate that they are not one and the same. Tabbi's articulation of the "processual page" marks one attempt to consider the radical changes of the material page in tandem with the semantic and semiotic changes to writing in general. The processual page: an intentionally vague metaphor, it can refer, on the one hand, to the migration of literary media from print to digital forms, and all of the cultural transformations of the "page" as we know it. On the other hand, it refers to the dynamic movement of a specific, electronically animated onscreen text—literally, a page in process.

Tabbi's elaboration of the "Processual Page" in his eponymous (2003) essay goes hand in hand with that of theorist Hanjo Berressem. In an essay titled "Data Dance" (2002) Berressem provides a brief historical overview of hypertext theory and the misguided appropriation of spatial rhetoric, namely its celebrated "three-dimensionality," in an attempt to conceptualize network structures. Three-dimensionality, as more recent digital discourse makes clear, merely extends the practice of mapping space onto the stable planes of Cartesian geometry. Berressem defends the use of a topological rhetoric, which stems from the inherent topology of network systems. Most examples of topologically informed poetics postdate the creation of the most popular and celebrated works of network fiction. Michael Joyce, for instance, explores the scientific and sensual connotations of topology in *Otherminded-ness*, but the work was published in 2000, at least two years after he completed his last major work of digital literature (*Twilight, a Symphony*) and two years before he announced his withdrawal from the field. The convergence of topology and poetics might be best understood as a characteristic of second-wave digital literature and second-wave digital-literary criticism. Both Tabbi and Berressem recognize the need for a "processual" and "emergent" hermeneutics (Berressem 2002, 42) in light of a text comprising dynamic signifiers. "Instead of an object," writes Tabbi (2003), "the page is to become a description of a possible object, reflecting only what the author makes of materials that the reader can, in turn, cast into further potentials."

The same hermeneutics, however, must affirm its utility without misconstruing the ontological status of digital texts. Berressem's critique lapses briefly in this respect when he refers to the "immateriality" (2002, 29) of the computer screen, recalling a similar expression of immateriality in the "flickering signifiers" of Hayles's (2000) electronic text. When he describes the materiality of the "computer screen" as "made up purely of light and electricity," surely this represents an incomplete list of materials. Putative immateriality—of screens *or* texts—ultimately proves misleading, feeding a problematic opposition of print versus digital text and contributing to over-inflated claims for the fluidity and ethereality of all things "virtual." *Meaning*, I would emphasize, is immaterial; the text that conveys meaning, regardless of its medium, is not and cannot be such. The development of processual criticism might benefit by following Brian Massumi (2002) in redefining the *virtual* not as the "immaterial" but rather as the "changeable," thereby grounding the "virtuality" of digital text in what Aarseth (1997, 43) calls "a concrete phenomenon" of topological structures, one that is "defined formally and not metaphorically, in terms of nodes and links." Even though a processual text is changeable in a way that eludes our familiar systems of reference, readers attend to a defamiliarized materiality of network texts, not a radical immateriality of text.

Terminological miscues aside, what makes Berressem's and Tabbi's discussion that much more significant is the fact that both have created and put into practice their own conceptions of the processual page. Invoking the Deleuzian notion of "folding," Berressem creates a theoretical (and inevitably reflexive) essay in which microtexts or subtexts (though they are not "sub-" in the sense of *under* or *below*) are brought in and out of the reader's frame of reference.[5] In "Poeto:pologies: Folded Space, Traversal Machines and the Poetics of 'Emergent Text'" (Berressem 2001) these microtexts are brought directly into the text present onscreen whenever the reader activates the links to a number of "folds." Despite the fact that the folds are set apart by different font styles and weightings, the design of the page, which also includes a number of hyperlinks interspersed throughout the text, can overwhelm the uninitiated reader. The point, however, is to create the effect that the reader is moving (indeed, not *moving through*) a unilateral text-space,[6] one in which the notion of text/subtext or macro-/micro-text is lost in the process of topological enfolding. With his textual topology Berressem puts into practice a conceptualization of reading and writing native to its medium rather than one inherited from common conventions of print.[7]

Tabbi's processual page, or pages, can be found in the interface of the *electronic book review*, which employs the metaphor of weaving to convey its processuality. Authors, readers, and editors can all assume the role of weaver, contributing to the active page in the form of marginal glosses (activated via rollovers) and lateral linkages, either inbound to other *ebr* essays or outbound to other essays or sites in the greater Web environment. Or, one can write a full-length response to an existing essay or review (a "riPOSTe") that appears chronologically after the piece to which it responds. As Tabbi (2003) writes, "With such activity there is certainly the suggestion of openness, that the connections and potential readerly associations are infinite. Authors are made aware, explicitly, that their production will undergo continued threading, weaving, and glossing at the hands of readers, and this activity will be made visible, cumulative, and public over time with the author's own text."

The ordinarily static attributes of the printed page acquire mobility and mutability in the Weave, and the responsibility for their creation is *distributed*, both in authorial and temporal terms.[8]

If Berressem and Tabbi take the concept of the processual page into the realm of critical discourse and academic publishing, then Morrissey instantiates the concept in a fictional form with *The Jew's Daughter*. As Morrissey and Talley (2002) write, "The work in its current incarnation . . . is a narrative that unfolds through subtle textual transformations in a fluid rectangular text-space. The reading experience is unlike any other in that the page appears to be constantly weaving itself together in response to the decisions of the user." In an interview with Mirapaul (2000) Morrissey adds, "Because it takes the paradigm of the page, you can see that it's not a page. . . . I wanted a fluidity that I haven't seen in hypertext." The fluidity of the text works in two ways, both of which underline discrete paradigms of textual kinetics. Literary criticism must differentiate between texts that move with the reader's intervention and those that move without it. Therefore, Morrissey and Talley's reference to "decisions" is misleading, since there is really only one decision: continue or cease. They should refer instead to the reader's *action* or *intervention*.

In Aarseth's (1997) cybertextual typology, transiency refers to texts whose signifiers move independently of the reader's actions; conversely, intransient texts are static. *The Jew's Daughter* contains isolated instances of transiency. Pages 34 through 134 and pages 173 through 203, for example, involve segments where the text is generated spontaneously, appearing one word after another until the segment is complete and the page returns to an intransient state. The narrator in the first instance, a writer and literature student who serves as the authorial consciousness for a substantial portion (but not all) of the narrative, alludes to an experience in which his partner witnessed a woman in Indonesia commit suicide by placing her head over a railroad track. One word at a time appears on the screen, generated automatically with a short pause between each. The generation of the text involves a repetition of the sentence, "She had laid her head on the tracks and the train cut cleanly through her neck," even though she could only have done this once. Furthermore, when it has ceased, a macabre play of words reinforces the act of detaching a woman's head. *She,* the word itself, is severed: "(She had laid her head on the tracks and the train cut cleanly through her neck. Sh she had laid her head on the tracks and the train cut cleanly through her neck. e had laid her head on the tracks and the train cut cleanly through her neck. In Java she had seen a woman decapitated)" (34–134). The staccato manner of the retelling—a grammatical choppiness, so to speak—comments reflexively on the diegesis. In language, of course, one is always already detached from the act itself. More generally, the suicide account announces a decapitation motif that recurs throughout the narrative in both a thematic and linguistic mode; readers are in turn repeatedly reminded of the suicide, much as the experience of witnessing a horrific scene can resurface continually in one's consciousness.

The unnamed student has several encounters with homeless men while walking the streets of Chicago, where he is currently renting an apartment. Another instance of transient text reproduces the dialogue of one such encounter: "Hey. Was up? I know you gots change. You got a dime or smoke to spare?" (173–203). The steady rhythm of words coming into view has the effect of acutely focusing the reader's attention, as if calling out to her or him in an act of interpellation. The majority of the text, however, remains still until the reader rolls over the linked text. The processuality of *The Jew's Daughter* emphasizes not a hyperkinetic "data dance," to borrow Berressem's title, but rather the ability of the digital medium to stage and animate transitions in an innovative way.

Transitions occur in several locations across the space of the page. Page 8, for example, begins with the fragment, "closed in with isolating weight" and concludes with "a ship's horn," which is also the linked phrase.[9] In order to locate transitions, the start of the page can be called A, the end of the page called Z, and the linked word or phrase called L. The first transition involves a recursive fold whereby readers follow the end of the page back to its beginning (Z back to A): "In one of the newer establishments, a sound like a foghorn bellowed whenever someone pushed the button on the drinking fountain, a ship's horn / closed in with isolating weight." (The backslash in the citation marks the "processual page break.") Quite obviously, one does not read a printed page in this manner, but many transitions in the narrative—though they often imply a dramatic and disorienting perspectival rupture—are carefully crafted so that they are grammatically fluid. What comes next is always, to an extent, what came before, and the transitions across the page have the effect of prose refrains.

Other transitions occur in the movement of one page to the next. The phrase "echoing among the shrouds" appears at the beginning of page 9. Therefore, one can identify the new transition that reads "a ship's horn / echoing among the shrouds." Adding page numbers to the lettered locations, the transition is simultaneously Z8 to A9 as well as the new Z9 to A9, since the description of the water fountain concluding with the "ship's horn" remains the same in page 9. Thematically, the ship's horn remains, but is read again as it is heard again, repeating with a difference as an echo of itself. But

□

closed in with isolating weight. A morning that asks too much, but its urgent pressing (one, frayed and tired, would hope) consolidates, transfigures, and, in doing so, places its need in more capable hands. It takes security, is its own haltless guarantee, arouses someone and puts him to work. Words are always only real-time creation, realized under the pressure of days, just as this once should have been realized under the pressure of days. Incipit. Three knocks.

Who gets what? I'm sure that a year has passed, since I was walking (that was the year that I never stopped walking), watching the lake boil in its pot, and two men were passing together, but when one spoke to another, he looked directly into me, placing his words there were they resounded. I proceeded, coiling and uncoiling, with my year-long walk, turning over words like wager, deadline, loan and extension. Complete the task.

To master her and yet to preserve her, I had thought to myself, seated in a confined space in one of the old hotels, the famous rooms of the Drake, the ornate ballrooms of the Midland on Lasalle. Beard sculpted, curls constrained. In one of the newer establishments, a sound like a foghorn bellowed whenever someone pushed the button on the drinking fountain, a ship's horn.

close

Figure 4. *The Jew's Daughter,* page 8 (the linked word appears here in gray). © Judd Morrissey. Reproduced with permission.

more of the text has changed: everything from the new beginning at "echoing" (A) to the phrase "Real-time creation" has been replaced by new material. The phrase, "real-time creation" marks the place—or the *crease*—where new and extant material has been brought together (while "Real" has been capitalized in page 9 to maintain the fluidity of the narrative).

The entirety of new material introduced into each page can be referred to as the fold (F). The further distinction is necessary given that the crease does not always occur at or near the linked text (L), nor is it always confined to the beginning (A) or end (Z) of the page. Complexity arises in that the beginning and the end of each fold are also transitional points in the processual text. Thus another level of transitions can be named at (1) the new end of the

□

echoing among the shrouds. Frigid nights when mists ascended the
white castle, diffusing the white horn-glow of the invisible tower.
The fog-breath of the carriage horse on Michigan Avenue would
rise impenetrably to obscure the city.

Real-time creation, realized under the pressure of days. just as it
once should have been realized under the pressure of days. Incipit.
Three knocks.

What has already not yet happened? What losses are taken and
who keeps what? I'm sure that a year has passed, since I was
walking (that was the year that I never stopped walking), watching the
lake boil in its pot, and two men were passing together, but when
one spoke to another, he looked directly into me, placing his
words there were they resounded. I proceeded, coiling and
uncoiling, with my year-long walk, turning over words like wager,
deadline, loan and extension. Complete the task.

To master her and yet to preserve her, I had thought to myself,
seated in a confined space in one of the old hotels, the famous
rooms of the Drake, the ornate ballrooms of the Midland on
Lasalle. Beard sculpted, curls constrained. In one of the newer
establishments, a sound like a foghorn bellowed whenever
someone pushed the button on the drinking fountain, a ship's horn

close

Figure 5. *The Jew's Daughter,* page 9 (the linked word appears here in gray). © Judd
Morrissey. Reproduced with permission.

preexisting material and the beginning of the new fold (F^A), and (2) the end
of the new fold (F^Z) and new beginning of the preexisting material. These
transitions may or may not be concomitant with the transitions at A and Z.
In this case A9 is concomitant with the *beginning* of the fold, F^{A}9. The transition to F^{Z}9 becomes a sequence of two new sentences: "The fog-breath of
the carriage horse on Michigan Avenue would rise impenetrably to obscure
the city. Real-time creation, realized under the pressure of days, just as it once
should have been realized under the pressure of days." The text reflects the
student's observations as he walks. But just as the fog physically obscures his
observations, the text obscures the reader's view of these observations. Our
view is partial and prismatic, refracted through textual repetitions and ob-

fuscations. These textual movements—in tandem with the movements of the interface—approximate those of the character's thought.

A final transition, albeit one of a more lyrical nature, occurs with the linked words and phrases themselves. On page 8 "a ship's horn" (L8) is foregrounded as the link but then recedes from view as the next page highlights "Three knocks"(L9), which is previously part of the background text. "Three knocks" in the narrative tends to mark beginnings in a number of ways, following, as it does here, the word *Incipit*—from the Latin for "here begins."[10] At this point the three knocks will begin the next page, but the knocks themselves, at other points in the story, belong to the student's partner trying to see him in order to make amends, the neighbor from downstairs, or—and these three knocks are for him the most unnerving—the psychologically unstable landlord angry about the partner extending her stay indefinitely without paying rent.

The linked words inevitably draw the reader's immediate attention, before he or she (re)reads from the "beginning" of the page, and also before he or she attempts to identify only the material that belongs to the new fold (which is often the case as the narrative—and the reader's familiarity with it—progresses). For this reason the linked words can be read as a succession that is meaningful in and of itself; that is, as our eyes immediately register a series of blue-lit words, we can more gradually read them as a metonymy of images. For example, the movement of pages 8, 9, and 10 forms not only images but also "sounds": "a ship's horn" (L8), "Three knocks" (L9), and "Somnambulistic murky muddled sinking speech" (L10, where *Somnambulistic* is the linked word). The links imply more subtle transitions and associations as well. On page 230 the linked text is the single letter *j* in the word *joined*. In the next page the student is intercepted at his front gate by a homeless man who asks to be invited in for coffee or beer. The man introduces himself as "J." (230), after the linked text effectively "introduces" him three pages earlier. In another instance the student recalls a dream in which his perspective shifts to that of his partner: "And then I could see through your eyes" (239). The word *eyes* contains the linked text but only partially in "yes." The implication is that "her eyes say yes"—an association that takes on a pointed relevance when the possibility arises of her unfaithfulness to him. Thus, the links in the narrative provide another site for electropoetical transformations.

For all the grace of the interface, not all of the foldings in *The Jew's Daughter* result in clean creases; that is, there is not always a discernible transition from Z to A or from L1 to L2, and at times the textual fold confounds grammar or syntax to the extent that no meaningful transition is apparent, and one must wait until that fold smoothes itself out in the pages that follow. The syntactic awkwardness that arises at these transitionary moments can have a dramatic effect on a work that aspires to "fluidity," and despite the relevant tension that arises between seamlessness on one hand and decapitation on the other—a thematic justification for disjunction—the result is an occasionally disjunctive reading experience. That said, if the transitions of this processual page are not seamless, then neither is the transition from the printed page to the digital one.

Remixing Narration

Despite the attention it has gained, the material innovation of *The Jew's Daughter* does not overwhelm the discursive depth and density of the narrative itself, and Morrissey undoubtedly makes good on his statement that "the responsibility is always to the writing, in whatever media" (Pressman 2003, 1). In terms of its materiality *The Jew's Daughter* is dynamic but stable. In terms of its discourse the work is highly unstable and ultimately indeterminate.

Morrissey employs diverse modes of discourse to convey the story, and the volatility of the discourse and the diversity of narrative technique produce the indeterminacy of the text. We know that the story begins and ends with a first-person narration by an unnamed male narrator, the student who recounts not only his thoughts and observations as he walks but also conversations with his partner (referred to at one point as Eva), his neighbor (Richard Nuxman), his landlord (Josephine, an Italian countess) and her hired hand (John Austin), and various homeless men he meets in passing. From these conversations we know that the student has recently returned to his home in Chicago after a trip to England. His relationship with his partner is strained and insecure, and their future together is uncertain. His relationship with Josephine and John, who live in the estate house they rent to him, is also tense and made worse by his partner's decision to stay in the apartment without their permission while he is away in England. Not only are the landlords overly particular and protective of the old house, but John also appears to have a violent and obsessive temperament.

We know, moreover, that the student describes himself as an "Irish-Jew" (23), that he has blue eyes and (from the compliment of a homeless man) that he has a beard—much like many of the other male characters in the story, including a terrier named Uncle, which belongs to John but is later adopted by Eva. Based on his role in opening and closing the narrative, and the proportionally significant amount of the story told from his point if view, it is possible to see the student, according to Genette's terminology, as not only a homodiegetic narrator (a character in the story) but also an autodiegetic narrator—the protagonist of his own story. The narrative begins with a question, "Will she disappear?" which can be read, retrospectively, as an expression of the narrator's insecurity about his partner. Page 1 continues:

> That day has passed like any other. I said to you, "Be careful." Today is a strange day and that was the end of it. I had written impassioned letters that expressed the urgency of my situation. I wrote to you that that [*sic*] it would not be forgivable, that it would be a violation of our exchange, in fact, a criminal negligence were I to fail to come through. To hand to you the consecrated sum of your gifts, the secret you imparted persistently and without knowledge, these expressions of your will that lured, and, in a cumulative fashion, became a message. In any case, the way things worked. Incorrigible. Stops and starts, overburdened nerves, cowardice (Is this what they said?), inadequacy, and, as a last resort, an inexplicable refusal. You asked could I build you from a pile of anonymous limbs and parts. I rarely slept and repeatedly during the night, when the moon was in my window, I had a vision of dirt and rocks being poured over my chest by the silver spade of a shovel. And then I would wake up with everything. It was all there like icons contained in a sphere and beginning to fuse together. When I tried to look at it, my eyes burned until I could almost see it in the room like a spectral yellow fire.
> A street, a house, a room. (1)

The first-person pronoun establishes the homodiegetic narrator, and the "she" becomes the "you" of the direct address. From here the narrative situation moves from direct discourse ("I said to you, 'Be careful'") to indirect discourse ("I wrote to you that . . . it would not be forgivable"), where the narrator is citing his own letter and, again, ("You asked could I build you from a pile of anonymous limbs and parts"), where the narrator is recounting a question put to him by his partner. In both cases, however, the narrator's retelling leans more toward the impressionistic or even the surreal than it does toward the journalistic.

The speaker of the narrative changes. In addition to the many homeless men who assume the first-person pronoun throughout the narrative, the speaking "I" belongs to a number of other characters. At one point the "I" belongs to a bartender, named Annie, nervous about a drunk and belligerent patron (who may be the erratic John Austin):

I told him to leave. You better leave, I says. He came in here, his hands was shakin' like a tremor. I told him where he could go right away. And he says to me, he says Annie, give me one on the house. My throat's dry like sandpaper. Can you believe it? I told him all I gots just gonna make you thirstier. I can't help your thirst, I says. I said get out. Believe that, her wide eyes insisted. She pushed her dumb blue gaze first at the man in the brown fedora and then at me, seeking our approval. (134)

This example moves from indirect discourse ("I told him to leave") to direct discourse ("You better leave, I says") and to more direct discourse ("And he says, Annie, give me one on the house"), all with Annie as the speaker. The entire scene, however, appears to be focalized by the student narrator, presumably sitting at the bar observing the exchange; the phrase, "She pushed her dumb blue gaze . . . back at *me*" returns the first-person diegesis to him. In this interpretation all of the direct and indirect discourse in the bar scene is, in fact, embedded in what can be accounted for as free indirect discourse of the student narrator—it is he who consciously renders these events. That is, even though Annie speaks in the first person, she does not focalize the narrative; on the contrary, it is clear that the student is refracting Annie's locution in the text ("You better leave I says. He came in here, his hands was shakin'"). His rendering falls in line with his subsequent description of her "dumb" gaze.

Mirapaul alludes to such narrative complexity when he describes *The Jew's Daughter* as "an impressionistic journey" that is "told from multiple viewpoints" (2000), and Morrissey himself describes the "shifts in voice or place, intrusions, antennae transmissions, thematic and linguistic associations rendered in transitional mutations at the sentence-level" (Pressman 2003, 1). His reference to "transitional mutations" gestures toward a discussion of how the interface itself destabilizes the narrative situation. But if the narrative, as Mirapaul rightly suggests, is *told* from multiple viewpoints, it is also *seen* from various viewpoints. The narrative employs variable focalization, which shifts the narrative consciousness—the seeing "I"—completely away from the student in several different cases. One passage appears to reflect Eva thinking about how she wound up staying in the apartment after her partner left for England: "The possibility of living there had just seemed somehow too appropriate to resist. Resist? We coerced our way in. We bartered and argued. I was not wanted, but obstinately and with your assistance, I usurped that room. There was no place else I could have gone. And even with the lack of privacy and the possible threat of homicide, I could not leave. I woke up taut with the shrill train cutting through me" (262). This violent image,

though quite possibly originating from the sound of a train physically passing nearby, arises from her fear of John's violent temper and calls to mind
(hers and the reader's) the decapitation she witnessed in Java.

Other cases of focal shift are less determinate and ultimately lead to alternative interpretations of the narrative situation:

> It seems to me that he was training her. I don't quite understand him.
> He seems to have been removing himself from her incrementally, and
> then when the distance was nearly consummate, he would recoil, return
> his affection to her, remind her of the importance of strengthening the
> bond between them through trial and endurance, and yet, from what
> I gather, his own suffering was tapered by light distractions, delight-
> ful conversations, which in turn, served to heighten her experience of
> pain for once when he left for England as though). She knocked on his
> door and he didn't respond. Again she knocked and again he did not
> answer. She knocked and he stood with the door open at a slight angle,
> and stared at her and did not speak. (274)[11]

This could be Richard, the neighbor, commenting on the student and his
relationship with Eva. The fact that "*he* left for England" makes it unlikely
that the student is speaking of himself in the third person here, and it is just
as unlikely that he would be present to overhear someone speaking of him
in this manner. The phrase "from what I gather" also implies what could be
Richard's limited knowledge of their arrangement (and runs counter to the
assumption of an omniscient perspective). The same passage, however, would
require that Richard somehow witnesses the exchange where Eva knocks
(three times) on her partner's door and he stands, staring at her, not speaking. Or it is possible that the knocking signals the beginning of yet another
narrative shift. After all, these turns of consciousness are not limited to the
turning of digital pages; rather, they can occur from one sentence to the next.
But if it is someone else who sees here, then who is it?

It would appear that, in addition to the first-person narrative situations
(both homodiegetic and, in the case of the student, arguably autodiegetic),
there *is*, at times, also a narrator external to the storyworld. In this interpretation the narrative does not simply switch from one homodiegetic (character-
bound) narrator to another but rather stems from a heterodiegetic narrator
who employs figural narration and introduces free indirect discourse into
the text. Specifically, the free indirect discourse includes first-person positions, which variously tell and see the story in different cases. Monika Fludernik (2003, 123) accounts for this case with what she calls "reflector-mode"

narration, which sits in a simplified binary opposition to "teller-mode" narration. In "reflector-mode" narration a figural, heterodiegetic narrative can exploit first-person perspectives of various characters without being *told* by any one of them.

In this reading the student also loses his position as the dominant teller of the story. Granted, the interpretation of student as teller gains force given that the lyrical prose could well have been composed by a writer and student of literature. That the student evaluates events retrospectively throughout the text also supports any interpretation that positions him as the dominant narrative consciousness—though temporal frames prove elusive even for the student himself, who at one point asks, "What has already not yet happened?" (9). Nevertheless, the many scenes rendered in a similar style, but seen from either a cognitive or a physical perspective logically inaccessible to him, ultimately make the equation of the student to a singular narrative consciousness problematic. The resulting indeterminacy of the narrative situation goes hand in hand with the indeterminacy of story events.

That rereading can both clear up and compound this indeterminacy is a comment on medial mobility and the process of interpretation.[12] Typically, rereading moves one toward greater determinacy, even if, paradoxically, an interpretation suggests indeterminacy. That is, just as certain grammatical and syntactical constructions can yield ambiguous or indeterminate meanings, it is possible to *determine*—which is to say *argue* or *decide* if not prove— that certain narratological factors (in this case the overall narrative situation) remain indeterminate as well. In *The Jew's Daughter,* however, the processuality of the interface complicates movement toward determinacy given that signifiers can change at any time, undermining elements that might have offered stable ground for interpretation by recombining them—revealing new connections and associations while closing off others. Metonymically, the text suggests how a medial process can revise the interpretative process in narrative fiction.

To read *The Jew's Daughter* is also to reinforce certain ironies evoked by its digital environment. Readers are continually reminded that, on a material level, they *cannot* go back (at least in the familiar mode of an interfacial "Back" button); at the same time, on a discursive level, they *must* go back. The irony evokes a parallel to lived experience: just as we can never go back temporally, we often must go back psychologically. The act of reading the text evokes another parallel between the storyworld and the embodied reader. The physical movement of the reader, shifting the mouse control in order to move the story forward, often corresponds to the shifting perspective of the narrative consciousness. We literally and figuratively reposition ourselves in relation to the text.

Repeated shifting can suggest discomfort, and in the narrative it is indeed symptomatic of an increasing uneasiness. The indeterminacy at the level of the storyworld gives rise to an emergent paranoia that infects the mood of the characters—and, potentially, that of the reader. Both the student and his partner, whether each alone behind the apartment door or in the room together, live in constant fear of John's next knock. While Eva weighs the "possible threat of homicide" (262), her partner's fears are more difficult to measure: "I often wonder, looking back to that time, why it seemed to me that everyone who came to my door was like a co-conspirator, a knowing demon that I had summoned" (11). Paranoia also infects their relationship to one another, and at times their mutual distrust manifests itself in dramatic fashion. The student recalls one such instance when Eva confronts him, then breaks down: "Who are you? Who are you? Where is your heart? Where is your mind? the days crept by and I felt like pieces of me were . . . O god the letters I wrote you and I knew I knew all the time. What am I to you? one in hundreds, in thousands. Who are you? And then her voice broke. You've lost me" (250). The loss appears to be temporary, for not only does she return to him on several occasions (she is "always leaving a trail of things: a scarf, wallet, or glove. They all come back. To go away quietly" [12]), but the narrative ends where it begins, and we are left once again with his *present* concern, "Will she disappear?" (1).[13] Morrissey accomplishes this return by linking the concluding text on the concluding page with the text of page one—enacting a Z-to-A transition on a macrostructural scale. The linked text is "WiP," which denotes a "Work in Progress." Indeed, the processual text of *The Jew's Daughter* is a work "in progress" in many ways.

In addition to its demonstration of the page in transition—on the broader cultural level of medial transformations and the semiotic level of its own dynamic pages—*The Jew's Daughter* is itself undergoing another radical transition. Morrissey, along with Lori Talley and computer scientist Lutz Hamel, is moving the project toward its "next stage," which will integrate principles of artificial intelligence and "machine learning" into their narrative interface: "The ambition of the next phase of this project is to automate the metamorphic activity of the text, and to create a literary work that is a hybrid of experimental narrative and machine-writing. . . . Our goal will be the creation of a software engine that will enable the text to evolve dynamically, in response to user interaction, and in accordance with a set of semantic and syntactic restraints. The product of our collaboration will be both a literary work and an evolved tool for architecting and composing narrative in a new form" (Morrissey and Talley 2002). The act of rolling over linked text would no longer yield one and only one result; in effect, the linear succession of linked pages would be broken, and the narrative itself would more closely resemble a structurally *networked* text. Unlike the highlighted links in the network fictions discussed in the earlier chapters,[14] however, the linkages would no longer be predetermined and *fixed* by the author; that is, they would "evolve dynamically" as a product of a reader intervention and computer-generated algorithmic response. True, the algorithms are predetermined, but the transition that occurs during the reading act arises from an unfixed and unpredictable machinic response. Morrissey and Talley (2002) explain:

> Our system will be a radical departure from others that have been developed for digital literature in several important ways. The most obvious of these is that there will be no outbound links, no windows launched, and the reading experience will be continuous and fluid. Less obviously, the changes that occur on the page will not be the result of rigidly determined links. The text that appears will be selected dynamically from an internal database, out of a pool of semantically appropriate options. Once selected, the new text will be *syntactically assimilated* by the page, and this will sustain the intelligibility of the reading. These are the basic goals of our system, but more advanced compositional rules and algorithms will be developed during our period of research and development.

Issues of authorial, readerly, and machinic control are foregrounded by the text's next phase of production, which is not to say that they are resolved in any way. Composition and control aside, the work itself, *The Jew's Daughter,* as it has been read on the Web by critics and students, the work *as we know it,* would be reconfigured or even simply replaced. Since this artist statement was presented in 2002, however, Morrissey, Talley, and Hamel have taken the creative infrastructure of *The Jew's Daughter* as the foundation for an entirely different new text, called *The Error Engine* (see Morrissey, Talley, and Hamel 2004). This departure could actually preserve the textual integrity (real or imagined) that readers associate with the text titled *The Jew's Daughter.*[15]

With the narrative mood brought to the fore, details of the story recede beyond the reader's reach. Even though the narrative proceeds linearly, its plot does not gain momentum through the forward progression of events directed toward an end. In this regard *The Jew's Daughter* resonates with the network aesthetic described by Laura Trippi (2003): "Instead of driving the narrative forward, plot to a greater or lesser degree follows mood, which rides and also guides the network's volatility. In some cases, plot gives way altogether to the ambient interplay of pattern/randomness anchored in mood." Even for the student the need to express his state of mind overcomes the desire to recount events: "She rested her head in the cliff formed by my ribs and stomach, and her oriental green eyes danced beyond my comprehension. But who remembers these things and why the hell should they matter?" (141).

Remixing Myth

If indeterminacy dictates the narrative mood, then it also dictates the mythological framework implied by the text. In his interview with Jessica Pressman, Morrissey writes of the "language and rhythm" of *The Jew's Daughter* and notes that it is "especially preoccupied with voices and their signature cadences, and, from time to time, breaks into song" (Pressman 2003, 1). Morrissey speaks here of the musicality of the prose and the occasional lyrical interpolation it contains. The inclusion of lyrics from Cole Porter's jazz song "Night and Day" (1932), in particular, elicits the dreaded knocking ("like the beat beat beat of the tom tom"),[16] while, intertextually, other lyrics from the same song also characterize the manic state of Eva alone in the apartment: "In the silence of my lonely room I think about you night and day, night and day, night and day." But when Morrissey speaks of *The Jew's Daughter* in terms of "breaking into song," he also evokes the broader motivations of the work. "Sir Hugh, or the Jew's Daughter" is an anti-Semitic Scottish-English ballad dating back to the twelfth century. Significantly, the ballad from which *The Jew's Daughter* takes its name is the same song that Stephen Dedalus "breaks into" in the company and home of Leopold Bloom in the "Ithaca" chapter of James Joyce's *Ulysses*.

　　Not surprisingly, the exact origins of the ballad itself remain unknown, and popular accounts trace its first appearance, in print at least, as far back as Chaucer's "Prioress' Tale" in the fourteenth century.[17] It relates the story of a young boy, Sir Hugh, playing ball with his friends. Hugh kicks the ball over the garden wall belonging to a neighboring Jew. The Jew's daughter comes out of the house and refuses to return the ball unless Hugh follows her back inside. She eventually entices him inside and then murders him—in different ways depending on the version, often by stabbing him in the heart, but always in a manner heavy in ritualistic overtones. According to the manuscript introduction included with Thomas Percy's version of the ballad, printed in 1765 and reprinted in 1996 (and also included in both Child collections), the story relates the "supposed practice of the Jews in crucifying or otherwise murdering Christian children, out of hatred of the religion of their parents: a practice, which has been always alleged in excuse for the cruelties exercised upon that wretched people, but which probably never happened in a single instance" (Percy 1765/1996, 32).[18] The manuscript suggests that the stories of ritual child murders may have been fabricated either to justify further religious persecution or simply out of an irrational fear and paranoia that the Jews' otherness evoked. Hence, both the ballad and its subject matter are of dubious origin.

But if the ballad breeds multiplicity and uncertainty, so too does the discussion of Joyce's appropriation of it. The ballad in *Ulysses* refers to "Little Harry Hughes," a name that appears in only one version of the Child ballads (155N) and is considered a "corruption" by Helen Child Sargent (Sargent and Kittredge 1904, 368). According to Don Gifford's *Ulysses Annotated* (1988, 579), ballad 155N is closest to the variant Joyce uses. But if the use of "Harry Hughes" is evidence for Joyce's citing variant 155N, then there is also evidence to the contrary. Ballad 155N substitutes "Duke's daughter" for "Jew's daughter," most likely to avoid the anti-Semitic implications. Joyce's ballad, however, which appears both italicized in the text and also as an image of musical annotation occupying the top half of the page, does not make this substitution (Joyce 1986, 565–67). After all, the same implications of anti-Semitism are relevant to the awkwardness felt by Bloom, an Irish Jew, in response to Stephen's choice of song. There are other suggestions as to Joyce's source. A much more recent account appears on the Web site of the Irish Public Service Broadcasting Organisation, Radio Telefís Éireann (RTÉ). In a section of the site celebrating the one hundredth anniversary of Bloomsday (a national holiday that occurs every year on June 16, the day in 1904 on which *Ulysses* is set), Gerry O'Flaherty (2004) provides a synopsis of each chapter. In his summary of "Ithaca" O'Flaherty includes a footnote about the ballad: "The song 'Little Harry Hughes,' sung by Stephen, is a version of an ancient ballad called 'Sir Hugh, or, the Jew's Daughter.' In the recently unveiled 'Paris-Pola commonplace book' at the National Library of Ireland, there is evidence that Joyce took his version from Sir Thomas Percy's" *Reliques of Ancient English Poetry,* volume 1. The Paris-Pola, a notebook Joyce began keeping on his first visit to Paris in 1903, may indeed contain evidence that Joyce consulted Percy's version of the ballad, but even a cursory comparison of the texts shows that this is not the version *he cites:* Percy's ballad begins differently, ends differently, and contains no mention of "Harry" (Percy 1765/1996, 32–35).

What is clear is that Morrissey's title alludes to the version of the ballad reproduced in *Ulysses*. In Joyce's version the Jew's daughter kills Little Harry Hughes by cutting off his head:

> She took a penknife out of her pocket
> And cut off his little head.
> And now he'll play his ball no more
> For he lies among the dead. (Joyce 1986, 567)

The detail does not appear in any of the eighteen versions originally collected by Child, nor does it appear in any of the twenty-one versions in Sargent and Kittredge's volume. Though he does not name a source, Gifford (1988, 579) adds that Joyce "apparently recalled his version from memory." Thus, one can only speculate as to Joyce's own source with regard to Harry's beheading. We do know, however, that a similar image haunts his protagonist, Stephen Dedalus, in *A Portrait of the Artist as a Young Man*. In the diary that fills the concluding pages of the novel Stephen's March 21 entry reads, "Thought this in bed last night but was too lazy and free to add to it. Free, yes. The exhausted loins are those of Elisabeth and Zachary. Then he is the precursor. Item: he eats chiefly belly bacon and dried figs. Read locusts and wild honey. Also, when thinking of him, saw always a stern severed head or death mask as if outlined on a grey curtain or veronica" (Joyce 1993, 270). Stephen is recalling a conversation he has had with his friend Cranly earlier in the day. Cranly has told Stephen that when he was born, his father was sixty-one years old, though he has never mentioned the age of his mother. In his previous diary entry on March 20, Stephen wonders if Cranly's mother is "Very young or very old" and concludes, "Old then. Probably, and neglected. Hence Cranly's despair of the soul: the child of exhausted loins" (270). If Cranly is the "child of exhausted loins" in the March 20 entry, then the "child of exhausted loins" in the March 21 entry that follows refers to John the Baptist, for he is the son of "Elisabeth and Zachary" in the Scriptures and is regarded as the "precursor" of Christ. On the order of King Herod John the Baptist was beheaded.

Stephen's association of Cranly and a severed head (Cranly's name itself suggests a play on *cranium*) grows out of his fixation with skulls and religious iconography, likely rooted in an unsettling memory of the ever-present skull on the desk of Father Conmee at his Jesuit school (Joyce 1993, 58). Cranly is not only Stephen's confidant but also, in his eyes, a "priest-like" friend, which is why he calls up the same repressed, traumatic image: "Why was it that when he thought of Cranly he could never raise before his mind the entire image of his body but only the image of the head and face? Even now against the grey curtain of the morning he saw it before him like the phantom of a dream, the face of a severed head or death-mask, crowned on the brows by its stiff black upright hair as by an iron crown. It was a priest-like face, priest-like in its palor" (192). The reader can understand or at least contextualize the association even if Stephen cannot.

In *The Jew's Daughter,* even though it is Eva who witnesses the decapitation of the woman in Indonesia firsthand, the image haunts the student narrator as well, coloring his conscious encounters. In one instance a woman's head acts as an obstruction: "I walked into a public library to read another portion of a certain biography and was disturbed to see that the book was already in use by a bird-like woman who sat intently reading and jotting in her journal. I stood over her sh" (151). The sentence breaks at *sh,* enacting a linguistic severance, and it remains broken until page 153, where the sentence resolves itself: "I stood over her shoulder to see if I could decipher what she had written but it was illegible" (153). The *sh* recalls the image of the suicide ("Sh she had laid her head on the tracks") and recasts it in a different, and somewhat ironic, context. He would likely be able to read the text if her head were not in the way; inversely, she would likely have an easier time reading if it were not for the man standing over her. The "sh" doubles as her attempt to silence the disturbance originating from directly behind her.

In another instance, just after pacifying another homeless man with spare change, the student sees himself as a madman: "Impressed by his straight-forward persistence, I yielded some small change and continued walking, hungerless, a madman, jaw-clutching, beating my chest, the little book in a bag under my arm, wandering the unfolded streets of this city (so inspiring in its architecture and history), a decapitated head" (Morrissey 2000, 223). The reference to a "decapitated head" is syntactically ambiguous—it can refer to the city or even the speaker himself—but it most plausibly describes the bag he carries, which contains notes for the book that he is working on (see Morrissey 2000, 21). It makes sense that he would see himself "carrying" his consciousness, externalized in this way, for a book is a product of an intense cognitive process, a product that might seem consubstantial with one's own *head.* Soon after, however, the image is transposed. The phrase "A decapitated head" remains static for several pages, while subsequent folds have altered the text immediately surrounding it. "A decapitated head," now devoid of any coherent referent, is still present on page 230, the same page that subtly "introduces" the student's next encounter with "J," the homeless man who greets him at the gate. The introduction, by way of the linked *j* in the word *joined*, takes on an added irony when juxtaposed with an image of a severed head.

The student proceeds to fixate on the homeless man's head: "He asked me my name and I answered him without thinking, but when I returned the question, he paused suspiciously, and then with his head tilted, his eyebrows tight, and his dark eyes looking at me as though they were sincerely curious, even bewildered" (234). The page's linked text, which is located at the word *head*, underscores the narratological potential of links. That linking in a network fiction suggests a distinct rhetorical register is already clear, whether or not this register differs from that implied by the narrator and narration. But rather than simply superimposing a commentary on and often against the narrative discourse, links can directly reflect a character's consciousness. In this case the link at *head* suggests focalization, a representation of the student's conscious preoccupations rather than a detached commentary by an external narrator. More generally, the example might suggest an added variant of the familiar narratological frames—"Who speaks?" and "Who sees?"—by posing a question unique to the network environment: "Who links?" The question takes on added significance in *The Jew's Daughter* as a possible indication of implicit agency when problems of infidelity, and perhaps violence, arise.

The rhetorical register that mediates the links does not remain constant throughout. The previous link at *joined*, for example, serves a different rhetorical function, closer to that of a heterodiegetic narrator who knows that "J" will approach before he actually does. Thus, the homeless man not only figures as a severed head, but he also recalls the martyred saint, John the Baptist, as "J" marks the linguistic decapitation of "John." Of course, whereas John the Baptist was imprisoned in the walls of Herod's kingdom, "J" is a prisoner of a twenty-first-century city.

The broader mythological parallels between *The Jew's Daughter, Ulysses*, and, by extension, Homer's *Odyssey* are transparent. Odysseus returns home to Ithaca; Leopold Bloom returns home to 7 Eccles Street, Dublin; and the protagonist of *The Jew's Daughter* returns home to his troubled apartment in Chicago. But whereas Odysseus returns to a wife who has been faithful, and Bloom to a wife who certainly has not, the student (and, for that matter, the reader) simply does not know what has transpired in his absence. Certain scenes open the possibility of Eva's infidelity. In one Eva has an unannounced visitor: "Sharp knocking at midnight, and the door, creaking, sweeps the shadows into the wall. Long straggly goatsbeard and taut eyes that swell even larger (impossible) when he begins to speak, and scratching his stiff-dirty head, asks Did you think it was going to be me? It occurred to me that it might be. It looks like I've interrupted you. What is it that you were reading? Home?" (142). The identity of the visitor is not revealed, only the fact that he has a beard, much like most if not all of the male characters in the story. So this could be either John Austin the hired hand or Richard Nuxman the neighbor calling in. "Gangen Richard Nuxman" is, in fact, seen (by an indeterminate someone) walking "[o]nto the street and around the block" immediately afterward (144). It is not definitively clear, however, that this scene is rendered from Eva's point of view—despite its being followed by a sampling of Patsy Cline lyrics that seem to reflect Eva's melodramatic state of mind: "I fall to pieces / Each time I see you again" (141). (The lyric also recalls the odd question put to her partner on page 1, or at least his odd paraphrase of it: "You asked could I build you from a pile of anonymous limbs and parts".) It is just as likely that the student focalizes this scene—and that he greets the bearded man at the door. It makes sense that a student of literature would be reading at midnight, and the visitor's guess as to the title of the book might be the result of an obstructed view of "Homer." Morrissey's choice of titles would thus suggest a near metalepsis, inverting the conception of a text called *The Jew's Daughter,* which is embedded in *Ulysses,* which is embedded in the *Odyssey.* Instead, Homer's *Odyssey* is embedded in *The Jew's Daughter.* After moving "down" two levels, we somehow wind up where we began, in the manner of a strange loop. The detail thematizes a transgression of narrative levels, but it remains a *near* metalepsis since we have not "entered" the text being read by the student; then again, if, by way of the represented point of view, we are already inside the student's mind, then we too are already inside the textual world that occupies it.

Other details suggest that Eva is not present here. The reply, "It occurred to me that it might be [you at the door]," implies a degree of familiarity between the two people and conveys the impression that a similar encounter has happened before. Such a scenario would run counter to the possibility of Eva's opening the door to John Austin, who is not likely to have a positive or accommodating reaction to her presence in the room. Richard is also the only male character who does not, as far as the reader is told, definitely have a beard, another factor that complicates reading this scene from Eva's point of view. Perhaps the homeless man, who has persisted in asking for an invitation up to the house, has somehow devised a way to get beyond the gate to the house. Perhaps he has climbed over it, or picked its lock, and now stands at the student's door, "scratching his stiff-dirty head" (142).

But once we rule out the possibility of Eva's infidelity in one instance, we are reminded of the possibility in another, and the process of interpretation cycles. For example, later on in the narrative, the fragment, "His smell, his touch all over me," immediately follows "Precious time away" and "Where is my body?" (242). The next fragment in this succession, "Kept a log for him of letters sent," suggests that the pronoun *him* refers to her partner during their "precious time away." But it is not necessarily the same male referent of "His smell, his touch all over me"—which might in any case seem an unflattering way to refer to one's own partner. Rather, this could be an expression of regret: an unsettling memory of an uncomfortable sexual encounter with someone else prompts her to think of her partner and the letters she wrote to him while he was away. Moreover, the transition from page 242 to 243 (specifically, at the end of the fold) substitutes the fragment, "Excuse bad writing," for "Precious time away" (242–43). The phrase reproduces the request made by Milly, daughter of Leopold and Molly Bloom, in a letter to her father in the Calypso episode of *Ulysses*. The allusion to Milly, herself a Jew's daughter, casts the scene into an elaborate web of potential indiscretions.

In Joyce's novel, while Molly spends an adulterous day with Dublin impresario Blazes Boylan, Bloom himself indulges in fantasies over a young girl at the beach in the Nausicaa episode, and he also struggles to repress an unsettling attraction to Milly, who is coming to resemble a young Molly as she approaches womanhood. While some critics have read Bloom's torment as guilt over an indiscretion with Milly he has *actually* committed,[19] the arguments for and against this possibility are ultimately inconclusive, and it remains likely that Bloom's alleged indiscretions are simply in thought rather than deed. Similarly, Eva's infidelity could be imagined, a product of paranoia—perhaps the same paranoia that feeds her fear of a homicidal landlord. Significantly, the succession of suspicious fragments also follows the evocative text link at "yes" contained by the word *eyes*, which is embedded in one of the protagonist's descriptions of his partner (239). But this accumulation of details is not enough to confirm or deny Eva's infidelity. Though her partner can see her eyes, we do not know if he can see eyes that are capable of saying *yes*, repeatedly, in the manner of Molly Bloom.

The intertextual parallels with the folk ballad are just as unstable as the parallels with *Ulysses*. If we know nothing else of the Jew's daughter of the ballad, we at least know that she is seductive, and there is an unmistakable connection between her green dress (a constant in most all of the versions) and the seductive green eyes of Eva that "dance beyond comprehension" (141). But if one pursues the parallel further, Eva becomes not the potential victim of violence but instead herself a vicious and manipulative murderer. In a narrative that conceals so much within its folds, the suggestion is not as convoluted as it first may seem. There is a reference to her "flailing arms" and the mention of a specific incident ("although I did not witness the act"), which is followed by further mention of a judge and prosecuting attorney (282).

One can also return to the narrative's mythological framework to support the claim for a violent or potentially violent Eva. In the biblical text that tells of the beheading of John the Baptist, the order arises from the request of Salome, who "danced before the guests, and Herod was so delighted that he promised on oath to give her anything she asked for. Prompted by her mother, she said, 'Give me here on a dish the head of John the Baptist'" (Matt. 14:5–8).[20] In the biblical myth, just as in *The Jew's Daughter*, there is a "dance" of seduction and a potential indiscretion. At the very least there is an attraction between an older man and a younger woman and, more specifically, between a father figure and a daughter figure. Joyce's *Portrait* adds a layer to this web: Stephen describes Cranly's father as having an "Unkempt, grizzled beard"; he is, furthermore, someone who "Sometimes talks to girls after nightfall" (270). Nevertheless, the reason for or cause of the violence in *The Jew's Daughter*, much like that in the biblical story, cannot be determined with any real clarity or attributed to any one source.

In fact, other evidence points to the possibility that the protagonist *himself* is the source of the story's subterranean violence, and while the student has reason to direct aggression toward John Austin in light of his unrelenting harassment, he may be harboring a much less rational aggression toward his own partner. One passage portrays Eva as a demanding and uncompromising partner who holds firm to her notion of an ideal relationship and expresses her steadfast intention to pursue it. The narrator moves from a mundane description of a woman who "won't rest until she has everything she wants" to a mythologized depiction of a woman who—ideally and ultimately—"knits her heavy gray hair in a chair on the porch, and life ends like a sweet yarn" (283). The passage continues: "If by that providence that so often guided these liovers [*sic*] / in life, they are returned to this world for another round, the stick is divided again. . . . She is tired and dreams of a happy repetition" (283). The sentence is formed by reading from the bottom of the page back to the top in the manner of a Z-to-A transition. It is the result of the fold from page 282, which contains a text link located at the word *lover*. On page 283 text is replaced at both the top and bottom of the page, revealing the new sentence. Once the thought of "lovers" has been highlighted—indeed, literally—in the text, the transition to the misspelled "liovers" arouses some suspicion.

If the "Irish-Jew" protagonist is the source of this passage—albeit again referring to himself in the third person as one of "these lovers"—then the same mistake has been made before and by another Irish Jew. According to Richard Ellman's authoritative biographical account of James Joyce, the name of Joyce's protagonist, Leopold Bloom, is a composite of two Blooms who actually lived in Dublin during the author's lifetime. One was a dentist Joyce personally knew. But, as Ellman notes, Joyce at least *knew of* another Bloom, a man who was committed to a mental institution for the murder of a girl who worked with him in a photographer's shop. As Ellman writes, "He had planned a double suicide; after having killed her and, as he thought, himself, he scrawled the word LOVE (but misspelt it as LIOVE) with his blood on the wall behind him" (1982, 375).

Is the protagonist doing more here than simply focalizing the narration of the passage? That is, does he (re)take control of the text as a first-person narrator, not only telling the story but also writing it, and thus misspelling *lovers* in a manner chillingly reminiscent of Mr. Bloom's suicidal scrawl? Is Ellman's text the "certain biography" the protagonist of *The Jew's Daughter* attempts to read over the shoulder of a "bird-like woman" in the public library, encouraging his own intentional interpolation? (151).[21] Could this final act of violence be the "completion of the task" the student so cryptically alludes to at the start of the narrative (6–9)? And is it the same task he mentions just before recalling the scene in the library: "I remember that once at what seemed then to be an extremely crucial time in relation to the failed completion of my task, I walked into a public library" (151–52)? If it is, this task would seem markedly incongruent with the "new task" he mentions later on, which involves "moving photo albums and designing a layout for the house which starts with ripping up the carpet in the master bedroom and tiling it" (243–44).

The interpolation would enact a dramatic ontological shift: it would suggest that despite so much evidence to the contrary, there remains a possibility that we have before us a first-person narration that is confined to the student's world and his world only. It would suggest that, quite possibly, despite all of the references to "pages" (23) and "notebooks" (223) without a single computer screen in sight (his neighbor even writes on a typewriter [23]), and despite all of the scenes rendered from a point of view logically inaccessible to him, what we have before us is not simply a text but a writing process—a reflexive narrative called *The Jew's Daughter*. It would be a work in progress written by a student who usurps not only an apartment but also, solipsistically, the thoughts and dreams of all those around him. After all, ironic as it sounds, only a student of literature—indeed, *a student of Joyce*—would misspell *lovers*.

The reader, in turn, occupies a paradoxical position in relation to the text's unfolding: in effect, one feels neither inside nor outside of the text. If one conceives of the text as a unilateral form, then the concept of inside and outside no longer applies. Topological figures can be folded and unfolded in such a way as to reverse inside and out or even render them simultaneous, co-extensive, and indistinguishable. Here again, however, one must differentiate between the material and the discursive and, at the same time, be reminded of the fact that the reader's position in relation to both the fictional story-world and the digital text involves a relation to an abstract spatiality. The narrative text, on the one hand, can represent discursive folds that are temporal, perspectival, or ontological. On the other hand, the text itself can provide the structural fodder that is shaped and reshaped to create an array of inscribed surfaces. The innovative technological folds of *The Jew's Daughter* contribute to the dialogue on reading network fiction by way of defamiliarizing a traditional literary-critical trope. When a narrative "unfolds," typically it means that the plot progresses to the point at which a story, and perhaps its themes and overall significance, comes into view for the reader—that which was concealed is gradually revealed. *The Jew's Daughter* enacts a reversal of this trope: often refolding follows unfolding, and often the more the reader folds, the more complex the figure that is shaped.

In *The Jew's Daughter* ambiguous narratological positions go hand in hand with the ambiguous subject positions assumed by the characters. The narrative situates itself as one among many layers of a mythological palimpsest, an "intertext" that both represents and produces a complex array of psychological forces from a limited set of archetypes—that of father, daughter, and lover. But the same framework does not conclusively remedy the indeterminacy of the story events. Rather, its intertextual ties to Joyce's *Ulysses*—itself a "book of many happy returns"[22]—and the multiplicity of the eponymous ballad underscore the need to return, even manically, to *The Jew's Daughter*. Morrissey sees this process of repetition and return not as a choice for the reader but rather a responsibility. He challenges each reader "[t]o read. To write. To repeat. To become the ear of the poet-sleuth who excavates the poem, stirs up history, only to become implicated in a new repetition" (Pressman 2003, 1).

Mnemonic Devices

All in all, even though the structure of the text follows a linear progression, we do not know if we are on a line approaching greater determinacy or greater confusion, and with each shift of the page comes the prospect of reprocessing the text. Like the lover in the story who knits her hair as it grays, we grow tired and dream of a "happy repetition." Or, like the student entangled in his own telling, we do not know "what has already not yet happened." Perhaps the most appropriate figure for the condition of the text, however, is "J," the amnesiac homeless man who appears at the gate: "What do you study? He asked. Literature Oh yes. I see. So, what are you doing today? He continued. I reminded him that I was making my way to the library, and the conversation proceeded this way, like a persistent interview about nothing in particular, consisting of a few questions that repeated in a sort of cycle" (232). Like the amnesiac, the reader only has a few questions, but they too cycle interminably. Once answered, they become unanswered, and must be reframed and asked again.

"J" might be the ghost of John the Baptist. Or he might be just another homeless man. But there is a third possibility to consider. In Joyce's *Portrait* Stephen too is confused by a doubling of J's—more specifically, by the two Saints that take the name of *John:* "Puzzled for the moment by saint John at the Latin Gate. What do I see? A decollated precursor trying to pick the lock" (270). Stephen first pictures St. John the Evangelist, one of the twelve disciples of Christ, who was sent to Rome in chains to be martyred before the Latin Gate at the entrance to the city. He was cast into a cauldron of boiling oil, but legend has it that he emerged unscathed and even refreshed from the bath. (The image recalls the student narrator "watching the lake boil in its pot" as he wanders the streets of Chicago [8].) Stephen, however, muses that it was not divine intervention that saved John the Evangelist but instead the presence of the other John, St. John the Baptist, the "decollated precursor" who "picks the lock" of the Latin Gate.[23] Both John the Evangelist and "J" the homeless man seek to escape a city that would otherwise bring them death. John the Evangelist escapes through the gate and finds freedom outside of the city walls. "J," by contrast, escapes through a gate but (assuming he has made his way up to the student's apartment) finds his freedom deeper inside the city.

Thus, inside and outside each offer an escape—a paradox that might also comment on the reader, who is neither trapped nor set free by the text. Ultimately only Judd Morrissey—the authorial J.—has the power to pick the lock. But whom would this set free? The reader from the machine? The writer from his prison house of language? Which writer? It is not possible to offer answers with any degree of certainty. What is certain, however, is that implicit in the processuality of *The Jew's Daughter* is the desire to be set free from the process, the desire for fluidity to crystallize, if only briefly, into some observable entity, the desire for all motion to simply come to a halt.

Concluding Movements

[T]o return is never to repeat
the memories cluster round a key
becomes a shell becomes a thorn

to return is never to rewind
the tape will stretch beyond its reach
as voices shift from place to space

to return is always to rejoice regret
as covered pathways hum like ghosts
and footprints decorate your steps
—Hazel Smith and Roger Dean, *Returning the Angles*

Hazel Smith and Roger Dean's *Returning the Angles* (2001) shares many qualities of network fictions but takes a linear form rather than that of a navigable
network.[1] Further, it is designed first and foremost not to be read but to be
heard; in addition to appearing onscreen, it is published on an audio CD as
what its creators call a "sound technodrama." Despite the fixed order of the
text's presentation, *Returning the Angles* does not necessarily entail a progression of any one narrative line. Instead, it traces a number of geographical returns that establish a central theme: the "impossibility in a mobile and globalized world of calling any place 'home'" (Smith and Dean 2003, 115). The
work is organized principally around the voice of character Helen Simmons,
a native of Britain who has relocated to Sydney ("One thing I do know—It's
not hip to be British in Australia" [Smith and Dean 2001]). She has since revisited London and, in a series of emails to an Australian friend, recorded the
changes she observes ("Everything is familiar but different, and everyone is
a little greyer" [2001]). But Helen's voice is one among many in an often chaotic audial mix: voices overlap and repeat, are distorted in time and timbre,
and are sometimes replaced entirely by musical instruments. The complex
polyvocality signals migrations of place and, at times, shifts between actual
and fantastical places. The soundscape of *Returning the Angles* therefore dis-
rupts any sense of the landscape, which in turn complicates any sense—for
Helen and for the audience—of feeling at home.

Smith and Dean's text illustrates that the foregrounding of returns in technoliterary domains is by no means exclusive to narrative fiction, and an analogous foregrounding is evident in other forms of digital literature that are not necessarily networked or, for that matter, predominantly narrative. But *Returning the Angles* also underscores a subtext that threads through the art and theory of network culture: when considering a broad historical continuum of writing technologies, it is possible to suggest that no one is quite at home yet in digital environments and, until the collective fascination with "new media" has ebbed, no one will be. Any study of digital literature, after all, is at once radical and conservative, depending on which term of the compound phrase one emphasizes: *digital* literature might sound overwhelmingly radical, even futuristic, to those traditionally grounded in print-based scholarship of literary texts, whereas digital *literature* might sound hopelessly conservative for those convinced that digital art must have its own indigenous forms and that digital environments make poor hosts for literature. Either way, for the time being, writing in or about literature in digital environments involves some measure of idealism and anxiety, and amid an atmosphere of accelerated enthusiasm—and accelerated obsolescence—there is no way of knowing whether this study arrives at the beginning or end of something that best describes itself as network fiction.

There is also no simple way to state what the Web itself means for the future of narrative literature. The migration of digital literature to the Web has created a venue for publication and critique no longer subject to the control of the traditional gatekeepers of the literary establishment. It is an incredibly powerful mass-marketing machine and has greatly improved the odds of serendipitous success in much the same way that anonymous musicians climb the charts after releasing their songs for free on the Internet. This development might be bad news, however, for more than just the gatekeepers. The second wave of Web fiction has undoubtedly brought with it some severe flooding, which has left behind a wasteland of inane blogs, broken hypertexts, and a plague of commerce-crazed Web pages and pop-up windows. There is even a practice of "spam fiction" that involves pasting— typically copyrighted—fictional excerpts into spam messages to trick email filters into allowing them into your inbox. Add to this an ever-growing appetite for streaming audio and video along with an increasing domestication of broadband access, and the Web becomes a strange, unlikely stage for the literary arts.

I like to think that all in all narrative fiction stands to benefit from hypertext technology and the digital medium, for all the technical, theoretical, and poetical implications of digital text. I also like to think that online forums and journals of high standards and quality will continue to build reputations and audiences. At the same time, even something as debased as spam fiction remains significant as a cultural fact—what Barth (1967/1982, 11) has called a "historical datum"—and can be turned against itself, creatively appropriated by the same community it seeks to exploit *and* via the same medium. One needs to look no further than "spam fiction contests" or online poets who treat these excerpts as "found art" for examples of this response. Furthermore, even though an emphasis on newer and more sophisticated forms of *interaction* is likely to overshadow an emphasis on *writing*, at least in the short term, our cultural production will include digital literatures that continue to demonstrate the mutual dependence of these two qualities, in the way network fiction already has.

As for the steady succession of critical debates on terminology and technological determinism, on the empowered reader and the dead, distributed, or automated author, debates polarized by utopian claims for the promise of hypertext and apocalyptic claims for the demise of the book, it is still doubtful that there has been enough interpretive engagement with the works that supposedly give rise to them. As David Miall (2004) writes, "[T]he surprise for me, contemplating the critical literature on hyperfiction, is how few systematic accounts have been provided of the experience of reading it. . . . By reading, I don't mean proposals such as those of Jim Rosenberg [1996], who elaborates a valuable theoretical description of readerly functions, . . . but phenomenological accounts of the flows and disruptions of reading as these unfold in relation to a specific hyperfiction." In responding to the call for systematic interpretation, this study affirms not only the discursive complexity and conceptual depth of individual works but also that of a larger body of writing created for the surface of the screen.

In moving beyond reflex reactions to the topologies of network fiction, which would include anything from "frustration" (Phelan and Maloney 2000, 277) to "textual claustrophobia" (Aarseth 1997, 79), I have aimed to afford the comprehensive treatment of textual repetition and recurrence that is warranted in light of digital media. This is not to say that the recurrence of nodes is an essential quality of narrative fiction in network environments; rather, such recurrence is a defining trait of network fiction that can prompt the recognition of recursive constructs and encourage a distinctive form of hypertextual comprehension. But even if the mode of recurrence is peculiar to network fiction, its effects recall the question posed by the Russian formalist Shklovsky nearly a century ago: What is the critical role of art itself if not to impede familiar acts of perception—to encourage the viewer or reader to perceive something again in a different way or in a different context?[2]

On a metacritical level network fictions exploit the digital environment to reanimate certain aspects of reading and writing. They exemplify the manner in which, as John Cayley (2005) puts it, "new tools may allow existing but latent tropes and forms to emerge, and emerge in unfamiliar contexts." In the most apparent sense new technologies change the meaning of words; just as a *computer*, before the 1940s, used to refer to "one who computes," digital writing technologies have changed the meaning of terms such as *orientation* and *movement* in relation to narrative texts. More specifically, I've endeavored to advance the discourse of orientation by proposing a mode of reading network space appropriate to textual topologies; add clarity to the discourse of "immersion and interactivity" in network environments and to the notion of immersive reading itself; identify the problem of excess and the value of selectivity as significant aesthetic and pragmatic issues of digital textuality; and determine with precision the implications of material mobility for the process of interpretation.

It remains the task of literary theory and narratology to attend to further narrative experiments and innovations in digital environments, beyond those that fall under the distinction of network fiction. Digital textuality can in turn encourage a retroactive attendance not only to the materiality of the print medium but also to the ways in which repetition and recursion function there. Digital media do not dispossess us of an interpretive reading practice. In fact, the future of literary and narratological discourse—and reading itself—will inevitably depend on what we are beginning to learn from digital literatures such as network fiction.

Appendix

On the Critical Analysis of Judd Morrissey's *The Jew's Daughter*

For some critics and theorists of creative media, probing the underlying mechanics of an artwork is common practice, and since network texts rely on computer programs, this often involves analyses of computer code. The example of Espen Aarseth exporting all 539 nodes of Joyce's *afternoon* into a single text file and reading them linearly is well known among early hypertext critics. Raine Koskimaa (2000, sec. 8) refers to the practice as "resistant reading," and he alludes to another example in which "Nancy Kaplan told how one of her students had . . . 'opened' a hypertext, but then . . . put it together again, changing the link structure according to the modification dates found in each lexia: she had added new links so that the text could be read in the order in which the lexias were included in the text." The practice might also be thought of as *transgressive* in the same way that the reader is encouraged to "crash" John McDaid's *Uncle Buddy's Phantom Funhouse* (1992) by running one of its nodes as code, thereby subverting the boundaries that separate its systemic levels (see "Textual Kinetics" in chap. 2 above). As Koskimaa (2000, sec. 8) notes, such transgressions are by no means contrary to the writerly ethos crucial to many proponents of digital literature.

My own transgressive reading of *The Jew's Daughter* yielded an unexpected and significant result. From the task bar that runs along the top of the browser page, I selected "View," then "Source" from the drop-down menu. (This option is available in some platforms and not others. For example, on PC computers that I've used, the page window of the text takes up the entire screen, including the browser task bars, and it is not possible to minimize the window. In the Mac computers that I've used, the task bar remains visible.) The "Source" option, I thought, would give me an idea of how HTML tags were used to prepare the Flash site for presentation on the Web. In addition, much like Aarseth's "linear" reading of *afternoon,* the source view would give me an alternative—which is to say, more static—perspective on the textual material.

In surveying the textual material, however, I noticed content that I had not seen in the initial 351 pages (as mentioned in chapter 6, "A Processual Page," given the transient text that comprises pages 34 to 134 and pages 173 to 203, a count of full pages is closer to 221). In fact, there was a significant amount of "extra" material. For example, assuming that a hypothetical page of the text averages two hundred words, and there are approximately 220 pages, the text would consist of forty-four thousand words. A word count of the material in the "Source" window yields more than 130,000 words, roughly three times as much as appears in the initial cycle with "page 1" and "page 351" as its parameters.

Because the text is created using Flash, an animation program, it is possible to "Play" the text, even though the interface of *The Jew's Daughter* makes no provision for this. On a Mac computer the 'open-apple' key + one mouse click will open a pop-up window that allows users to select "Play" from the menu (PC platforms open the same menu by right-clicking the mouse control). In effect, this transforms the entire text to a transient state. "Playing" the text in this mode makes it move too quickly to read each page carefully or in its entirety; nonetheless, the result confirms the presence of material that does not appear otherwise. As discussed in chapter 6, "Remixing Narration," the text-link at "WiP" on page 351 returns readers to an identical page 1, which contains the same link as it does when readers view it the first time around. The only visual difference is the fact that, for whatever (technical) reason— and likely related to the failure of the new text to appear at this point—the page counter that appears at the top of each page does not reset itself; instead it remains blank.

The observation has profound implications in terms of the structural integrity of the work. Specifically, as it appears, the formal constitution of *The Jew's Daughter* is a loop. If, however, when readers return to page one, there is a new or different text-link present, which in turn introduces a new fold (in a new location and containing new material), then the formal constitution of the text is not a loop but rather a spiral, with the parameters of "page 1" and "page 351" now serving as the points demarcating recursive levels. Furthermore, the estimated total word count of 130,000 words would suggest that the text's structural spiral consists of three revolutions. After that point, it may indeed begin again from the first level, which would mean that the formal recursions are embedded in a macrostructural loop. Or, in a manner that might even seem radical for a network text, it may simply come to an end.

It remains unclear exactly how the text is supposed to function, but what is clear is that—contrary to the ethos of the interactive or even interventionist hypertext reader—Morrissey did not intend for the reader to peruse the textual material in the source code view. Following an email correspondence with the author (September 2004) in which I mentioned the observations recorded here, he made changes so that the source code is no longer visible in this way. The dys(functioning) of the textual loops, however, does not appear to have changed since this time. Either way, *The Jew's Daughter* is, indeed, a work in progress in many ways for its readers and creators, some of which may have been more expected than others.

Notes

Introduction

1. Critics divide the first and second wave of digital literature at different points and in different ways. Hayles (2002, 37), for example, sees the "second generation" as marking the parity of and interplay between image and text in onscreen narratives. For Hayles, Jackson's *Patchwork Girl* (1995) ushers in the transition to the second wave. There are other ways to distinguish or divide movements, and there have been several characterizations of the aesthetics of the Storyspace School: Aarseth (1997, 76–96) discusses its engagement with modernist poetics. More specifically, Michael Joyce, in *Of Two Minds* (1995, 105–17) and *Othermindedness* (2001, 150–78), and Mark Bernstein, in "Hypertext Gardens" (1998a), provide the theoretical underpinnings of the Storyspace School's preoccupation with the "topography" of hypertext; and Stuart Moulthrop (2001) explores the obsession with the "crash" and other moments of "breakdown" in "Traveling in the Breakdown Lane." Ultimately, however, Hayles's division is too arbitrary (involving a relative *degree* of image incorporation pre-1995), and aesthetic discussions tend to reveal as much continuity as discontinuity and likewise do not offer a reliable way of defining a break.

2. There are precedents: Noah Wardrip-Fruin refers to his *Book of Endings* as a "network fiction" (1994). In an introductory node to the work, he writes, "By this I mean that . . . [it] is organized as a network. It co-exists, and interacts, with other information that is part of a common network. It grows and changes. Over time, the network will continue to expand, connections will be re-routed in response to stimuli, particularly reactions from the Web community" (http://www.cat.nyu.edu/~noah/theBook/About.html). The idea that the work changes not only for the reader in the course of reading(s) but also over the course of its existence in a broader discourse community is underscored in Wardrip-Fruin's usage.

3. For example, for the e-poet Loss Pequeño Glazier (1996), any text that constitutes "an internal system redefining the notion of a bibliographical unit" is an example of hypertextuality.

4. Landow credits Tom Meyer with introducing the ideas of Deleuze and Guattari into one of his earliest classroom discussions on hypertext theory. Meyer's "Plateaus" appears in Landow 1995. Moulthrop's 1994 "Rhizome and Resistance" is simultaneously an appropriation and critique of Deleuze and Guattari's notion of smooth vs. striated space. The concept, however, is also one of many misappropriated by hypertext theorists who saw hypertext as "the linguistic *realisation* of Deleuze and Guattari's 'rhizomatic' form" (Snyder 1997, 53; my emphasis).

5. Categorical differences are apparent, however, when considering the level of IF discourse in relation to other digital fictions with arborescent structure; that is, IFs always position the user—or "interactor" (Montfort 2003)—in the first-person role of protagonist or player-character. In addition, rather than choosing among linked words or phrases, the player-character in IFs enters *textual* input (in the form of diegetic "commands"), which in turn call on an algorithmic engine to generate a textual output.

6. The music analogy is encouraged by AI scientist Herbert Simon's discussion of nonrepresentational patterns in prose (1995, part 5). Simon writes, "It is a matter of terminological preference whether we want to use the word 'meaning' broadly enough to encompass the nonrepresentational components of pattern. Apart from the question of terminology, there are no particular problems in seeking out such patterns in a work of art, whether it be music, painting, or literature. It is really the representational component in painting and literature, rather than the nonrepresentational component, that is problematic."

7. Texts such as Pavic's *Dictionary of the Khazars* might be considered network fiction as well, and it is indeed often placed in the stable of "hypertextual" works in print, though this would similarly require a broadening of terms given that its "networked" elements remain in a static relation to one another by virtue of the print medium.

8. The directory (http://directory.eliterature.org/) is in development and by no means constitutes an exhaustive list of works that use hypertext to create narrative fiction; however, it is suggestive of the distribution of techniques included within the "technique/genre" of "hypertext."

9. The use of *discourse,* rather than the originary term *dungeon,* is mentioned by Aarseth (1997, 143) as a possible alternative. It is useful in referring more broadly to synchronous textual environments that do not necessarily adopt adventure themes and are not necessarily strategic and outcome-based but rather are organized around collaborative social dynamics. The most well-known example of these social MUDs would be the still-active LambdaMOO that gained international media attention after a "virtual rape" transpired in its textual world (see Dibbell 2001).

Chapter 1

1. The implication of an unanchored agency mirrors a rhetorical quality evident in Deleuze's broader tropology, in which the distributed function of a concept not only affords agency but also seems to assume it.

2. Bruce Kawin (1972, 7) makes this point with regard to literature: "The growth of the work, even from one identical line to another, makes exact repetition impossible. . . . Repetition is a nonverbal state; it cannot be committed to any art that occurs in time"; and Søren Kierkegaard's *Repetition* (1843) demonstrates the impossibility of pure repetition in lived experience. (Kierkegaard's narrating persona, the aptly named Constantin Constantius, returns to Berlin in hope of rehearsing an earlier visit with utter exactitude. The attempt fails for reasons that include anything from the coffee tasting different in a familiar café to something less discernibly different about his same hotel room. He realizes that the repeated experience introduces difference, wherein lies its value for Kierkegaard.)

3. In Deleuze's *Difference and Repetition* the concept of complex repetition goes hand in hand with his concept of pure or absolute difference, since the "perpetual divergence and decentering of difference correspond closely to a displacement and a disguising within repetition" (xx). Complex repetition, in his terms, can "comprehend" the movements of a difference that continually displaces and diversifies and, in the most extreme sense, comprehends a difference that seems otherwise incomprehensible. As purity connotes sameness, the phrase "pure difference" is itself paradoxical if not oxymoronic. But Deleuze sees such paradoxes as inevitable in forcefully articulating a philosophy that finds no precedent in traditional metaphysics. Connor adopts Deleuze's rhetoric when he writes, "In order to be recognizable as such, a repetition must, in however small a degree, be different from its original. This 'difference' is invisible except in the fact of its *pure differentiality*" (Connor 1988, 7; my emphasis). The two concepts thus coalesce in a model in which repetition repeats and difference differentiates.

4. Although the possibility that the earth seesaws from a habitable to an uninhabitable state over vast sweeps of time is by no means inconceivable, some critics assert that after satisfying himself that such a hypothesis was not borne out by any known facts of natural science, Nietzsche resolved to deal with the eternal return as a philosophical speculation. Others believe that its formulation was in fact *compelled by* the scientific possibility of the eternal recurrence of cosmic events, and he simply applied the idea to human experience (see Kaufmann in Nietzsche 1883–92/1995, 236).

5. As Higgins (1988, 143) writes, "The overman is the ultimate concern of humanity because he is to be our descendent. When Zarathustra calls for self-sacrifice in the name of the overman he is speaking of the kind of self-sacrifice that parents would make for their children." The idea that the Overman can guide the human will in a Godless world is crucial to the affirmative force of Nietzsche's doctrine.

6. In the visual arts the work of Andy Warhol is most certainly a meditation on this theme.

7. Suleiman (1983) defines ideological fictions as realist works that seek, often didactically, to demonstrate "the validity of a political, philosophical, or religious doctrine" (7). In describing repetition (or "redundancy") as a significant "criterion of [this] genre" (171), her study is similar to my own in at least one regard: though I do not describe network fiction as a *genre*—a difficult term perhaps made even more so

by the hybridity common to digital art—the play of repetition is certainly a defining criterion of the form.

8. For a full-length treatment of this field of writing see Stark 1974.

9. For Deleuze, Menard's writing is a demonstration of *complex repetition:* "In this case, the most strict repetition has the maximum of difference" (Deleuze 1994, xxii). But if this repetition evokes Deleuze's ideal, it does not constitute it, for this would amount to a conflation of a theme with an artifact. Borges does not compose chapters of *Don Quixote;* the fictional Pierre Menard does, and Borges's reproductions of Menard's reproduction appear only as a few fragments. For now, at least, we live in a world in which we can imagine an author such as Pierre Menard but not one in which his work would be met with the same approval as that of Borges's narrator—a world in which Borges's fiction succeeds precisely because Menard's would fail. Borges does not demonstrate or instantiate Deleuze's theory; he rearticulates it as a parable.

10. The phrase is evoked by Matthew Kirschenbaum's (2001) "Materiality and Matter and Stuff: What Electronic Texts Are Made Of."

11. Kawin's discussion of film at one point invokes the material properties of the medium to ground his conception of cinematic aesthetics, but his description of "a ribbon of frames that goes properly in only one direction" (1972, 104) similarly marks its datedness.

12. Janet Murray (1997, 65–66) makes a parallel claim when she writes of the introduction of the film medium and the legend of a Parisian café where the audience is said to have run screaming from the room when the lifelike image of a locomotive engine appeared to be rushing toward them from the screen. Murray suggests that the legend is conveniently satisfying in that "it falsely conflates the arrival of the representational technology with the arrival of the artistic medium, as if the manufacture of the camera alone gave us the movies."

13. Although associated predominantly with early hypertext theorists, the "literalist" approach continues to color more contemporary accounts. Ilana Snyder (1997, 119) claims that "because hypertext *embodies* postmodern theories of the text, it makes it easier to study them" (her emphasis), and Ryan (1999, 101) suggests that "the aspects of contemporary literary theory that find their fulfillment in hypertext hardly need explanation at all." These perspectives resonate with Richard Lanham's earlier contention that "it is hard not to think that, at the end of the day, electronic text will seem the natural fulfillment of much current literary theory, and resolve many of its questions" (1993, 130). Diane Greco (1996, 87) echoes these claims when she describes hypertext as "a literal embodiment *not only of postmodern fragmentation but also its possible resolution.*" In short, such a view posits that hypertext not only asks the same questions as contemporary literary theory but also holds unprecedented promise to answer them.

14. My use of the term *node* rather than *lexia* is prompted by the same disjunction between a poststructuralist concept on one hand and a technological medium on the other. The appropriation of Barthes' *lexia* in defining the reading and writ-

ing units of the network text is common but misguided: the crucial difference between a Barthesian lexia and a hypertextual lexia is that the former is an operation of the reader, whereas the latter is an operation of the writer. With regard to Barthes' theory, readers of print fiction break the text into what they see as discrete units of meaning, whereas readers of network fiction encounter hypertextual nodes *already established*.

15. The role of repetition in signaling artifice and, more generally, in the spatial construction of the network text is the topic of the next chapter.

16. The other factor that counteracts time in Rimmon-Kenan's model involves "the existence of quasi-spatial patterns which establish supra-linear links, e.g. analogy" (Rimmon-Kenan 1983, 137n). I discuss this mode of print-based spatiality in chapter 2.

17. This point departs in one respect from Jill Walker's (1999) understanding of nodal repetition. Walker claims, "The knowledge that you are reading the same node as before gives a feeling of materiality to this repetition that is not exactly repetition, but re-vision. It is being re-read, but not re-narrated." The distinction of rereading/renarrating is necessarily an arbitrary one, especially given the possibility of constraints that allow authors to plot narrative recursions. Readers have no way of knowing which retellings are planned and which are not.

18. I present an extended example of the first case, reading a node in a different "semantic neighborhood," in chapter 4, on *Victory Garden*.

19. Default paths are a feature of the Storyspace application that allows readers to move through sequences of preordered nodes instead of choosing a text link.

20. I discuss Hanjo Berressem's "text ergodic geometry," which appropriates Guattari's concept of *folding* as a basis for understanding text-topological movement, in chapter 6.

21. In rhetorical grammar *tmesis* refers to the separation of the parts of a compound word. It comes from the Greek word for an "act of cutting."

22. In addition, because the network text is capable of both remembering and responding to a reader's choices, not only do we read the text, but the text, simultaneously, reads us. "History" functions, whether an aspect of a specific software program or a function of a Web browser, provide ways of "remembering," whereas a preprogrammed conditionality based on the choices made during a given reading would constitute a "response" peculiar to a given reader. Storyspace software, in particular, to some extent allows authors to choreograph the reading experience using "guard fields," which force readers to encounter some nodes (or scenes) before others and make some nodes conditional. Thus, when recalling Barthes' description of reading for Bliss, where "we boldly skip descriptions, explanations, analyses, conversations" since "no one is watching" (11), one can say that in network narratives, someone, or rather something, *is* watching.

23. Eskelinen describes how cybertexts expand the category of duration by providing quantifiable text-time measures through dynamic time-constrained interfaces. Moulthrop's *Hegirascope* is one example.

24. With regard to Frequency in network narratives, Eskelinen acknowledges that Genette's category can be "modified both by quantitative and qualitative analysis of link structures," but he sees little benefit in working from or with Genette's model: "I'm not too interested in expanding narratives to *infect* too many cybertextual possibilities" (Eskelinen 2001; my emphasis). His main concern appears to be the "purification" of cybertext.

25. The Nietzschean repetition discussed by Miller (1982) informs Walker's critique.

26. The recurrence of hypertextual nodes can facilitate interpretative acts analogous to Freud's retroactivity, but, contrary to the inclinations of the "literalist" critique, there is no way to concretize this (psychic) phenomenon with a computer interface.

27. In prefacing her comprehensive reading of *afternoon,* J. Yellowlees Douglas (1994) questions, against the arguments of Joseph Conrad and Walter Benjamin, how essential closure is to the satisfactions of reading narratives (159–65).

28. The idea recalls Laura Trippi's (2001) comments about "disentangling" *story* from the concept of *narrative* that encompasses it.

Chapter 2

1. With regard to frontier rhetoric, a competing but by no means dominant discourse in the formative years of network culture, one finds a telling example of auto-deconstructive writing in Mitch Kapor and John Perry Barlow's "Across the Electronic Frontier" (1990): "In its present [i.e., 1990] condition cyberspace is a frontier region, populated by a few hardy technologists who can tolerate the austerity of its savage computer interfaces, incompatible communication protocols, propriety barricades, cultural and legal ambiguities, and lack of useful maps and metaphors" (cited in Mitchell 1995, 110). The authors complain here about the lack of useful metaphors, but the frontier imagery is a foregone conclusion.

2. There are several examples of hybridized discourse. See, e.g., Amerika (n.d.), where the "feeling of blue despair colors the mode of perception. A field of action motorizes itself into the *topological plain* as HTC burrows for more connectivity" (my emphasis); and Roger Chartier (1995, 18), who writes that "in place of the immediate apprehension of the whole work, made visible by the object that embodies it, [the electronic text] introduces a lengthy navigation in *textual archipelagos that have neither shores nor borders*" (quoted in Riess 1996; my emphasis).

3. Kierkegaard paints his aesthete, a young romantic whom he designates *A,* in contradistinction to the ethical man, a married judge named Wilhelm, designated *B.* The judge welcomes a state of commitment and obligation over time, specifically through marriage and public service, whereas the aesthete exists outside of time and in relation only to Beauty.

4. "Hypertext fictions are rife with collision, impact, and the scattering of 'motor parts' all over the imaginary roadway. Perhaps these images are so pervasive pre-

cisely because hypertext fiction enacts and incorporates the principle of breakdown" (Moulthrop 2001). Moulthrop's own *Victory Garden* (1991b) features a near collision during a car chase in the node titled "No Coincidence."

5. I am using the term *instrumental* to connote utility—serving as a means to an end. Artists of digital media, such as Moulthrop and Wardrip-Fruin, have more recently used the term to describe certain performative art works that users can "play."

6. Bernstein writes on the topic earlier on in "The Navigation Problem Reconsidered" (1991), which was written the same year a panel at the 1991 ACM hypertext conference, considering the "status of the navigational problem," decided that there might not be any problem at all (see Bernstein et al. 1991). The panel, which included the theorists George Landow, Mark Bernstein, Peter Brown, Mark Frisse, Robert Glushko, and Polle Zellweger, marked a turn away from a first wave of critical literature on hypertext that identified disorientation and cognitive overload as the two most crucial challenges to overcome in order to implement successful hypertext systems. Of course, the benchmarks for a successful hypertext system in the educational or commercial sector differ dramatically from the aesthetic questions that arise when appropriating hypertext technology for works of art. Landow (1997, 117–23) addresses the issue of disorientation as an aesthetic device.

7. Tolman's work planted the seeds of environmental and cognitive psychology. In the 1970s neurobiologists discovered that certain "place cells" in the hippocampus of rodents would fire preferentially when the animals were moving through a given environment, a finding that "located" the production of the cognitive map posited by Tolman.

8. For Ryan literary cartography is a means to the end of "immersion" in the fictional world. I treat the concept of immersion in relation to network fiction at length in chapter 4.

9. The claim can be understood as a variant of the broader popular analogy of *mind* and *machine* (read: digital computer). Neurobiology likewise exposes the flaws in this comparison. As Gerald Edelman (2004b) says, "The most important thing to understand is that the brain is 'context bound.' It is not a logical system like a computer that processes only programmed information; it does not produce preordained outcomes like a clock. Rather it is a selectional system that, through pattern recognition, puts things together in always novel ways." Edelman debunks the mind-as-computer analogy more thoroughly in *Wider Than the Sky* (2004a, 28–30).

10. Joyce's desire to shape space "proprioceptively and sensually" anticipates the elaboration of his poetics of "contour" in *Othermindedness* (2000), which is a response to the challenge of "reading" topological structure.

11. Sanford Kwinter (1992, 53) explains that the "classical grid system does not, strictly speaking, limit one to static models of form, but it does limit one to *linear* models of movement or change. A linear model is one in which the state of a system at a given moment can be expressed in the very same terms . . . as any of its earlier or later states."

12. Even though exposure to computer networks has foregrounded theoretical discourse on topology in the humanities, the concept is by no means new to artists and critics. Umberto Eco (1993, 81) described topological space decades ago in a parodic essay, "Paradox of Porta Ludovica," which is a purported phenomenon of urban space that leaves the inhabitants of Milan in a perpetual state of bewilderment: "It is therefore a topological space, like that of a microbe that chooses as its dwelling place a wad of chewing gum for the period of time . . . in which the gum is chewed by a being of macroscopic dimensions." In addition, in "Cybernetics and Ghosts" Italo Calvino (1987, 25–27) cites an essay by the German poet and critic Hans Magnus Enzensberger ("Topological Structures in Modern Literature") that discusses the significance of topology as a theme in modern fiction. Enzensberger's essay was published in Spanish in the Buenos Aires magazine *Sur* in 1966 and has not been released in an English translation.

13. Joyce (2000, 15n) credits Sandra Braman's reading of Kwinter's essay for his own discussion of topology.

14. "Strange Horizon: Buildings, Biograms, and the Body Topologic" appears as chapter 8 of Massumi's *Parables for the Virtual* (Durham, NC: Duke University Press, 2002). An earlier version, published in the conference proceedings of *Chaos/Control: Complexity,* ed. Philipp Hofmann (Hamburg: Lit Verlag), is cited here.

15. Olson wrote a series of chartlike prose pieces first published in 1961 and 1962. The citations come from the opening piece, "Proprioception." Olson is known to have been familiar with the work of Norbert Wiener, who led the way in establishing the field of cybernetics in the late 1940s, and Olson is likely to have appropriated the term from him.

16. In Massumi's terms, "we orient with two systems of reference used together. The contradiction between them is only apparent. Pragmatically, they co-function. Visual cues and cognitive mappings function as storage devices allowing us more ready reaccess to less habituated proprioceptive patches" (2002).

17. There is, however, a form of "embodied reading" in digital media that is quantifiably absent in the space of print: the ability of the computer mouse to make an analog translation of human movement (the hand of its holder) into graphical space. As Thierry Bardini (1997) writes, this translation introduces "a direct connection between the topographical space of the interface and the human gesture of the user."

18. The notion of the text-from-within evokes the "internal perspective" discussed by Ryan in the context of the opposition of *map* and *tour* strategies of discourse analysis. As Ryan writes, in the *map* strategy "space is represented panoramically from a perspective ranging from the disembodied god's-eye point of view of pure vertical projection to the oblique view of an observer situated on an elevated point." The *tour,* by contrast, "represents space dynamically from a perspective internal to the territory to be surveyed. . . . The tour thus simulates the embodied experience of the traveler" (2003, 218). But again, Ryan remains focused on the perspec-

tives of the spatial relations in the represented world rather than the spatial relations that might constitute a hypertextual form.

19. Moulthrop (1994, 303–4) carries the notion of "local coherence" into hypertextual discourse.

20. See Teemu Ikonen (2003) for a listing of e-poetry genres and a classification of types of motion in contemporary poetry.

21. Eco's stance has since softened; speaking at the 1994 symposium "The Future of the Book" at the University of San Marino, he issued a qualified endorsement of what he sees as the potential of hypertext: "We may conceive of hypertexts which are unlimited and infinite. Every user can add something, and you can implement a sort of jazzlike unending story. At this point the classical notion of authorship certainly disappears, and we have a new way to implement free creativity. As the author of *The Open Work* I can only hail such a possibility. However there is a difference between implementing the activity of producing texts and the existence of produced texts. We shall have a new culture in which there will be a difference between producing infinitely many texts and interpreting precisely a finite number of texts" (Eco 1996, 303).

22. Hofstadter's (1979) *Gödel, Escher, Bach: An Eternal Golden Braid* is a powerful demonstration of recursion in varied contexts, treating the mathematician, the visual artist, and the musician of his title as "shadows cast in different directions by some central solid essence" (28).

23. As Bal (1981, 58) notes, however, "the 'priority' of the first level is neither chronological (the text can begin with a hypo-text) nor primary in importance."

24. Marsh's use of "paragram" follows from Julia Kristeva:

> In the Kristevan model . . . any work which explores the "internal orders" of print text . . . could be described as a "paragrammatic" text whose ambivalence lies in its functioning as both text (linear and monological) and hypertext (tabular, spatial and dialogical). Such an equation would perhaps oversimplify the dynamics of both the paragram and the hypertext; nonetheless, it is clear that both terms describe an engagement in language which foregrounds the "beyond" of textuality. . . . Elsewhere Kristeva defines the paragram as a "moving gram" ("gramme mouvant") . . . and so brings us closer to a literal sense of the term as suggested by its etymology—"beside-" or "beyond-letter"—which proves useful with regard to the "hyperlink" in web-based writing. (Marsh 1997)

See also Marsh's footnotes 4 and 5 on the etymologies and appropriations of the paragram.

25. The term *tangle* takes on a specific denotation in Mark Bernstein's (1998b) hypertextual lexicon: "The *tangle* confronts the reader with a variety of links without providing sufficient clues to guide the reader's choice. . . . [T]angles can help inten-

tionally disorient readers in order to make them more receptive to a new argument or an unexpected conclusion."

Chapter 3

1. From the archives of Eastgate's *HypertextNow,* http://www.eastgate.com/HypertextNow/archives/Twilight.html (accessed March 2006).

2. As both Douglas (2001) and Hayles (2002) point out, despite the many alternative scenarios portrayed in the narrative regarding the central scene of the car accident, one node ("White Afternoon") is privileged in the text by virtue of its role as a prominent navigational juncture, accommodating many links and recurring often for the reader. The privileged node suggests that the protagonist, Peter, is in fact responsible for causing the accident he spends so much time investigating. In effect, both Douglas and Hayles read *afternoon* as a network fiction, where conflicting events or accounts of events can be reconciled and explained in some way.

3. Intertextually, that fabric extends further to include another narrative that plays heavily on the Goldberg Variations: Richard Powers's *The Gold Bug Variations,* which was published in 1991, several years before *Twilight.* The novel also braids together two narrative strands—two love stories—that occur around the dates of Gould's recordings, one in the 1980s and the other, in flashback, in the 1950s.

4. The interrelationship of theme-and-variation, orientation, and return is established in a passage from H. T. David and A. Mendel's *The Bach Reader* (1966) on the aspects that unify Bach's music: "His form in general was based on relations between separate sections. These relations ranged from complete identity . . . to the return of a single principle of elaboration or a mere thematic allusion. . . . The resulting patterns were often symmetrical, but by no means necessarily so. Sometimes the relations between the various sections make up a maze of interwoven threads that only detailed analysis can unravel. Usually, however, a few dominant features afford people orientation at first sight or hearing" (quoted in Hofstadter 1979, 28). The description, which strikes overt literary parallels, has clear relevance to the form of network fiction. Hofstadter (1979, 10) also discusses the recursive movement of strange loops in Bach's music.

5. The works consulted for Gould's background include Friedrich (1989) and Girard (1993). Joyce makes reference to the creation of Girard's film in *Twilight.*

6. Powe's essay is a contribution to *Noise of Time,* a hypermedia project on Glenn Gould created by French Canadian artist Henry See. Joyce makes several references to the work and its creators in *Twilight.* "A Return to Gould" (1989) can be found through the National Library of Canada's Glenn Gould Archive (www.collectionscanada.ca/glenngould/028010-502.10-e.html).

7. By some accounts Gould suffered from chronic afflictions; by other accounts he was a hypochondriac. Either way, he was known to take a lot of pills.

8. Underscoring Gould's emphasis on the expanded role of the listener/consumer, Joyce cites him directly in *Twilight:* "All the music that has ever been can now become

a background against which the impulse to make listener-supplied connections is the new foreground—Glenn Gould *The Prospects of Recording*" ("Prospects").

9. Goldberg and Gould provide only one mythical genealogy for Joyce's protagonist. Hugh's name also marks one of many returns to the work of James Joyce who, as an accomplished Irish tenor, also demonstrated musical ability. Hugh Colin Enwright is another possible incarnation of the protagonist of James Joyce's *Finnegans Wake*: Humphrey Chimpden Earwicker. The initials H. C. E. invite the comparison of Hugh to an everyman, just as James Joyce's Earwicker sounds the universal appeal of "Here Comes Everybody." Hence, we can read Hugh as the embodiment of any number of mythical and archetypal figures who live in the past, present, and future, just as Earwicker fuses together folk hero Tim Finnegan, the gallant Tristan of medieval Irish lore, the legendary giant Finn MacCool, Huck Finn, and Humpty Dumpty to name a few. By creating a homonym for *you* with *Hugh*, Michael Joyce adds "you," the reader, to this list of metafictional characters, a move that recalls Moulthrop's character Boris Urquhart—commonly known in *Victory Garden* as "U."

10. *Ekphrasis*, broadly speaking, is "the verbal representation of a visual representation" (Mitchell 1994, 152). It also refers specifically to a genre of poetry reserved for the description of works of visual art. A classic example is Keats's "Ode on a Grecian Urn" (1820).

11. Murphy and Smith cite Deleuze and Guattari (1987, 137–38).

12. See Moulthrop (1992a) for a response to and critique of the appropriation of Deleuze and Guattari's notion of "smooth space."

13. This is accomplished by using an "anchor" that links directly to another string of text rather than simply another node.

14. Works published in Storyspace are republished in updated editions (for Mac and PC) as the software is upgraded, and there are a number of versions of the software in between Storyspace I and II. Joyce's *afternoon* itself has been published in at least a half dozen versions/platforms and editions since its original 1987 release. It is clear that the presence of variations from edition to edition has implications for any aesthetic discussion, especially among operating systems, but it is entirely viable to discuss aesthetics based on continuities across platforms and systems.

15. It is true that these nodes are *fixed* only insofar as this is how Joyce presents them, for the reader can manipulate the placement of the nodes in the Storyspace map overview and peruse them in a slightly modified topography. There is no compelling reason, however, why this might be useful without the Storyspace software installed as well, which allows readers to make changes to the linking structure. If anything, such modification would further complicate the directional cues provided by Joyce's thematic arcs.

16. In the map view (both windows are always "open"—one just eclipses the other on the screen) readers can enact the same above and below movement graphically, by using different commands. For example, readers can "double-click the body of a writing space in the map to zoom the map view in, showing the spaces contained in that space." Or they can "click the *close box* in the upper-left corner of the map window

to replace that map by a map one level up the hierarchy, showing the neighborhood containing the space that had been in the map" ("Instructions").

17. The text of "Our story so far" scrolls onward for another six paragraphs. Scrolling nodes (common to the World Wide Web) were introduced as an added feature of Storyspace II and raise key questions concerning network aesthetics. For instance, how can a node be a self-contained semantic entity if there exists no set measure or means of "containment"?

18. Confusion remains even for some who assume they have overcome the initial inscrutability of the maps. For example, in a review of *Twilight* Susana Pajares Tosca (1997) goes so far as to describe Joyce's work as a "perfect symbiosis" of technology and storytelling and a "mastery of the technical hypertext environment." When explaining the navigational palette, however, Tosca incorrectly describes the left arrow on the compass tool as what takes us "to the space we've read before," whereas the right arrow on the compass tool takes us "to the next space." This misrepresents the function of the compass arrows by confusing them with the function of the bidirectional default/backtrack arrow located below the compass on the palette, which she does not mention. The left arrow takes us to the space located to the left (west) of the current node; the default arrow + shift will take us back one node, to "the space we've read before." The right arrow takes us to the "next space" only if *next* refers to the node located immediately to the right (east) of the current node. The default arrow will take us to the next node in the default path.

19. Elsewhere Joyce says that the "visual form of electronic texts" can include the following: (1) "the apparent content of the text at hand," (2) "its explicit or available design," or (3) "implicit and dynamic designs" such as "patterns, juxtapositions, or recurrences within the text or as abstractions situated outside the text" (2000, 22). When we begin to consider also those "abstractions situated outside" of the text, we approach a more comprehensive phenomenology of reading. In fact, in a later "Intermezzo" piece in *Othermindedness* the contour becomes nothing short of an encompassing totality: it is "how the form of things mean, . . . the totality of the work" (130). Setting aside what Joyce's notion of contour includes, we might ask instead, What does it exclude?

20. With his poetics of contour Joyce also articulates what has been the most visible emergence of an erotics of hypertext. Joyce does not, however, set out to do with literary hypertext what Barthes does with his "text of Bliss" (Barthes uses *contour* at one point in his *Pleasure of the Text* to link our physical body to the body of the text, describing a medial "body of bliss" that "consists solely of erotic relations" [see Barthes 1980, 16]). The two articulate different, even incompatible, textual pleasures. Barthes' *jouissance* calls up a rapturous, climactic, or even violent bliss in which cultural codes and forms are fractured or transgressed. Joyce, by contrast, invokes contour to apprehend forms readers create but cannot see: "I had in mind . . . the sense of a lover's caress in which the form expresses itself in successiveness without necessarily any fixation" (Joyce 2000, 167). Both seek a pleasure devoid of intention—arising from the text as it exists, not as it intends. But Joyce plays more to the tune of the never-

ending story in that, unlike Barthes', the pleasure of his text comes without necessarily any climax—from a succession and recurrence that is stable and sustained.

21. Other theorists of digital media have made a similar observation. Sean Cubitt (2001, 2), for instance, writes of "the movement through disorientation to new orientation" as one of the "characteristic emotions of digital artworks."

22. Michael Joyce, email correspondence with the author, July 14, 2003.

23. See Eastgate's catalog listing at http://www.eastgate.com/catalog/Twilight.html (accessed March 2006).

Chapter 4

1. Moulthrop, *Victory Garden,* from the node, "Balanced Coverage."

2. See, e.g., Lisbeth Klastrup's (1997) "Hyperfiction in Practice: Walking in the Garden of Forced Paths."

3. See "Victory Gardening in America," *Victory Seed Company* multimedia, www.victoryseeds.com/TheVictoryGarden/index.html (accessed March 2006).

4. As Robert Coover (1993, 8–12) writes, "What Jude is trying to do (she recognizes her desire as both 'deeply symbolic' and 'radically perverse') is 'to create a link that would unite all three of them, a symbolic link outside of bodies and time,' a desire shared in some respects by Mr. Moulthrop and exhibited in his multidirectional, atemporally linked hypertext structure. Jude's three-way link is in some manner made—with the help of set, costumes, wig and mirror; the late Emily Runbird invades the lovemaking (love *is* strange) of Jude and Victor; later both confess that they loved Emily (the verb is now past tense), and their last candle goes dark."

5. The errors are Emily's and are indicative of hastily written letters. The font used to present them in the narrative is also suggestive of typewritten documents, with signatures that appear handwritten.

6. Robert Selig (2000, 657) discusses this development.

7. The document cited in the Department of Defense (2000) article is George N. Lewis, Steve Fetter, and Lisbeth Gronlund, *Casualties and Damage from Scud Attacks in the 1991 Gulf War,* appendix (Cambridge, MA: MIT Center for International Studies, March 1993).

8. There are, of course, limits to this technique of identification, and irreconcilable splits between you the character and you the reader arise. Such a split is evident even in the second sentence, especially if one does not own a television or is reading outside: "Best to close the door; the TV is always on in the next room" (3). In addition, despite Gaggi's politic reference to the "he or she" that is also a character in the novel, Calvino's narratee is unavoidably male. Eventually he meets the "Other Reader," who is female, and falls in love.

9. These and other graphical or typographical elements that often solicit the reader's participation have contributed to a description of *Tristram Shandy* as the first "interactive" novel. But there are more specific parallels. Iser (1988, 62) discusses Sterne's use of typographical marks in the novel as structural elements that explic-

itly invite the reader to "complete the text." If, as Sterne's protagonist suggests, writing is simply "a different name for conversation," then his use of the dash is a significant indication of this exchange. Iser writes, "[The dash] marks the openness of speech, which can branch off unexpectedly, go forwards or backwards, turn to the other characters or to the reader, and generally allow the flexibility necessary for conversation as the process of exploration. Syntactically the dash is an interruption, but as such it permits new links, thereby granting access to new territories" (1988, 62). Although there is no direct equivalence between Iser's semantic gaps and the "spaces" between hypertextual nodes, hyperlinks enact an analogous interruption of the text, redirecting the reading and granting access to new territories of the network text.

10. There are ways out, of course, such as using the back arrow or the Links menu or even turning off the computer—a surefire route to "disconnect."

11. The passage is also cited in the node "Swarming."

12. Coover (1993) describes the work's subject matter as that of a "typical academic novel," and its dense and highly allusive layering has led other critics to describe it as modernist. According to Mark Amerika (1998), "most of the early practitioners of hypertext employ a more Modernistic writing style that attempts to use [it] as a technology that creates stories whose top priority is to make us feel whole again (a priority not too dissimilar from the conventional novels of the past)." Similarly, Aarseth writes, "Hypertext fictions are novels, both narratologically and sociologically" (quoted in Moulthrop 2001).

13. The authors of *The Unknown*, the subject of chapter 5, demonstrate that it is possible to pursue excess in many ways other than the creation of an alephic text.

14. The list does not claim to be definitive. Not only do some nodes with different material carry the same title, but conversely, some of the same nodes with the same material carry different titles. In addition, different versions of *Victory Garden* contain different numbers of nodes. The 1991 version for Windows used here has 993, whereas Selig refers to a 1993 Windows version that has 1,025. Exact quantities, nonetheless, are not necessary to make the comparison.

15. As I mentioned in my introduction, network fictions, as defined in this study, always maintain the distinction of reader and writer, which means they do not accommodate Ryan's "strong" form of interactivity.

16. A transparent work is not necessarily immersive. As Charles Bernstein (1992, 26) reminds us, "transparency is not the equivalent of absorption" [read: immersion]; rather "transparency is but one technique for producing absorptive works." The converse scenario, an immersive work that is not necessarily transparent, is also possible and is discussed in greater detail below (see "Garden Care").

17. From Bob Perelman's *The First World* (1986), cited in Bernstein (1992, 33).

18. The role of weblogs (or "blogs") has been a dramatic application of participatory media in the coverage and criticism of the war in Iraq.

19. Moulthrop's comments coincide with his own movement away from narrative fiction in digital realms to artistic experiments that probe what he calls the "middle space in between the literary and the ludic" (2003c). His statement regarding "the

prime agenda of art" is of course predicated on the assumption of an artistic agenda that is already instrumental or politically motivated in some way.

20. In one of the most lucid contributions to the early discourse of digital textuality, Richard Lanham (1993) discusses the formalist notion of looking "AT" a text's "opaque" structural artifice versus looking "THROUGH" to its "transparent" story-world, and he applies the distinction to digital media. He describes a process of oscillation between the two as "the most powerful aesthetic attribute of electronic text" (43).

21. In "Artifice of Absorption" Bernstein discusses poems "that ask the reader to do something, such as those poems by Jackson Mac Low that have accompanying instructions" (34). This strikes a parallel to most early works of hypertext fiction, and still many Web-based works, which include instructions on everything from how to install the work on one's computer to how to go about "reading" it. Both have an immediate anti-immersive effect, and complicate Genette's (1997) notion of the "paratext."

22. Schema theory is a branch of cognitive science that studies the way in which we revert to categorical rules or scripts on receiving new information, interpreting it in terms of how it fits or fails to fit an existing schema.

23. Critics fault Hargadon and Douglas on other grounds. Drawing on the work of Rand Spiro (1982), David Miall (2004) states that schema theory does not adequately explain affective responses to reading:

> First, as Spiro showed in the case of a short story by James Joyce, we can understand a story (experiential understanding) without knowing what it is about (schema-based understanding). Secondly, during reading the informational, situational aspects of a text can become "overlearned" and relegated to the background; what captures attention is our feelings about the text. Spiro's account implies that schemas and feelings are thus separate sources of meaning. He proposes that reading involves two levels: first, the comprehension process of assigning events to types, second, the invocation of personal meaning. . . . [T]he two levels may often occur concurrently, a suggestion that would allow us to infer that feeling as well as schemas contributes to textual coherence. In fact, the relation of feelings and schemas may often be the reverse of that proposed by Douglas and Hargadon.

Adrian Miles (2004), furthermore, identifies a strand of technological determinism that may inform Hargadon and Douglas's argument:

> Their claim that given "the enhanced immersive possibilities of full motion video, not to mention virtual reality, coupled with hypertext fiction's complex possibilities for engagement, future interactives could easily enable casual readers to experience . . . flow" . . . sets off warning bells. This could well be the case, but surely this is close to some sort of technological determinism

where an imagined lack is "corrected" by more technology to generate immersion. Surely print, film and video have already taught us that immersive works are immersive in spite of, not because of, their technical constraints. There are poorly printed books that are immersive, there are low budget, dark and poorly acted films that are immersive, just as there are well printed books and well made films that require engagement.

More generally, both Miall and Miles see the essay cornering itself into some form of high-low cultural divide through its distinction of "engagement" and "immersion."

24. The idea that hypertext media can accommodate or encourage immersive reading runs counter to empirical studies conducted by David Miall and Teresa Dobson (2001), who show that "hypertext discourages the absorbed and reflective mode that characterizes literary reading" (1). Their findings support common characterizations of digital literature as a defamiliarizing art form that forces readers to attend to its "opacity" or structural artifice. At this early stage in the development of digital literature, however, it is best not to put too much confidence in empirical studies at the risk of curtailing the aesthetic potential of digital writing technologies. Studies of readers unacquainted with literary works in network environments have little value insofar as they affirm only initial reactions of confusion or disorientation experienced by those who are as yet unable to look beyond the medium. This is the case with Miall and Dobson's study, which included readers who had only cursory knowledge of the form, as is evident in some of their readers' comments: "Reading this story off the computer was kind of confusing at first because as I went to different screens I realized the story wasn't in order" (2001).

But their study is problematic for other reasons. It involves adapting short stories originally published in print into a hypertext format so that a control group can read the original print version. Although they acknowledge this limitation, it is actually a much bigger problem than they let on, given that (1) the story was not composed in self-contained nodes and (2) Miall and Dobson effectively become the authors of the semantic network of the new text by retroactively and somewhat arbitrarily installing links. Significantly, despite these problematic factors, some readers were able to conceive of an emergent coherence; to cite a remark from a reader that recalls Ryan's (2001a) narrative jigsaw puzzle, one was "able to put the puzzle together, so to speak."

25. Boris is actually dressed as "Uqbari the Prophet," which is his deliberate invocation of Uqbar, a land described by Borges in his short fiction "Tlön Uqbar, Orbis Tertius." During one of his tormented personal musings, Boris explains, "Borges referred to a place called Uqbar, supposedly 'a region of Iraq or Asia Minor' which was in fact unreal. Uqbar is brought to you by the people who invented Tlön, a conspiracy to replace the bad old world with a *novus ordo saeculorum*. There's a lot of that going around" ("Story of My Life"). The *novus ordo saeculorum* refers to the phrase "New World Order," which found its way into several Gulf War speeches by President H. W. Bush.

26. The nodes on the default path are "Ring," "Help Mister Wizard," "Fool's Errand," "Ring Cycle," "Errant Fool," "In Need of Help," "Ring Around," "Arrant Fool," and "Helpful."

27. Of course, repetitions do not necessarily always build *toward something*. One can think of popular music, which relies on formulaic repetitions of themes, as well as musical patterns, the melodies and harmonies designed to arouse and heighten emotion toward extremes such as elation, longing, or rage. Pop songs end in one of two formulaic ways: after repeating the chorus however many times, they either reach a *fine*, or they simply fade out. The same general idea can apply to a network fiction: repetition can move toward cohesion, confirmation, reinforcement, and emphasis. These are generative forms of repetition, repetitions that build on one another. By contrast, repetition can move toward redundancy, fragmentation, erasure, and neurosis. These are all repetitions that degenerate, often by creating an unreleased or unreleasable tension, or tiredly canceling itself out in a process of dissolution.

28. Bernstein again echoes Moulthrop's aesthetic when he writes that "such textures may be particularly vital at a time when readers are skeptical of the transparency effect, whether it is used to reveal unmediated inner states or external narrative spaces" (1992, 29).

Chapter 5

1. The sampler is available at www.eastgate.com/VG/VGStart.html (accessed Dec. 12, 2006).

2. In an exclusively instrumental sense hypertext technology is meant to combat informational excess, as in, for example, a hyperlinked airplane repair manual designed to expedite the repair process.

3. The artists of the Oulipo (Ouvroir de littérature potentielle—or "Workshop of Potential Literature") have perhaps found more virtue in the aesthetics of constraint than any other group in literary history. They popularized the concept of "constrained writing" in the latter half of the twentieth century. This mode of writing involves a specific application of a given—typically announced—constraint as a generative concept during the process of composition (a well-known example is Georges Perec's novel, *La Disparition*, written without the letter *e*).

The Oulipian conception of constraint has been carried enthusiastically into digital forms, in works such as Nick Montfort and William Gillespie's *2002: A Palindrome Story*, a narrative palindrome 2002 words in length written with the assistance of a computer program.

For a discussion of constraint and "machinic" composition techniques in modernist and postmodernist poetry see Brian McHale's "Poetry as Prosthesis" (2000); see also the "writing under constraint" thread in the *electronic book review* (www.electronicbookreview.com). This section of the journal was introduced in the winter of 1999/2000 and employs a constraint of its own in restricting all essays in the millennial collection to between 1999 and 2000 words.

4. All citations of *The Unknown* are abbreviated, assumed to follow the domain name "www.unknownhypertext.com" unless otherwise indicated. Note the suffixes "html" and "htm" are also included as they differ throughout. Linked words or phrases in citations appear underlined.

5. See, e.g., Miller (1998); for a riposte see Swiss (1998–99).

6. The press kit is available at www.spinelessbooks.com/unknown/presskit/index.html (accessed Dec. 12, 2006).

7. By opting to include *The Unknown* in a book on digital literature, it would appear that I, too, have decided to take the work seriously. But rather than attempt the requisite clarification of what exactly constitutes literary "seriousness," the intention is that this chapter as a whole will both justify and qualify the work's inclusion. To put it another way, in terms of both (1) a theoretical model of digital narrative and (2) the broader community of digital discourse, it is necessary to put *The Unknown* in its place.

8. The "Anthology" link, however, which appears under the navigational buttons on each node, offers the reader an opportunity to purchase the 240 printed pages of *The Unknown: An Anthology* for $14.

9. A system whose components produce something with an organization and structure other than itself is by contrast not autopoietic but *allopoietic* (such as an automobile factory and most other industrial processes, but also biological reproduction, given that offspring are materially distinct from their parents).

10. The equation of *narrative* to a *system* is common in narratology. Bal (1990, 737), for example, assumes that "narrative is a system, but it is not ahistorical, collective but not unchangeable, regulated by abstract rules but not uninformed by concrete uses and adaptations of those rules." Since narrative, by narratological definition, must involve a narrator and narratee, it is possible to suggest that the social system to which Clarke alludes is assumed and implied. It is also possible to argue that narratology embraces the systematic theoretical study of narrative and narrativity even though it lacks the terminological precision of the systems theoretical discourse with which it overlaps.

11. The poem itself does little to justify the constraint (Ginsberg's rambling "Footnote" is fewer than three hundred words by contrast), unless one grants an equivalency to the images juxtaposed in the opening two lines, which move from the self-evident to the scatological: "unknown just wrote a poem and / unknown just took a dump" ("1000words.htm").

12. Despite some distinctively definitive attempts to complete their work, including an epilogical scene in which "The Unknown all died, of course, in the end" ("theend.htm"), the text still continues to grow. If one can trust the planned "Live Readings" listed in the Green Line, there looks to be an Australian tour in the works for 2009.

13. In fact, the decision to color-code the "lines" of the text can be said to mimic the decision by the Chicago Transit Authority, in 1993, to change the branch and ter-

minal names from those of the historical neighborhoods to a simple color-coded system. With an estimated five hundred thousand passengers on a given weekday, the change was intended to make navigation easier for new users.

14. Such debates must consider not only the qualities of the computer medium but also specific applications that allow for "second-order" programming in choreographing nodal progression, such as the guard fields in Storyspace or JavaScript techniques for HTML. Both contribute to a working definition of the "network environment." Rettberg (2003, 76) discusses the "conscious rejection" of using "rounded" characters in the hypertext novel: "Characterization in *The Unknown* is disingenuous to the extent that the novel's characters are often used as blunt instruments to explore styles of writing."

15. IRC is widely considered the most important "ancestor" of the related applications collectively known as instant messaging, offered by several organizations, including America Online (AOL), Microsoft's MSN, and Yahoo! The program allows users to send messages to one another in "real time." It differs from an email exchange since its users log in and "converse" in the same window without exiting the program. Correspondence scrolls from top to bottom, resembling a textual transcript of a phone conversation more than a typical—still somewhat epistolary—email exchange.

16. All citations of *water writes always in *plural* are abbreviated, assumed to follow the domain name "http://ensemble.va.com.au/water/" unless otherwise indicated. Linked words or phrases in citations appear underlined.

17. Judging by gamma's textual self-description, in which he "gently takes linda in *his* arms," gamma indeed appears to be male.

18. This is effectively the ethos Barth describes in his "Literature of Exhaustion" (1967).

19. The quote from Roland Barthes' *A Lover's Discourse: Fragments* is cited in "boredom.html."

20. The belief in the *potential* of a contemplative form of electronic fiction informed much of Michael Joyce's creative output in the field. In turn, what he sees as both an individual and collective failure to achieve it also influenced his decision to abandon the field in 2002.

21. In the embodied live readings of *The Unknown* the audience was asked to call out links, which would interrupt the performance so that it could restart with another path, and usually with another member of the Unknown reading. Rettberg (2002) discusses how the reactions to the live readings shaped his understanding of link poetics in general: "The link is likely pay off for the reader who favors the radical speed and dramatic shifts of hypertext, who focuses on the poetic moment of linkage, but it is however also likely to frustrate the more traditional, and in some ways more patient reader, who takes pleasure in the 'tyranny of the author,' and in reading as a contemplative act."

He also footnotes his statement: "Through analysis of log files and through correspondence with some of the most devoted fans of *The Unknown*, we've learned that while most of our readership is of the impatient variety that flings rapidly from scene to scene, rarely finishing an entire scene, those 'repeat visitors' who read the work in more depth tend to slow down, to choose links after reading entire scenes, as their reading of the work progresses." Rettberg thus draws an implicit but rather intuitive link between *repetition* and *patience*, which invariably requires some measure of waiting.

22. To hear *Fur Elise* the reader must have a Shockwave plug-in, which is an additional software component that enables Web browsers to play audio content. Ironically, if unwittingly on the part of the authors, readers who do not have the plug-in installed are subjected to a pop-up window that repeatedly alerts readers to the "Error" in failing to locate the application.

23. "The Vatican yesterday depicted what it claimed were women's characteristic traits: 'Listening, welcoming, humility, faithfulness, praise and waiting'" (Hooper and Revill 2004).

24. Landow (1997) examines the conception of Guyer's *Quibbling* (1993) as a "feminist rhizome narrative" (205) and the broader claim that hypertext "embodies some essential form of women's writing" (207).

25. See Joyce (1996) and Yaszek (1995) for a concise discussion of the development of postfeminist rhetoric and practice.

26. As N. Katherine Hayles (1999, xi) points out, though often overlooked by history, the question of gendered writing was in fact one focus of the famous "imitation game" of the Turing Test—the other being one's ability (or not), based on typed responses to questions, to tell the difference between the human and the machine respondent.

27. Irigaray (1985) charges that the difficulty of formulating an adequate scientific theory of turbulence and fluid mechanics arises not simply from the fact that turbulence requires a mathematically challenging nonlinear physics but from the fact that such physics has been undertaken traditionally by men, who have exhibited their bias toward a study of solid or solidified forms.

28. Carroli and Wilson also collaborate to produce another network fiction called *cipher* (1999); see http://ensemble.va.com.au/cipher/ (accessed March 2006).

29. The title of Carroli and Wilson's text is displayed incorrectly as *water always writes in *plural* (reversing *writes* and *always*) on some of the graphical pages that introduce the work. Carroli confirms that "the Duchamp reference is the correct one" (email correspondence, Aug. 4, 2004).

30. Text of "*The*" (1915), by Marcel Duchamp:

If you come into * linen, your time is thirsty because * ink saw some wood intelligent enough to get giddiness from a sister. However, even it should be smilable to shut * hair whose * water writes always in * plural, they have avoided * frequency, meaning mother in law; * powder will take a chance; and * road could try. But after somebody brought any multiplication as soon as * stamp was out, a great many cords refused to go through. Around * wire's people, who will be able to sweeten * rug, that is to say, why must every patents look for a wife? Pushing four dangers near * listening-place, * vacation had not dug absolutely nor this likeness has eaten. (Quoted in Octavio Paz, *Marcel Duchamp: Appearance Stripped Bare* [New York: Viking, 1978], 91)

31. See, e.g., Schwarz 1969, 584.

32. The allusion to Duchamp elicits other parallels. Just as hypertextual narratives place added demands on readers, Duchamp's poetics were driven by a desire to place great emphasis on the spectator. Furthermore, Duchamp's masterwork, *Large Glass* (also called *The Bride Stripped Bare by Her Bachelors, Even*) is a mixed media sculpture that reflects his attempt to portray what he called the "4th dimension," recalling many of the popular descriptions of hypertextual structure, including the definition offered by the Unknown authors: "Hypertext, to put it clearly, is a mapping of a text onto a four-dimensional 'space'" ("hypertext.htm").

Chapter 6

1. As the title page indicates, the work is "programmed and crafted by the author, Judd Morrissey" and the "mechanics of reconfiguration [are] designed in collaboration with Lori Talley."

2. I use *rollover* rather than the alternative *mouse-over* in order to focus more on what occurs on the screen and less on the hardware that enables it.

3. As Joseph Tabbi writes, "The visual artist Daniel Wenk and I came up with ["electropoetics"] when we were putting together the concrete poems that illustrate the Critical Ecologies and Electropoetics threads of *ebr*. It's possible too that Joel Felix, who guest edited the initial batch of Electropoetics essays, had something to do with the term" (email correspondence, Sep. 8, 2004).

4. As Tabbi (2003) notes, with regard to "nonlinearity" on a diegetic level, "the most we can say is that the literal nonlinearities in hypertext stimulated literary theorists to rediscover nonlinearity as the rule, rather than the exception, in print narratives."

5. Berressem (2002, 31) writes, "The idea of folding has been seminal in much of recent theory, for instance in the work of Jacques Derrida or Jean-François Lyotard. The most elaborate theory of folding, however, is provided by Deleuze in his book *The Fold: Leibniz and the Baroque* . . . in which he develops, on the basis of a reading of the works of G. W. Leibniz, a philosophy in which the main figure of thought is that of folding."

6. *Unilateral* is used here, as in Berressem's critique, to connote a continuous one-sidedness.

7. Berressem is invested in the material folding of digital text, and, for the same reason, his textual topology comes into conflict with the notion of moving through a text, whether that is a function of the text's spatial structure or the represented spatial topography of a fictional storyworld. In this regard Berressem's emphasis on the

movement *of* "digitaltext" departs from the conceptualization of network space put forth by Joyce, Hayles, and in this study in general (see "Movement beyond Mapping" in chap. 2).

As an abstract understanding of text-topological structure Berressem's conception is on the whole instructive, but I would argue that it remains inadequate to the experience of reading network *fiction*, which relies on deeply ingrained rhetorics of *embodied* movement. An exception to the instructiveness of his critique, furthermore, arises when he takes issue with popular descriptions of the Internet: "The reader/user 'enters' the information superhighway and is *literally* able to move around and to travel on it" (2002, 46; my emphasis). Clearly, Berressem does not mean *literally* literally, but the conclusion he draws later on is nonetheless problematic: "If one takes a closer look at how the internet works, however, the picture is quite a different one: the only thing that moves on the internet is data" (47). True, "there are no fixed places in cyberspace" (47), but with regard to *reading,* his comments do not establish a need to arrest (or elide) the *notional movement* of the embodied reader.

8. The movement from static to dynamic, however, does not rest on a strict binary of a print versus digital page. *Static* and *dynamic* can apply not only to a text's material substrate but also to its function in a broader network of discourse. The discourse network itself is dynamic and changeable, which allows for the continual processing and reprocessing of texts. Paradoxically, the text itself acquires stability through its processing—that is, stability becomes a function of usability and circulation rather than a strictly material durability. In this sense any text live in the network is in fact more stable than a hermetically sealed book in an environmentally controlled vault.

9. Note that since the work is composed in Flash, there are no Web addresses (or URLs—Uniform Resource Locators) for the individual pages; once the work is loaded online, it is available in its entirety and the network connection is no longer necessary.

10. Narratologists also use *incipit* generically to refer to the opening passage of a text.

11. The half parenthesis following "as though" here is closed in the transition to the following page: "(always the one who leaves always I have to vanish except for once he left for England as though)" (275). Significantly, the completed phrase is easily attributed to Eva, referring to her own "disappearing," but the interjection still remains nested in what appears to be a third person speaking analytically of their relationship.

12. As Morrissey notes, a text such as *The Jew's Daughter* does not always lend itself to *rereading* per se: "When the new text enters into one area on the page, it is assimilated visually and syntactically, leaving the rest of the page undisturbed. The effect upon the reader is a conflation of seeing and reading, and the engagement of memory and peripheral vision as one learns to adjust to the activity of the text, to register the remnants of past pages without always re-reading them" (Morrissey, Talley, and Hamel 2004, 2).

13. Elsewhere, in what appears to be a different encounter, "Her voice broke and

a tear moved along the curve of a long black eyelash. But she was already drawing me back to her. Her words were returning me to her. I told her that I had left her for a while but that I was coming back around" (162). Clearly, and especially in light of what may have been an extended stay in England, she harbors the same fear of her partner disappearing.

14. *The Unknown* does employ algorithmically generated material in limited ways. For a time one of the work's home pages would display an image of the Unknown authors selected at random while an audio track (the Unknown anthem?) played in its entirety.

15. There is still some degree of confusion with regard to the constitution of the text as it exists on the Web, which I discuss in the appendix.

16. The page on which the lyric appears is not numbered, as it falls outside the initial 351 pages (see the appendix).

17. Starting in 1882, Francis J. Child compiled what would come to represent a canon of folk lyrics, a five-volume work called *The English and Scottish Popular Ballads* (the project culminated in 1898, two years after his own death). In it Child collected eighteen versions of "Sir Hugh, or the Jew's Daughter." In 1904 his daughter, Helen Child Sargent, along with George L. Kittredge, followed with another edition of ballads based on the initial Child volumes. This work contained twenty-one versions of "Sir Hugh, or the Jew's Daughter," which is number 155 of what are now popularly known as the Child Ballads. See Child (1888, 243–54); and Sargent and Kittredge (1904, 368–71).

18. I have modernized the obsolete orthography of the manuscript.

19. See Ben-Merre (1981) for an outline of this debate.

20. *Oxford Study Bible* (1992), ed. Jack M. Suggs, Katharine D. Sakenfeld, and James R. Mueller (New York: Oxford University Press).

21. Ellman's biography uses "J" as shorthand for James Joyce in the index.

22. The phrase belongs to Leopold Bloom, one of his many passing thoughts as he attends the funeral of Paddy Dignam in the Hades episode of *Ulysses* (77). Brook Thomas (1986) borrows the same phrase for the title of his book, whose thesis is essentially that Joyce's text self-consciously encourages continual rereading.

23. The "decollation" is the Church's term for the beheading of John the Baptist.

Concluding Movements

1. Hazel Smith writes and performs the text, and Roger Dean does the sound. The work was released on CD by Soma Publications in Sydney (2001) and is also published online, with both text and audio available, at *Jacket Magazine*, no. 7, http://jacketmagazine.com/07/smith-hazel.html (accessed March 2006).

2. Shklovsky (1965, 4) defines art as "a way of experiencing the artfulness of an object. . . . [It] develops a variety of techniques to impede perception or, at least, to call attention to themselves."

References

Aarseth, Espen. 1994. "Nonlinearity and Literary Theory." In Landow 1994b, 51–86.
———. 1997. *Cybertext: Perspectives on Ergodic Literature.* Baltimore: Johns Hopkins University Press.
Achter, Jeffrey. 1992. "Topoliteracy or (Mis)uses of Topology in Literary Criticism and Theory." www.scholars.nus.edu.sg/cpace/science/topolit/Topology.html (accessed Dec. 9, 2006).
Amerika, Mark. 1998. "Triptych: Hypertext, Surfiction, Storyworlds." Amerika Online. www.altx.com/amerika.online/amerika.online.5.1.html (accessed Dec. 30, 2006).
———. 2000. "Designwriting: A Post-Literary Reading Experience." Amerika Online. www.altx.com/amerika.online/amerika.online.5.6.html (accessed Dec. 30, 2006).
———. n.d. *HyperTextual Consciousness.* www.grammatron.com/htc1.0/htc.html (accessed Dec. 30, 2006).
ANAT [Australian Network for Art and Technology]. 1998. "A Virtual Writers-in-Residence Project." www.anat.org.au/pages/archived/1998/waterwrites/waterwrites.html (accessed Dec. 13, 2006).
Bal, Mieke. 1981. "Notes on Narrative Embedding." *Poetics Today* 2, no. 2: 41–59.
———. 1990. "The Point of Narratology." *Poetics Today* 11, no. 4: 728–53.
Bardini, Thierry. 1997. "Bridging the Gulfs: From Hypertext to Cyberspace." *Journal of Computer-Mediated Communication* 3, no. 2 (Sep.): http://jcmc.indiana.edu/vol3/issue2/bardini.html (accessed Dec. 10, 2006).
Barth, John. 1967/1982. "The Literature of Exhaustion." Special bound edition. Northridge, CA: Lord John Press.
———. 1982. "The Literature of Replenishment." Special bound edition. Northridge, CA: Lord John Press.
———. 1984. "Tales within Tales within Tales." In *The Friday Book,* 218–38. Baltimore: Johns Hopkins University Press.
———. 1988. *Lost in the Funhouse.* New York: Anchor.

———. 1996. "The State of the Art." *Wilson Quarterly* 20, no. 2 (spring): 36–46.

———. 1997. "Click." *Atlantic Monthly*, Dec., 81–96. www.tnellen.com/cybereng/ barth.htm (accessed Dec. 30, 2006).

Barthelme, Donald. 1968. *City Life.* New York: Farrar, Straus and Giroux.

Barthes, Roland. 1974. *S/Z: An Essay.* Trans. Richard Miller. New York: Hill and Wang.

———. 1980. *The Pleasure of the Text.* Trans. Richard Miller. New York: Noonday Press.

Baudrillard, Jean. 1988. "Simulacra and Simulations." In *Selected Writings,* ed. Mark Poster, 166–84. Stanford, CA: Stanford University Press.

———. 1994. *Simulacra and Simulation.* Trans. Sheila Glaser. Ann Arbor: University of Michigan Press.

———. 1996. *The Perfect Crime.* Trans. Chris Turner. London: Verso.

Bedford, Martyn, and Andy Campbell. 2000. *The Virtual Disappearance of Miriam.* www.dreamingmethods.com/miriam/ (accessed Dec. 30, 2006).

Benjamin, Walter. 1968. "The Work of Art in the Age of Mechanical Reproduction." In *Illuminations,* ed. Hanna Arendt, trans. H. Zohn, 217–52. New York: Schocken.

———. 1999. *Walter Benjamin: Selected Writings.* Ed. Michael W. Jennings. Cambridge, MA: Belknap Press.

Ben-Merre, Diana Arbin. 1981. "Bloom and Milly: A Portrait of the Father and the 'Jew's Daughter.'" *James Joyce Quarterly* 18, no. 4: 439–44.

Bernstein, Charles. 1992. "Artifice of Absorption." In *A Poetics,* 9–89. Cambridge, MA: Harvard University Press.

Bernstein, Mark. 1991. "The Navigation Problem Reconsidered." In *Hypertext/ Hypermedia Handbook,* ed. Emily Berk and Joseph Devlin, 285–97. New York: McGraw-Hill.

———. 1997. "Chasing Our Tails." www.eastgate.com/tails/cycles.html (accessed Dec. 30, 2006).

———. 1998a. "Hypertext Gardens." www.eastgate.com/garden/ (accessed Dec. 30, 2006).

———. 1998b. "Patterns of Hypertext." In *Proceedings of ACM Hypertext '98*, Pittsburgh, PA, 21–29. www.eastgate.com/patterns/Patterns.html (accessed Dec. 30, 2006).

———. 1998c. "Recurrence Is Not a Vice." *HypertextNow.* www.eastgate.com/ HypertextNow/archives/Cycles.html (accessed Dec. 30, 2006).

———. 1999. "Structural Patterns and Hypertext Rhetoric." *ACM Computing Surveys* 31, no. 4 (Dec.): www.cs.brown.edu/memex/ACM_HypertextTestbed/ papers/45.html (accessed Dec. 19, 2006).

———. 2003. "A Romantic View of Weblogs." *HypertextNow.* www.eastgate.com/ HypertextNow/archives/WeblogHandbook.html (accessed Dec. 30, 2006).

Bernstein, Mark, Peter J. Brown, Mark Frisse, Robert Glushko, George Landow, and Polle Zellweger. 1991. "Structure, Navigation, and Hypertext: The Status of the Navigation-Problem." In *Proceedings of the Third Annual ACM Conference on*

Hypertext, San Antonio, TX, 363–66. New York: ACM Press. http://delivery.acm. org/10.1145/130000/123011/p363-bernstein.pdf?key1=123011&key2=1331675611&col l=&dl=ACM&CFID=15151515&CFTOKEN=6184618.

Bernstein, Mark, and Diane Greco. 2004. "Card Shark and Thespis." *electronic book review* (Nov. 6): www.electronicbookreview.com/thread/firstperson/hyperbaton (accessed Dec. 30, 2006).

Bernstein, Mark, Michael Joyce, and David Levine. 1992. "Contours of Constructive Hypertext." In *Proceedings of the 1992 European Conference on Hypertext*, Milan, 161–70. New York: ACM Press.

Berressem, Hanjo. 2001. "Poeto:pologies: Folded Space, Traversal Machines and the Poetics of 'Emergent Text.'" www.poes1s.net/poetics/symposion2001/ a_berressem.html (accessed Dec. 13, 2006).

———. 2002. "Data Dance." In *Chaos/Control: Complexity*, ed. Philipp Hofmann, 7–42. Hamburg: Lit Verlag.

Birkerts, Sven. 1994. *The Gutenberg Elegies: The Fate of Reading in an Electronic Age*. New York: Fawcett Columbine.

Bly, Bill. 1997. *We Descend*. Watertown, MA: Eastgate Systems.

Bolter, Jay David. 1991. *Writing Space: The Computer, Hypertext, and the History of Writing*. Hillsdale, NJ: Lawrence Erlbaum.

Bolter, Jay David, and Richard Grusin. 2000. *Remediation: Understanding New Media*. Cambridge, MA: MIT Press.

Borges, Jorge Luis. 1964. "The Library of Babel." In *Labyrinths: Selected Stories and Other Writings*. Victoria, BC: Penguin.

———. 1993. "Pierre Menard, Author of the *Quixote*," "An Examination of the Work of Herbert Quain," and "The Garden of Forking Paths." In *Ficciones*. London: Everyman's Library.

Braman, Sandra. 1994. "The Autopoietic State: Communication and Democratic Potential in the Net." *Journal of the American Society for Information Science* 45, no. 6: 358–68.

Brooks, Peter. 1984. *Reading for the Plot*. New York: Knopf.

Buchanan, Ian. 1997. "Deleuze and Pop Music." *American Humanities Review* (Aug.–Oct. 1997): www.lib.latrobe.edu.au/AHR/archive/Issue-August-1997/ buchanan.html (accessed Dec. 30, 2006).

———. 2000. *Deleuzism: A Metacommentary*. Durham, NC: Duke University Press.

Burbules, Nicholas. 1997. "Rhetorics of the Web: Hyperreading and Critical Literacy." In *Page to Screen: Taking Literacy into the Electronic Era*, ed. Ilana Snyder, 102–22. New South Wales: Allen and Unwin. http://faculty.ed.uiuc.edu/ burbules/papers/rhetorics.html (accessed Dec. 30, 2006).

Bush, H. W. 1991. "Radio Address to United States Armed Forces Stationed in the Persian Gulf Region." March 2: http://bushlibrary.tamu.edu/research/ papers/1991/91030200.html (accessed Dec. 20, 2006).

Bush, Vannevar. 1945/2001. "As We May Think." In Trend 2001, 9–13. Page references are to the 2001 reprint.

Calvino, Italo. 1981. *If on a Winter's Night a Traveler.* Trans. William Weaver. San Diego: Harcourt Brace Jovanovich.

———. 1987. *The Literature Machine.* Trans. Patrick Creagh. London: Secker and Warburg.

Carpenter, Scott. 2000. *Reading Lessons: An Introduction to Theory.* Upper Saddle River, NJ: Prentice-Hall.

Carroli, Linda. 1998. "A Couple of Chicks Shooting The Breeze." *Flytrap.* http://home.pacific.net.au/~lcarroli/hypertext/breeze.htm (accessed Dec. 30, 2006).

———. 2001. "Mindful of Multiplicity." *electronic book review* (Sep. 1): www.electronicbookreview.com/thread/criticalecologies/mindful (accessed Dec. 30, 2006).

Carroli, Linda, and Josephine Wilson. 1998. **water writes always in *plural.* http://ensemble.va.com.au/water/ (accessed Dec. 30, 2006).

Cayley, John. 2004. "Literal Art." *electronic book review* (Nov. 2004): www.electronicbookreview.com/thread/firstperson/programmatology (accessed Dec. 30, 2006).

———. 2005. Riposte to Stuart Moulthrop's "From Work to Play." *electronic book review* (May 2005): www.electronicbookreview.com/thread/firstperson/manovichian (accessed Dec. 30, 2006).

Charney, Davida. 1994. "The Impact of Hypertext on Processes of Reading and Writing." In *Literacy and Computers,* ed. Susan J. Hilligoss and Cynthia L. Selfe, 238–63. New York: Modern Language Association.

Chartier, Roger. 1995. *Forms and Meanings: Texts, Performances, and Audiences from Codex to Computer.* Philadelphia: University of Pennsylvania Press.

Child, Francis J., ed. 1888. *The English and Scottish Popular Ballads.* Part 5. Boston: Houghton, Mifflin.

Cixous, Hélène. 1986. "Sorties." In *The Newly Born Woman,* by Hélène Cixous and Catherine Clément, trans. Betsy Wing, 63–129. Minneapolis: University of Minnesota Press.

Clarke, Bruce. 2003. "A System of Systems Distinctions." Paper presented for the panel "Narrative, Media, Systems" at the 2003 meeting of the Society for Literature and Science, Austin, TX.

Conklin, Jeff. 1987. "Hypertext: An Introduction and Survey." *IEEE Computer* 20, no. 9 (Sep. 1987): 17–41.

Connor, Steven. 1988. *Samuel Beckett: Repetition, Theory, and Text.* Oxford: Basil Blackwell.

Coover, Robert. 1992. "The End of Books." *New York Times Book Review.* June 21.

———. 1993. "Hyperfiction: Novels for the Computer." *New York Times Book Review.* Aug. 29.

———. 1998. trAce/Alt-X Hypertext Competition 1998. www.spinelessbooks.com/unknown/presskit/trace.html (accessed Dec. 12, 2006).

———. 1999. "Literary Hypertext: The Passing of the Golden Age." Keynote address,

"Digital Arts and Culture" conference, Atlanta, GA, Oct. 29. http://nickm.com/vox/golden_age.html (accessed Dec. 30, 2006).

Corin, Lucy. 2004. "Form and Emotion." *electronic book review* (Oct. 2004): www.electronicbookreview.com/thread/criticalecologies/predictable (accessed Dec. 30, 2006).

Cramer, Florian. 2001. "On Literature and Systems Theory." http://cramer.plaintext.cc:70/all/literature_and_systems_theory/literature_and system_theory.pdf (accessed Dec. 30, 2006).

Cubitt, Sean. 2001. "As." *digitalsouls.com*. www.digitalsouls.com/2001/Sean_Cubitt_AS.html (accessed Dec. 30, 2006).

David, Hans T., and Arthur Mendel, eds. 1966. *The Bach Reader: A Life of Johann Sebastian Bach in Letters and Documents.* New York: Norton.

de Certeau, Michel. 1984. "Walking in the City." In *The Practice of Everyday Life.* Trans. Steven F. Rendall. Berkeley: University of California Press.

Deleuze, Gilles. 1994. *Difference and Repetition.* Trans. Paul Patton. New York: Columbia University Press. Originally published as *Différence et répétition* (Paris: Presses universitaires de France, 1968).

Deleuze, Gilles, and Félix Guattari. 1987. *A Thousand Plateaus.* Trans. Brian Massumi. Minneapolis: University of Minnesota Press.

Derrida, Jacques. 1978. *Writing and Difference.* Trans. Alan Bass. London: Routledge and Kegan Paul. Originally published as *L'écriture et la différence* (Paris: Editions du Seuil, 1967).

Dibbell, Julian. 2001. "A Rape in Cyberspace; or How an Evil Clown, a Haitian Trickster Spirit, Two Wizards, and a Cast of Dozens Turned a Database into a Society." In Trend 2001, 199–213.

Dillon, Brian. 2004. "Eternal Return: On the Philosophy of Repetition." Frieze.com. www.frieze.com/feature_single.asp?f=925 (accessed Dec. 30, 2006).

Don, Abbe. 1991. "Narrative and the Interface." In Laurel 1991, 383–92.

Douglas, J. Yellowlees. 1994. "How Do I Stop This Thing? Closure and Indeterminacy in Interactive Narratives." In Landow 1994b, 159–88.

———. 2001. *The End of Books—Or Books without End.* Ann Arbor: University of Michigan Press.

Dunn, John. 1994. "Hyperfiction: Moulthrop's Computer Novel Weaves a Web of Alternative Endings." *Georgia Tech Alumni Magazine Online* (summer): http://gtalumni.org/news/magazine/sum94/fiction.html (accessed Dec. 30, 2006).

Eco, Umberto. 1989. *The Open Work.* Trans. Anna Cancogni. Cambridge, MA: Harvard University Press.

———. 1993. *Misreadings.* Trans. William Weaver. San Diego: Harcourt, Brace. Originally published as *Diario Minimo* (Milan: Bompiani, 1963).

———. 1996. Afterword. In *The Future of the Book,* ed. Geoffrey Nunberg, 295–306. Berkeley: University of California Press.

Edelman, Gerald. 2004a. *Wider Than the Sky: The Phenomenal Gift of Consciousness.* New Haven, CT: Yale University Press.

———. 2004b. "Neural Darwinism." *New Perspectives Quarterly* 21, no. 3: www.digitalnpq.org/archive/2004_summer/edelman.html (accessed Dec. 30, 2006).

Enns, Anthony. 2003. "A Media Theory of Consciousness." *Iowa Review Web* (April 1): www.uiowa.edu/~iareview/tirweb/feature/tabbi/review.html (accessed Dec. 15, 2006).

Ellman, Richard. 1982. *James Joyce.* London: Oxford University Press.

Eskelinen, Markku. 1998. "Omission Impossible: The Ergodics of Time." Paper presented at the Digital Arts and Culture conference, Bergen, Norway, Nov. 26–28. http://cmc.uib.no/dac98/papers/eskelinen.html (accessed Dec. 19, 2006).

———. 2001. "Cybertext Theory: What an English Professor Should Know before Trying." *electronic book review* (Feb. 2001): www.electronicbookreview.com/thread/electropoetics/notmetaphor (accessed Dec. 15, 2006).

Federman, Raymond. 1975. *Surfiction.* Chicago: Swallow Press.

Felluga, Dino. 2004. "Modules on Brooks: On Plotting." Introductory Guide to Critical Theory. www.purdue.edu/guidetotheory/narratology/modules/brooksplot.html (accessed Dec. 30, 2006).

Fifield, George. 2002. *Web Racket: Contemporary Interactive Web Art.* June 8–Sep. 1, 2002. www.decordova.org/decordova/exhibit/2002/webracket/webracket.html (accessed Dec. 13, 2006).

Fludernik, Monika. 2003. "Chronology, Time, Tense, and Experientiality in Narrative." *Language and Literature* 12, no. 2: 117–34.

Foucault, Michel. 1972. *The Archaeology of Knowledge.* London: Tavistock.

Frank, Joseph. 1945. "Spatial Form in Modern Literature." *Sewanee Review* 53: 221–40.

Frasca, Gonzalo. 2002. "Ludology Meets Narratology: Similitude and Differences between (Video)Games and Narrative." www.ludology.org (accessed Dec. 30, 2006). Originally published in Finnish in *Parnasso* 3 (1999).

Freud, Sigmund. 1920/1987. "Beyond the Pleasure Principle." In *On Metapsychology: The Theory of Psychoanalysis.* Trans. James Strachey. New York: Penguin. Page references are to the 1987 edition.

Friedrich, Otto. 1989. *Glenn Gould: His Life and Variations.* Toronto: Lester and Orpen Dennys.

Gaggi, Silvio. 1997. *From Text to Hypertext: Decentering the Subject in Fiction, Film, the Visual Arts, and Electronic Media.* Philadelphia: University of Pennsylvania Press.

Genette, Gérard. 1972. *Narrative Discourse.* Trans. Jane E. Lewin. Oxford: Blackwell.

———. 1983. *Narrative Discourse Revisited.* Trans. Jane E. Lewin. Ithaca, NY: Cornell University Press.

———. 1997. *Paratexts: Thresholds of Interpretation.* Trans. Jane E. Lewin. Cambridge, UK: Cambridge University Press.

Gifford, Don. 1988. *Ulysses Annotated.* Berkeley: University of California Press.

Gillespie, William, Frank Marquardt, Scott Rettberg, and Dirk Stratton. 1998–2001. *The Unknown.* www.unknownhypertext.com (accessed Dec. 30, 2006).

Girard, François, dir. 1993. *Thirty-two Short Films about Glenn Gould.* Samuel Goldwyn.

Gitlin, Todd. 1989. "Postmodernism: Roots and Politics." *Dissent* (winter 1989): 100–108.

Glantz, Aaron. 2004. "Victory Rises above a Mass Grave." Inter Press News Service (IPS). May 3: http://ipsnews.net/interna.asp?idnews=23567 (accessed Dec. 11, 2006).

Glazier, Loss Pequeño. 1996. "Our Words Were the Form We Entered." *Witz: A Journal of Contemporary Poetics* 4, no. 2: http://wings.buffalo.edu/epc/ezines/witz/4-2.html (accessed Dec. 30, 2006).

Greco, Diane. 1996. "Hypertext with Consequences: Recovering a Politics of Hypertext." In *Proceedings of the Seventh ACM Conference on Hypertext,* Washington, DC, March 16–20, 85–92. New York: ACM Press. http://scholars.nus.edu.sg/cpace//ht/greco1.html (accessed Dec. 8, 2006).

Grusin, Richard. 1994. "What Is an Electronic Author? Theory and the Technological Fallacy." *Configurations* 3: 469–83.

Guyer, Carolyn. 1993. *Quibbling.* Watertown, MA: Eastgate Systems.

Haraway, Donna. 1991. "A Cyborg Manifesto: Science, Technology, and Socialist-Feminism in the Late Twentieth Century." In *Simians, Cyborgs, and Women: The Reinvention of Nature,* 149–81. New York: Routledge.

Hargadon, Andrew, and Douglas, J. Yellowlees. 2004. "The Pleasures of Immersion and Interaction." *electronic book review* (Nov. 2004): www.electronicbookreview.com/thread/firstperson/avecplaisir (accessed Dec. 30, 2006).

Harpold, Terry. 2003. "The Contingencies of the Hypertext Link." In *The New Media Reader,* ed. Noah Wardrip-Fruin and Nick Montfort, 126–38. Cambridge, MA: MIT Press.

Hayles, N. Katherine. 1993. "Virtual Bodies and Flickering Signifiers." www.english.ucla.edu/faculty/hayles/Flick.html (accessed Dec. 30, 2006).

———. 1999a. "Artificial Life and Literary Culture." In *Cyberspace Textuality,* ed. Marie-Laure Ryan, 205–23. Bloomington: Indiana University Press.

———. 1999b. *How We Became Posthuman: Virtual Bodies in Cybernetics, Literature, and Informatics.* Chicago: University of Chicago Press.

———. 2000. "Open-Work: Dining at the Interstices." *Riding the Meridian,* www.heelstone.com/meridian/templates/Dinner/hayles.htm (accessed Dec. 30, 2006).

———. 2001. "What Cybertext Theory Can't Do." *electronic book review* (Feb. 15): www.electronicbookreview.com/thread/electropoetics/ecumenical (accessed Dec. 15, 2006).

———. 2002a. *Writing Machines.* Cambridge, MA: MIT Press.

———. 2002b. " 'Materiality Has Always Been in Play': An Interview with N. Katherine Hayles." By Lisa Gitelman. *Iowa Review Web* (July 1):

www.uiowa.edu/~iareview/tirweb/feature/hayles/interview.htm (accessed Dec. 11, 2006).

Heim, Michael. 1993. *The Metaphysics of Virtual Reality.* New York: Oxford University Press.

———. 1998. *Virtual Realism.* New York: Oxford University Press.

———. 2001. "The Erotic Ontology of Hyperspace." In Trend 2001, 70–86.

Herman, David. 2000. "Narratology as a Cognitive Science." *Image & Narrative* (Sep.): www.imageandnarrative.be/narratology/davidherman.htm (accessed Dec. 15, 2006).

Higgins, Kathleen M. 1988. "Reading *Zarathustra.*" In *Reading Nietzsche,* ed. Robert C. Solomon and Kathleen M. Higgins, 132–51. New York: Oxford University Press.

Hofstadter, Richard. 1979. *Gödel, Escher, Bach: An Eternal Golden Braid.* Hassocks: Harvester Press.

Hooper, John, and Jo Revill. 2004. "A woman's place is to wait and listen, says the Vatican." *Observer* (London), Aug. 1, www.guardian.co.uk/religion/Story/0,,1273858,00.html (accessed Dec. 13, 2006).

Ikonen, Teemu. 2003. "Moving Text in Avant-Garde Poetry: Towards a Poetics of Textual Motion." *Dichtung-digital.* www.dichtung-digital.com/2003/issue/4/ikonen/index.htm (accessed Dec. 10, 2006).

Irigaray, L. 1985. "The 'Mechanics' of Fluids." In *This Sex Which Is Not One,* 106–18. Ithaca, NY: Cornell University Press.

Iser, Wolfgang. 1980. "The Reading Process: A Phenomenological Approach." In *Reader-Response Criticism: From Formalism to Post-Structuralism,* ed. Jane P. Tompkins, 50–69. Baltimore: Johns Hopkins University Press.

———. 1988. *Sterne: Tristram Shandy.* Cambridge, UK: Cambridge University Press.

Jackson, Shelley. 1995. *Patchwork Girl.* Watertown, MA: Eastgate Systems.

Jameson, Fredric. 1983. "Postmodernism and Consumer Society." In *The Anti-Aesthetic: Essays on Postmodern Culture,* ed. Hal Foster, 111–25. Port Townsend, WA: Bay Press.

———. 1993. "Postmodernism, or the Cultural Logic of Late Capitalism." *Postmodernism: A Reader,* ed. Thomas Docherty, 62–92. New York: Columbia University Press.

Johnson, Laurie. 2002. "Agency: Beyond Strange Cultural Loops." *M/C Journal* 5, no. 4: http://journal.media-culture.org.au/0208/agency.php (accessed Dec. 15, 2006).

Johnson-Eilola, Jhondan. 1991. "Trying to See the Garden: Interdisciplinary Perspectives on Hypertext Use in Composition Instruction." *Writing on Edge* 2, no. 2: 92–111.

Joyce, James. 1959. *Finnegans Wake.* New York: Viking.

———. 1986. *Ulysses.* New York: Vintage.

———. 1993. *A Portrait of the Artist as a Young Man.* New York: Penguin.

Joyce, Lisa. 1996. "Writing Postfeminism." *electronic book review* (Sep.):

www.electronicbookreview.com/thread/writingpostfeminism/postfeminism (accessed Dec. 30, 2006).

———. 2005. "Writing as a Woman: Annie Abrahams' e-writing." *electronic book review* (Jan.): www.electronicbookreview.com/thread/writingpostfeminism/womblike (accessed Dec. 30, 2006).

Joyce, Michael. 1990. *afternoon, a story.* Watertown, MA: Eastgate Systems.

———. 1995. *Of Two Minds: Hypertext Pedagogy and Poetics.* Ann Arbor: University of Michigan Press.

———. 1997. *Twilight, a Symphony.* Watertown, MA: Eastgate Systems.

———. 2000. *Othermindedness: The Emergence of Network Culture.* Ann Arbor: University of Michigan Press.

———. 2001. *Moral Tales and Meditations: Technological Parables and Refractions.* Albany: State University of New York Press.

Kaplan, Nancy, and Stuart Moulthrop. 1994. "Where No Mind Has Gone Before: Ontological Design for Virtual Spaces." *ECHT '94: European Conference on Hypertext Technology,* Edinburgh, Sep. 19–23. New York: ACM Press.

Kapor, Mitch, and John Perry Barlow. 1990. "Across the Electronic Frontier." Washington, DC: Electronic Frontier Foundation. www.eff.org/Misc/Publications/John_Perry_Barlow/HTML/eff.html (accessed Dec. 9, 2006).

Kawin, Bruce. 1972. *Telling It Again and Again: Repetition in Literature and Film.* Ithaca, NY: Cornell University Press.

Keller, Julia. 1999. "Hypertext Novel Offers Easily Accessible Exits." *Chicago Tribune,* Oct. 4: www.unknownhypertext.com/presskit/trib991004.html (accessed Dec. 12, 2006).

Kendall, Robert. 2001. "Hypertext: Foe to Print." Word Circuits. www.wordcircuits.com/comment/htlit_8.htm (accessed Dec. 30, 2006).

Kierkegaard, Søren. 1946a. *Either/Or: A Fragment of Life.* Vol. 1. Trans. David F. Swenson and Lillian Marvin Swenson. London: Oxford University Press.

———. 1946b. *Either/Or: A Fragment of Life.* Vol. 2. Trans. Walter Lowrie. London: Oxford University Press.

Kirschenbaum, Matthew. 2001. "Materiality and Matter and Stuff: What Electronic Texts Are Made Of." *electronic book review* (Oct. 1): www.electronicbookreview.com/thread/electropoetics/sited (accessed Dec. 30, 2006).

Klastrup, Lisbeth. 1997. "Hyperfiction in Practice: Walking in the Garden of Forced Paths." www.itu.dk/people/klastrup/dischap2.html (accessed Dec. 30, 2006).

Koskimaa, Raine. 1997. "Visual Restructuring of Hyperfiction Narratives." *electronic book review* 6 (winter): www.altx.com/ebr/ebr6/6koskimaa/6koski.htm (accessed Dec. 30, 2006).

———. 1998. "From Afternoon till Twilight." *electronic book review* 7 (summer): www.altx.com/ebr/reviews/rev7/r7koskimaa/west.htm (accessed Dec. 30, 2006).

———. 2000. *Digital Literature: From Text to Hypertext and Beyond.* www.cc.jyu.fi/~koskimaa/thesis/thesis.shtml (accessed Dec. 15, 2006).

Kwinter, Sanford. 1992. "Landscapes of Change: Boccioni's *Stati d'animo* as a General Theory of Models." *Assemblage* 19: 52–65.

Landow, George. 1994a. "What's a Critic to Do? Critical Theory in the Age of Hypertext." In Landow 1994b, 1–48.

———, ed. 1994b. *Hyper/Text/Theory*. Baltimore: Johns Hopkins University Press.

———, ed. 1995. *Writing at the Edge*. Watertown, MA: Eastgate Systems.

———. 1997. *Hypertext 2.0: The Convergence of Contemporary Critical Theory and Technology*. Baltimore: Johns Hopkins University Press.

———. 1999. "Hypertext as Collage Writing." In *Digital Dialectic: New Essays on New Media*, ed. Peter Lunenfeld, 150–70. Cambridge, MA: MIT Press.

Lanham, Richard. 1989. "The Electronic Word: Literary Study and the Digital Revolution." *New Literary History* 20: 265–90.

———. 1993. *The Electronic Word: Democracy, Technology, and the Arts*. Chicago: University of Chicago Press.

Laurel, Brenda, ed. 1991. *The Art of Human-Computer Interface Design*. Reading, MA: Addison-Wesley.

LeClair, Tom. 1987. *In the Loop: Don DeLillo and the Systems Novel*. Urbana: University of Illinois Press.

———. 1989. *The Art of Excess: Mastery in Contemporary American Fiction*. Urbana: University of Illinois Press.

———. 2000. "False Pretenses, Parasites, and Monsters." *electronic book review* (Dec.): www.electronicbookreview.com/thread/webarts/noisy (accessed Dec. 30, 2006).

Le Guin, Ursula. 2002. "Rhythmic Patterns in *The Lord of the Rings*." In *Meditations on Middle-earth*, ed. Karen Haber, 101–16. New York: Earthlight (Simon and Schuster). Excerpt available at www.lordotrings.com/books/meditations.asp (accessed Dec. 30, 2006).

Liestøl, Gunnar. 1994. "Wittgenstein, Genette, and the Reader's Narrative in Hypertext." In Landow 1994b, 87–120.

Lombreglia, Ralph. 1996a. "The End of the Story: Excerpts from a Recent E-mail Exchange with Michael Joyce." *Atlantic Online*, Nov., www.theatlantic.com/unbound/digicult/dc9611/joyce.htm (accessed April 2004 [subscription required]).

———. 1996b. "So Many Links, So Little Time." *Atlantic Online*, Nov., www.theatlantic.com/unbound/digicult/dc9611/dc9611.htm (accessed April 2004 [subscription required]).

Luhmann, Niklas. 2000. *Art as a Social System*. Stanford, CA: Stanford University Press.

Lynch, Kevin. 1960. *Image of the City*. Cambridge, MA: MIT Press.

Lyotard, Jean-François. 1984. *The Postmodern Condition: A Report on Knowledge*. Trans. Geoff Bennington and Brian Massumi. Minneapolis: University of Minnesota Press.

Manovich, Lev. 2001. *Language of New Media*. Cambridge, MA: MIT Press.

Marsh, William. 1997. "Paragram as Is Hypertext." *Witz: A Journal of Contemporary Poetics* 5, no. 1: http://wings.buffalo.edu/epc/ezines/witz/5-1.html (accessed Dec. 30, 2006).

Marshall, Catherine C., and Russell A. Rogers. 1992. "Two Years before the Mist: Experience with Aquanet." In *Proceedings of the 1992 European Conference on Hypertext,* Milan, 53–62. New York: ACM Press.

Marshall, Catherine C., and Frank M. Shipman. 1993. "Searching for the Missing Link: Discovering Implicit Structure in Spatial Hypertext." In *Proceedings of the Fifth ACM Conference on Hypertext,* Seattle, WA, 217–30. New York: ACM Press.

———. 1999. "Spatial Hypertext: An Alternative to Navigational and Semantic Links." *ACM Computing Surveys* 31, no. 4es (Dec.): 1–5.

Massumi, Brian. 2002. "Strange Horizon: Buildings, Biograms, and the Body Topologic." *Chaos/Control: Complexity,* ed. Philipp Hofmann, n.p. Hamburg: Lit Verlag.

Mazza, Cris. 2000. "Editing Postfeminist Fiction: Finding the Chic in Lit." *symploke* 8, no. 1–2: 101–12.

McDaid, John. 1992. *Uncle Buddy's Phantom Funhouse.* Watertown, MA: Eastgate Systems.

McGrath, Timothy. n.d. "Fact or Fiction? Historical Narratives in Borges." Modern World, www.themodernword.com/borges/borges_papers_mcgrath.html (accessed Dec. 30, 2006).

McHale, Brian. 1987. *Postmodernist Fiction.* New York: Methuen.

———. 2000. "Poetry as Prosthesis." *Poetics Today* 21, no. 1 (spring 2000): 1–32.

Miall, David. 2004. "Reading Hypertext: Theoretical Ambitions and Empirical Studies." http://computerphilologie.uni-muenchen.de/jg03/miall.html (accessed Dec. 30, 2006).

Miall, David, and Teresa Dobson. 2001. "Reading Hypertext and the Experience of Literature." *Journal of Digital Information* 2, no. 1: http://jodi.ecs.soton.ac.uk/Articles/v02/i01/Miall (accessed Dec. 12, 2006).

Miles, Adrian. 1998. "Hypertext Should." Department of Communication Studies HyperText Working Web. http://hypertext.rmit.edu.au/online_hypertext/hypertext_should.html (accessed Dec. 30, 2006).

———. 2002. "Hypertext Structure as the Event of Connection." *Journal of Digital Information* 2, no. 3. (March): http://jodi.tamu.edu/Articles/v02/i03/Miles (accessed Dec. 12, 2006).

———. 2004. "Adrian Miles Responds to Hypertexts and Interactives." *electronic book review* (Oct.): www.electronicbookreview.com/thread/firstperson/aeffect (accessed Dec. 30, 2006).

Miller, J. Hillis. 1982. *Fiction and Repetition: Seven English Novels.* Oxford: Basil Blackwell.

Miller, Laura. 1998. "www.claptrap.com." *New York Times Book Review.* March 15.

Mirapaul, Matthew. 2000. "Pushing Hypertext in New Directions." *CYBERTIMES:*

New York Times on the Web, July 27, www.nytimes.com/library/tech/00/07/
cyber/artsatlarge/27artsatlarge.html (accessed Dec. 30, 2006).

Mitchell, W. J. T. 1994. *Picture Theory: Essays on Verbal and Visual Representation.*
Chicago: University of Chicago Press.

———. 1995. City of Bits: Space, Place, and the Infobahn. Cambridge, MA: MIT Press.

Montfort, Nick. 2000. "Cybertext Killed the Hypertext Star." *electronic book review.*
www.electronicbookreview.com/thread/electropoetics/cyberdebates (accessed
Dec. 30, 2006).

———. 2003. "Toward a Theory of Interactive Fiction." http://nickm.com/if/toward.
html (accessed Dec. 30, 2006).

Morrissey, Judd. 2000. *The Jew's Daughter.* www.thejewsdaughter.com (accessed
Dec. 30, 2006).

Morrissey, Judd, and Lori Talley. 2002. Visiting Artist and Writer (Statement).
CrudeOils (June): www.crudeoils.us/artwrite/June2002/index.html (accessed
Dec. 30, 2006).

Morrissey, Judd, Lori Talley, and Lutz Hamel. 2004. "The Error Engine." Documen-
tation for upcoming project, received in correspondence with author, Sep. 12,
2004. (Published as "The Error Engine." *Performance Research* 9, no. 2, Dec.
2004).

Moulthrop, Stuart. 1989a. "Hypertext and 'the Hyperreal.'" In *Hypertext '89: Proceedings,* Pittsburgh, PA, Nov. 5–8, 259–68. New York: ACM Press.

———. 1989b. "In the Zones: Hypertext and the Politics of Interpretation."
http://iat.ubalt.edu/moulthrop/essays/zones.html (accessed Dec. 30, 2006).

———. 1991a. "Beyond the Electronic Book: A Critique of Hypertext Rhetoric."
In *Proceedings of the Third Annual ACM Conference on Hypertext,* San Antonio, TX, 291–98. New York: ACM Press.

———. 1991b. *Victory Garden.* Watertown, MA: Eastgate Systems.

———. 1992a. "No War Machine." In *Reading Matters: Narratives in the New Media
Ecology,* ed. Joseph Tabbi and Michael Wutz, 269–92. Ithaca, NY: Cornell University Press, 1997. http://iat.ubalt.edu/moulthrop/essays/war_machine.html
(accessed Dec. 9, 2006).

———. 1992b. "The Shadow of an Informand: A Rhetorical Experiment in Hypertext." *Perforations* 3: http://iat.ubalt.edu/moulthrop/hypertexts/hoptext/ (accessed Dec. 30, 2006).

———. 1994. "Rhizome and Resistance: Hypertext and the Dreams of a New Culture." In Landow 1994b, 299–319.

———. 1995. *Hegirascope.* http://iat.ubalt.edu/moulthrop/hypertexts/hgs/HGS0B3.
html (accessed Dec. 30, 2006).

———. 1997a. "Pushing Back: Living and Writing in Broken Space." *Modern Fiction
Studies* 43, no. 3: 651–74.

———. 1997b. "Where To? A review of *Forward Anywhere,* by Judy Malloy and
Cathy Marshall." *Convergence* 3, no. 3 (fall): 132–38. www.eastgate.com/reviews/
Moulthrop.html (accessed Dec. 30, 2006)).

———. 2001. "Traveling in the Breakdown Lane: A Principle of Resistance for Hypertext." http://iat.ubalt.edu/moulthrop/essays/breakdown.html (accessed Dec. 30, 2006).

———. 2003a. "From Work to Play." *electronic book review.* www.electronicbookreview.com/thread/firstperson/molecular (accessed Dec. 30, 2006).

———. 2003b. "Electronic Books?" A Riposte in the *electronic book review,* www.electronicbookreview.com/thread/electropoetics/marginalized (accessed Dec. 30, 2006).

———. 2003c. "An Interview with Stuart Moulthrop by Noah Wardrip-Fruin." *Iowa Review Web* (Sep. 1): www.uiowa.edu/~iareview/tirweb/feature/moulthrop/interview.html (accessed Dec. 30, 2006).

Murphy, Timothy, and Daniel Smith. 2001. "What I Hear Is Thinking Too: Deleuze and Guattari Go Pop." *Echo* 3, no. 1 (spring): www.echo.ucla.edu/Volume3-Issue1/smithmurphy/smithmurphy1.html (accessed Dec. 30, 2006).

Murray, Janet H. 1997. *Hamlet on the Holodeck: The Future of Narrative in Cyberspace.* New York: Free Press.

Nell, Viktor. 1988. *Lost in a Book: The Psychology of Reading for Pleasure.* New Haven, CT: Yale University Press.

Nelson, Theodor H. 1981. *Literary Machines.* Swarthmore, PA: Mindful Press.

Nielson, Jakob. 1990. *Hypertext and Hypermedia.* Boston: Harcourt, Brace, Jovanovich.

Nietzsche, Friedrich. 1883–92/1995. *Thus Spoke Zarathustra: A Book for All and None.* Trans. Walter Kaufmann. New York: Modern Library. Page references are to the 1995 reprint.

O'Flaherty, Gerry. 2004. "Reading *Ulysses.*" RTÉ Radio. www.rte.ie/readingulysses/episode17.html (accessed Dec. 30, 2006).

Olson, Charles. 1997. *Collected Prose.* Ed. Donald Allen and Benjamin Friedlander. Berkeley: University of California Press.

Ong, Walter. 1982. *Orality and Literacy: The Technologizing of the Word.* London: Methuen.

Parker, Jeff. 2001. "A Poetics of the Link." *electronic book review* 12 (fall): www.altx.com/ebr/ebr12/park/park.htm (accessed Dec. 30, 2006).

———. 2003. "The Museum of Hyphenated Media." *electronic book review* (Jan.): www.electronicbookreview.com/thread/electropoetics/quilted (accessed Dec. 30, 2006).

Parunak, H. Van Dyke. 1989. "Hypermedia Topologies and User Navigation." In *Proceedings of the Second Annual ACM Conference on Hypertext,* Pittsburgh, PA, 43–50. New York: ACM Press.

Pavic, Milorad. 1989. *Dictionary of the Khazars: A Lexicon Novel in 100,000 Words.* New York: Vintage.

———. 2003. *The Glass Snail.* Word Circuits (Aug.): www.wordcircuits.com/gallery/glasssnail (accessed Dec. 30, 2006).

Percy, Thomas. 1765/1996. *Reliques of Ancient English Poetry*. Vol. 1. London: Routledge.

Phelan, James, and Edward Maloney. 1999–2000. "Authors, Readers, and Progression
in Hypertext Narrative." *Works and Days* 17/18, nos. 33/34, 35/36 (265–77).

Poster, Mark. 1995. *The Second Media Age*. Cambridge: Polity.

———. 1999. "Theorizing Virtual Reality." *Cyberspace Textuality*, ed. Marie-Laure
Ryan, 42–60. Bloomington: Indiana University Press.

Powe, Bruce. 1989. "A Return to Gould." *Noise of Time*. CD-ROM (Henry See, de-
veloper). www.collectionscanada.ca/glenngould/028010-502.10-e.html#a (accessed Dec. 30, 2006).

Powers, Richard. 1992. *The Gold Bug Variations*. New York: HarperPerennial.

Pressman, Jessica. 2003. "Flying Blind: An Interview with Judd Morrissey and Lori
Talley." *Iowa Review Web* (April 1): www.uiowa.edu/~iareview/tirweb/feature/
morrissey_talley/index (accessed Dec. 30, 2006).

Raley, Rita. 2002. "The Digital Loop: Feedback and Recurrence." *Leonardo Electronic Almanac* 10, no. 7 (July): www.shadoof.net/in/whitecubebluesky/rrloop.
html (accessed Dec. 30, 2006).

Rettberg, Scott. 2002. "The Pleasure (and Pain) of Link Poetics." *electronic book review* (Oct.): www.electronicbookreview.com/thread/electropoetics/pragmatic
(accessed Dec. 30, 2006).

———. 2003. "Destination Unknown: Experiments in the Network Novel." PhD
diss., University of Cincinnati. http://loki.stockton.edu/~rettbers/PDFS/
rettbergetd.pdf (accessed Dec. 30, 2006).

Riess, Daniel. 1996. "The Revolution May Not Be Computerized." Review of *Forms
and Meanings: Texts, Performances, and Audiences from Codex to Computer*, by
Roger Chartier. *electronic book review:* www.electronicbookreview.com/thread/
criticalecologies/revolutionary (accessed Dec. 9, 2006).

Rimmon-Kenan, Shlomith. 1980. "The Paradoxical Status of Repetition." *Poetics
Today* 1, no. 4 (summer): 151–59.

———. 1983. *Narrative Fiction: Contemporary Poetics*. London: Methuen.

Rosello, Mireille. 1994. "The Screener's Maps: Michel de Certeau's *Wandersmänner*
and Paul Auster's Hypertextual Detective." In Landow 1994b, 121–58.

Rosenberg, Jim. 1994. "Navigating Nowhere / Hypertext Infrawhere." *SIGLINK
Newsletter* 3 (Dec.): 16–19. www.well.com/user/jer/NNHI.html (accessed
Dec. 30, 2006).

———. 1996. "The Structure of Hypertext Activity." In *Proceedings of the Seventh
ACM Conference on Hypertext*, Washington, DC, March 16–20, 22–30. New York:
ACM Press.

Rosenberg, Martin. 1994. "Physics and Hypertext: Liberation and Complicity in Art
and Pedagogy." In Landow 1994b, 268–98.

Ryan, Marie-Laure. 1994. "Immersion versus Interactivity: Virtual Reality and Literary Theory." *Postmodern Culture* (Sep.): www.humanities.uci.edu/mposter/
syllabi/readings/ryan.html (accessed Dec. 30, 2006).

———. 1999. "Cyberspace, Virtuality, and the Text." *Cyberspace Textuality: Computer Technology and Literary Theory,* ed. Marie-Laure Ryan, 78–107. Bloomington: Indiana University Press.

———. 2001a. "Beyond Myth and Metaphor: The Case of Narrative in Digital Media." *Game Studies* 1, no. 1 (July): www.gamestudies.org/0101/ryan (accessed Dec. 30, 2006).

———. 2001b. *Narrative as Virtual Reality: Immersion and Interactivity in Literature and Electronic Media.* Baltimore: Johns Hopkins University Press.

———. 2003. "Cognitive Maps and the Construction of Narrative Space." In *Narrative Theory and the Cognitive Sciences,* ed. David Herman, 214–42. Stanford, CA: Publications of the Center for the Study of Language and Information.

———. 2004. "Cyberspace, Cybertexts, Cybermaps." *Dichtung-digital.* www.dichtung-digital.org/2004/1-Ryan.htm (accessed Dec. 30, 2006).

Ryman, Geoff. 1996. *253 or tube theatre, a novel for the Internet about London Underground in seven cars and a crash.* www.ryman-novel.com (accessed Dec. 11, 2006).

Sargent, Helen Child, and George Lynn Kittredge, eds. 1904. *The English and Scottish Popular Ballads.* London: George G. Harrap.

Schwarz, Arturo. 1969. *The Complete Works of Marcel Duchamp.* London: Thames and Hudson.

Selig, Robert L. 2000. "The Endless Reading of Fiction: Stuart Moulthrop's Hypertext Novel *Victory Garden.*" *Contemporary Literature* 41, no. 4: 642–59.

Shklovsky, Victor. 1965. "Sterne's *Tristram Shandy:* Stylistic Commentary." In *Russian Formalist Criticism: Four Essays,* trans. and ed. by Lee T. Lemon and Marion J. Reis, 25–60. Lincoln: University of Nebraska Press.

Shumate, Michael. 1998. "Whatever Happened to Editors Anyhow?" *Hyperizons.* www.duke.edu/~mshumate/hyperizons/original/winners3.html (accessed Dec. 30, 2006).

Siegle, Robert. 1999. "Twilit Ragas." *Blue Moon Review,* no. 4 (1998–99): www.thebluemoon.com/4/siegle.html (accessed Dec. 30, 2006).

Simanowski, Roberto. 2000. "When Literature Goes Multimedia." http://beehive.temporalimage.com/content_apps51/simanowski/f05.html (accessed Dec. 30, 2006).

Simon, Herbert. 1995. "Literary Criticism: A Cognitive Approach." In "Bridging the Gap," special issue, *Stanford Humanities Review* 4, no. 1: www.stanford.edu/group/SHR/4-1/text/simon1.html (accessed Dec. 30, 2006).

Sloane, Sarah. 2000. *Digital Fictions: Storytelling in a Material World.* Stamford, CT: Ablex.

Smith, Hazel. 1999. "From Cityscape to Cyberspace: Writing the City in Hypermedia." In *Australian Writing and the City,* ed. Fran de Groen and Ken Stewart, 164–72. Sydney: ASAL [Association for the Study of Australian Literature].

Smith, Hazel, and Roger Dean. 2001. *Returning the Angles.* CD version. Sydney: Soma Publications. Also available online: *Jacket Magazine*, no. 7, http://jacketmagazine.com/07/smith-hazel.html (accessed Dec. 30, 2006).

———. 2003. "Voicescapes and Sonic Structures in the Creation of Sound Techno-drama." *Performance Research* 8, no. 1: 112–23.

Snyder, Ilana. 1997. *The Electronic Labyrinth*. New York: New York University Press.

Spencer, Sharon. 1971. *Space, Time, and Structure in the Modern Novel*. New York: New York University Press.

Spiro, Rand. 1982. "Long-Term Comprehension: Schema-Based versus Experiential and Evaluative Understanding." *Poetics* 11: 77–86.

Stark, John. 1974. *The Literature of Exhaustion: Borges, Nabokov, Barth*. Durham, NC: Duke University Press.

St. Clair, Jeffrey. 2003. "Patriot Gore: The Fatal Flaws in the Patriot Missile System." *Dissident Voice*, April 19, www.dissidentvoice.org/Articles4/StClair_Patriot-Flaws.htm (accessed Dec. 11, 2006).

Stefans, Brian Kim. 2005. "Privileging Language: The Text in Electronic Writing." *electronic book review* (Nov.): www.electronicbookreview.com/thread/firstperson/databased (accessed Dec. 10, 2006).

Stephanson, Anders. 1988. "Regarding Postmodernism—A Conversation with Fredric Jameson." In *Universal Abandon: The Politics of Postmodernism*, ed. Andrew Ross, 3–30. Minneapolis: University of Minnesota Press.

Sterne, Laurence. 1759–67/1978. *The Life and Opinions of Tristram Shandy, Gentleman*. London: Penguin.

Strickland, Stephanie. 1999. "To Be Both in Touch and in Control." *electronic book review* (March): www.electronicbookreview.com/thread/electropoetics/perception (accessed Dec. 30, 2006).

Suleiman, Susan Rubin. 1983. *Authoritarian Fictions: The Ideological Novel as a Literary Genre*. New York: Columbia University Press.

Swiss, Thomas. 1998–99. "Reviewing the Reviewers of Literary Hypertexts." *electronic book review*: www.electronicbookreview.com/thread/electropoetics/corrective (accessed Dec. 12, 2006).

Tabbi, Joseph. 2002. *Cognitive Fictions*. Minneapolis: University of Minnesota Press.

———. 2003. "The Processual Page: Materiality and Consciousness in Print and Hypertext." *Journal of New Media and Culture* 2, no. 2 (fall): www.ibiblio.org/nmediac/fall2003/processual.html (accessed Dec. 30, 2006).

Thomas, Brook. 1986. *James Joyce's "Ulysses": A Book of Many Happy Returns*. Baton Rouge: Louisiana State University Press.

Tofts, Darren. 2001. "Opaque Melodies That Would Bug Most People: A Short History of Dislocation in Six Tracks." *Senses of Cinema*, www.sensesofcinema.com/contents/01/18/dislocation.html (accessed Dec. 30, 2006).

Tolman, Edward C. 1948. "Cognitive Maps in Rats and Men." *Psychological Review* 55, no. 4: 189–208.

Tolva, John. 1996. "*Ut pictura hyperpoesis:* Spatial Form, Visuality, and the Digital Word." In *Proceedings of the Seventh ACM Conference on Hypertext,* Washington, DC, March 16–20, 66–73. New York: ACM Press.

Tosca, Susana Pajares. 1997. "Crítica: Four Hypertexts from Eastgate." *Hipertulia.* www.ucm.es/info/especulo/hipertul/review.html (accessed Dec. 30, 2006).

———. 2000. "A Pragmatics of Links." *Journal of Digital Information* 1, no. 6 (June): http://jodi.ecs.soton.ac.uk/Articles/v01/i06/Pajares (accessed Dec. 30, 2006).

Trend, David, ed. 2001. *Reading Digital Culture.* Malden, MA: Blackwell.

Trippi, Laura. 2001. "Disentangling Play from Story." Entry in *net.narrative* weblog, posted Sep. 6. www.netvironments.org/blog/archives/2001_09_01_archives1_html (accessed Dec. 30, 2006).

———. 2003. "Networked Narrative Environments." www.netvironments.org/nne/Unit3/Presentation3/view (accessed Dec. 30, 2006).

Turkle, Sherry. 1995. *Life on the Screen: Identity in the Age of the Internet.* New York: Simon and Schuster.

Unknown, The. 1999. Radio Free Unknown. "The Unknown Interviews Itself for the AltX Publishing Network." Oct. 16: www.altx.com/hyperx/unknown/altxinterview.html (accessed Dec. 13, 2006).

———. n.d. Online Press Kit. www.unknownhypertext.com/presskit (accessed Dec. 13, 2006).

U.S. Department of Defense. 2000. "Information Paper: Iraq's Scud Ballistic Missiles." July 25: http://www.iraqwatch.org/government/US/Pentagon/dodscud.htm (accessed Dec. 20, 2006).

Van Dijk, Teun. 1980. *Macrostructures: An Interdisciplinary Study of Global Structures in Discourse, Interaction, and Cognition.* Hillsdale, NJ: Lawrence Erlbaum.

Virilio, Paul. 2001. "Speed and Information: Cyberspace Alarm!" In Trend 2001, 23–27.

Walker, Jill. 1999. "Piecing Together and Tearing Apart: Finding the Story in *afternoon.*" In *Proceedings of the Tenth Annual ACM Conference on Hypertext and Hypermedia,* Darmstadt, Germany, Feb. 21–25, 111–17. New York: ACM Press. http://huminf.uib.no/~jill/txt/afternoon.html (accessed Dec. 30, 2006).

Wardrip-Fruin, Noah. 1994. "The Book of Endings." www.cat.nyu.edu/~noah/theBook/About.html (accessed Dec. 30, 2006).

Wilson, Josephine. 1998. "Looking for Abalone." *Flytrap.* http://home.pacific.net.au/~lcarroli/hypertext/abalone.htm (accessed Dec. 30, 2006).

Woodbury, Chuck. 1990. "World War II Air Raid of Oregon Was a Real Bomb!" *Out West* 11 (July): www.outwestnewspaper.com/bomboregon.html (accessed Dec. 11, 2006).

Wordsworth, William. 1891. *The Complete Poetical Works of William Wordsworth.* London: Macmillan.

Yaszek, Lisa. 2005. "'I'll be a postfeminist in a postpatriarchy,' or, Can We Really Imagine Life after Feminism?" *electronic book review* (Jan.):

www.electronicbookreview.com/thread/writingpostfeminism/(fem)sci-fi
(accessed Dec. 30, 2006).

Žižek, Slavoj. 2001. "From Virtual Reality to the Virtualization of Reality." In Trend
2001, 17–22.

Zwaan, Rolf A. 1993. *Aspects of Literary Comprehension: A Cognitive Approach.* Amsterdam: John Benjamins.

Index